# SUCCESS

Success in coaching or playing should not be based on the
number of games won or lost, but rather on the basis
what each individual did in comparison with others when
taking into consideration individual abilities, the
facilities with which you had wo work, the caliber of your
opponents, the site of the contests, etc.

taking into consideration individual abilities, the
facilities with which you had wo work, the caliber of your
opponents, the site of the contests, etc.

True success comes only to an individual by self-satisfaction
in knowing that you gave everything to become the very best
that you are capable of.  As George Moriarty once said,
"Giving all, it seems to me, is not so far from victory."
Therefore, in the final analysis, only the individual himself
can correctly determine his success.  You may be able to
fool others, but you can never fool yourself.

It is impossible to attain perfection, but that should be
the goal.  Less than 100% of your effort toward obtaining

herefore, in the final analysis, only the individual himself
an correctly determine his success.  You may be able to
ool others, but you can never fool yourself.

t is impossible to attain perfection, but that should be
he goal.  Less than 100% of your effort toward obtaining
our objective is not success, regardless of how many games
ere won or lost.

thers may have far more ability than you have, they may be
arger, faster, quicker, able to jump better, etc., but no
ne should be your superior in team spirit,  loyalty,
ooperation, determination, industriousness, fight, and ch
cquire and keep these traits and success should follow.

# WOODEN
## ON LEADERSHIP

# WOODEN
## ON LEADERSHIP

Coach John Wooden
and Steve Jamison

## McGraw-Hill

New York   Chicago   San Francisco   Lisbon   London   Madrid   Mexico City
Milan   New Delhi   San Juan   Seoul   Singapore   Sydney   Toronto

The **McGraw·Hill** Companies

3  4  5  6  7  8  9  0    DOC/DOC    0  9  8  7  6  5

ISBN 0–07–145339–3

First Edition

Interior design by Nick Panos

McGraw-Hill books are available at special quantity discounts to use as
premiums and sales promotions, or for use in corporate training programs. For
more information, please write to the Director of Special Sales, Professional
Publishing, McGraw-Hill, Two Penn Plaza, New York, NY 10121–2298.
Or contact your local bookstore.

The authors wish to thank Benjamin Cummings Publishing (Allyn and Bacon)
for permission to use some original material from Coach Wooden's 1966
publication, *Practical Modern Basketball*.

*Library of Congress Cataloging-in-Publication Data*

Wooden, John R.
    Wooden on leadership / by John Wooden and Steve Jamison. — 1st ed.
        p.     cm.
    ISBN 0-07-145339-3 (hardcover : alk. paper)
    1. Leadership.   2. Management.   I. Jamison, Steve.   II. Title.
    HD57.7.W664 2005
    658.4'092 — dc22
                                                              2005003989

Thanks to

Nell—and our daughter, Nan Wooden Muehlhausen, and our son, Jim Wooden; and our wonderful grandchildren and great-grandchildren; also to coaches Ward "Piggy" Lambert, Glenn Curtis, and Earl Warriner; and the many fine players, assistant coaches, our trainer, and student managers who worked so hard with me on our journey in pursuit of success. I also want to wish INCH and MILES the best of luck as they take my Pyramid of Success to children around the world in the twenty-first century!

—*Coach John Wooden*


For

My parents, Mary Jean and Everett Edstrom, and my sisters, Pat, KRS, Kate, and Kim.

—*Steve Jamison*



*And thanks to Jeffrey Krames, whose coaching at crucial moments in the contest was most valuable.*

"*When it comes to building a winning team, John Wooden wrote the book. Now that book has a name:* Wooden on Leadership. *This is his personal blueprint for achieving success as a leader in business, basketball, or anything else. After all these years, I have finally come to learn what made Coach Wooden so special and why. I also have come to grips with his claim that I am his slowest learner ever.* Wooden on Leadership *tells the WHOLE story.*"

—Bill Walton

# CONTENTS

# PREFACE

D r. Albert Einstein and Coach John Wooden share a similar
brilliance; specifically, both mastered the complicated art of
keeping it simple. For Dr. Einstein, the complexities of nuclear
fusion were summed up in the elegance of a simple equation:
$E = MC^2$. For Coach Wooden, 10 national championships are
summed up in the simplicity of an elegant formula: $10 = C + F +
U$ (Conditioning + Fundamentals + Unity).

Simple as that. Only not so simple.

Having seen the equations of each man—one a master of science, the other of leadership—you are no closer to being able to
create atomic energy than to winning 10 national championships.
To truly comprehend the substance of what their formulas represent is perhaps a lifetime's work. Thus, this book will save you time
when it comes to identifying and implementing John Wooden's
leadership genius in ways that best suit your own organization.

Having worked with Coach Wooden for many years on several
books and projects, I hear this question: "What's his secret? How
did he do it—10 national championships (a record), including
seven in a row (a record); 88 consecutive victories (a record); 38
straight tournament playoff wins (a record); four perfect seasons (a
record) with only one losing year—his first—in 41 years of coaching? How did he do it? How did he set all those records?"

Here is the answer: Coach Wooden taught good habits. That's it—that's the answer.

John Wooden taught good habits to those under his leadership at Dayton [Kentucky] High School, South Bend Central High School, Indiana State Teachers College, and, of course, UCLA. All along the way he kept teaching good habits until eventually he became one of the best builders of winning teams the world has ever seen.

The exact nature of those "good habits" and how you can incorporate them with your organization is the subject of *Wooden on Leadership: How to Create a Winning Organization.*

As John Wooden takes us through the evolution of his education as a leader and the philosophy he developed for creating successful teams and organizations, you will see that, like the formula $10 = C + F + U$, it is straightforward—deceptively so.

Move past the equation, delve deeper, and the text of his good habits curriculum becomes the inculcation of values, knowledge, team spirit, discipline, consistency, standards, ideals, balance, character, details, hard work, love, self-control, loyalty, diligence, and more, including how to put on your socks in the most effective manner.

And that's what makes John Wooden's "secret" so compelling: The qualities and characteristics he possesses and has taught to his teams—those good habits and how you teach them—are available to everyone.

There is no patent pending, copyright law, or No Trespassing sign that prohibits use of his leadership "secrets." In the vernacular of the Internet, it's "open source code" or, as he writes so directly, "All you need is the will to look hard enough within."

What he taught and how he taught it is now available to all; and all of it is available in the pages of this book, *Wooden on Leadership.*

*Steve Jamison*

# PROLOGUE

# THE JOYS OF MY JOURNEY

Leadership offers its greatest reward beyond that of simply achieving supremacy over the competition. At least, this was true for me.

The joy and great satisfaction I derived from leadership—working with and teaching others, helping them reach their potential in contributing to the team's common goals—ultimately surpassed outscoring an opponent, the standings, even championships. It certainly surpassed the public attention that comes with achievement.

In fact, it was the hoopla and attention accompanying UCLA's success in basketball that perhaps drove me away from coaching.

On Saturday night, March 29, 1975, UCLA played Louisville in the semifinals of March Madness at the San Diego Sports Arena. Going into the game, I had every intention of remaining as head coach at UCLA for two, possibly three more years.

Some say they knew otherwise—that I'd indicated I would leave the Bruins at the end of the season. Well, maybe they knew, but I didn't. What happened happened quickly and with no warning.

After the final buzzer, when Louisville Coach Denny Crum and I had congratulated each other on a nearly perfect game, I turned toward the pressroom for the usual postgame interview.

But something came over me that I had never felt before in 41 years as a coach. I had the strongest feeling—almost revulsion—that I couldn't go through it anymore: the questions and answers, the never-ending speculation and examination; the crowds and all the folderol that had become such a disproportionate part of my daily life. Not just from reporters doing their job, but from the outside world.

While it's true I appreciate recognition for a job well done, just like anybody else, UCLA's success in basketball had created something I never aspired to, and didn't want, but eventually couldn't get away from, specifically, such overwhelming attention, inspection, and curiosity that it became more than an irritation. It was deeply disturbing.

I felt more and more that crowds were closing in and enveloping me. I seemed to be constantly surrounded. This great frenzy of activity and attention was more than unwelcome; it was unnatural.

At one coaches' conference I was asked to stand outside the meeting hall before I spoke, so as not to take attention away from the other coaches who were also guest speakers. I had become a distraction, a disruption, someone who needed special handling—a coach separate from other coaches. I was a celebrity who genuinely had never wanted to be one. I only wanted to be a coach among other coaches, a teacher among teachers. Now, I was being asked to stand outside the door while the coaches, teachers, and leaders gathered within, without me.

If this had happened in a dream, I would have said upon waking that I'd just had a terrible nightmare. What was happening, however, wasn't a dream.

What am I? Just a teacher—a member of one of the great professions in the world. My teaching had accomplished good things, but in the process it had created a level of attention that eventually drove me away.

I had to get out, but perhaps I didn't even know it until seconds after I shook Coach Crum's hand following that semifinal game. Minutes later I told our team that our upcoming game would be my last.

Many times I have suggested to interested observers that if I ever met a magical genie who could grant me two wishes, I knew what they would be. First, for those many coaches whom I respect and have warm feelings toward I would wish each one a national championship.

For those few coaches for whom I have less-than-warm feelings, my wish would be that they win many national championships. However, in truth, I'm not sure I would wish that on anybody.

Balance is crucial in everything we do. Along with love it's among the most important things in life. I strove for balance in my leadership and coaching and taught that balance was necessary for Competitive Greatness: The body has to be in balance; the mind has to be in balance; emotions must be in balance. Balance is important everywhere and in everything we do.

Unfortunately, over the last years of my coaching at UCLA things had gotten out of balance. Perhaps my subconscious mind figured out that the only way to regain the balance I required personally and professionally was to leave the game I love.

In fact, if the genie had given me a third wish, I might have requested that the folderol disappear but the practices remain. Those practices were where my teaching, coaching, and leadership existed in a wonderful and pure form, free from folderol.

What occurred in the practices is what gave me joy and satisfaction—teaching others how to bring forth the best of which they are capable. Ultimately, I believe that's what leadership is all about: helping others to achieve their own greatness by helping the organization to succeed.

How you accomplish that—at least, how I approached leadership—is the subject of this book.

It was a privilege to have been in a leadership position for 40 years. I miss the excitement of being on that practice court working hard with our team in pursuit of Competitive Greatness—"being at your best when your best is needed." To me, that is the most exciting part of being a leader: the journey to become the best of which you and your team are capable.

I miss the joys of that journey very much but take comfort in the fact that this book may provide some ideas useful in your own leadership journey. If it does, I'll be very pleased. I offer you best wishes all along the way.

*Coach John Wooden*

# THE
# FOUNDATION
## FOR MY
# LEADERSHIP

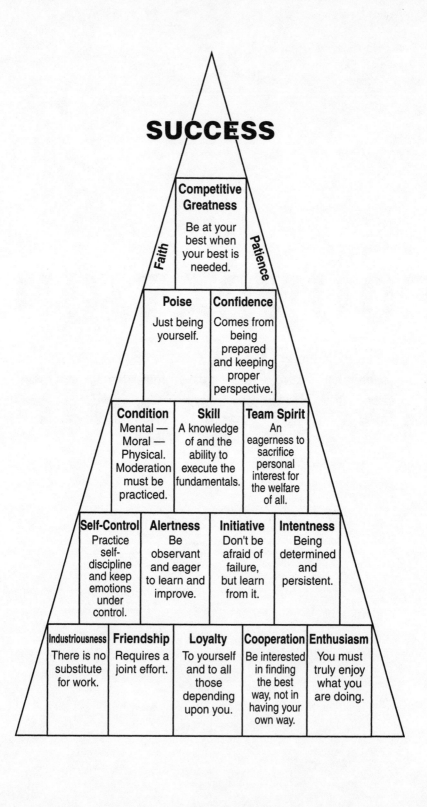

# INTRODUCTION

*"Success is peace of mind which is a direct result of self-satisfaction in knowing you made the effort to become the best of which you are capable."*

I OFFICIALLY BECAME "COACH" WOODEN on Monday afternoon, September 5, 1932—the first day of football practice at Dayton High School in Kentucky. I was 21, married a month, and recently graduated from Purdue University with a major in English and a minor in poetry.

The Dayton school board was paying me $1,500 annually and divided it up like this: $1,200 for teaching English classes; $300 for coaching football, basketball, and baseball. Despite the disparity in pay, everyone understood that I was hired primarily as a coach, not as an English teacher. That's how it was done in those days.

If pressed, school officials would have told you that Johnny Wooden, a three-time All-American and Big 10 scoring leader while a member of the national champion Purdue Boilermakers basketball team, was on the Dayton faculty not to teach English but because he knew all about coaching and leadership. They were wrong.

What I knew how to do was teach English, including Shakespeare and spelling, poetry and punctuation. As a matter of fact, just before graduation from Purdue, I was offered a fellowship with an eye toward my becoming an English professor and joining its faculty in West Lafayette, Indiana.

I would have accepted the offer except for one thing: Nellie and I were eager to get married and start a family, and the Purdue fellowship wouldn't pay enough for us to live on. Had I intended to stay single, however, I might have taken the offer, become a professor of English, and perhaps never become a full-time coach.

So when Dayton High School came calling with a pretty good sum of money for those days—$1,500 annually—we saw the preacher and headed off to my new job. What Dayton got for its money was a pretty fair English teacher and a pretty bad coach. However, on that first Monday afternoon in September, when I confidently blew my whistle to signal the start of practice, I thought I knew what I was doing.

Two weeks later, I quit coaching football.

## REMEMBER YOUR ROOTS

I am a competitive man. As far back as I remember there's been a fierce determination in me to win—whether as a young basketball player in Indiana or later as a coach leading teams into competition for national championships.

While I was blessed at birth with some athletic ability, my coaching skills were acquired later. In fact, I was so bashful as a young man that you would never have picked me as a future coach, a leader, who could stand in front of strong-willed, independent-minded individuals and tell them what to do—and how to do it. Overcoming shyness was something I had to learn.

I believe leadership itself is largely learned. Certainly not everyone can lead nor is every leader destined for glory, but most of us have a potential far beyond what we think possible.

Those who aspire to be leaders can do it; those who wish to become much better leaders can also do it. I know, because this has been true in my own life. Whatever coaching and leadership skills I possess were learned through listening, observation, study, and then trial and error along the way.

In my opinion, this is how most leaders improve and progress. For me, the process of learning leadership continued for 40 years until the day I walked off the court for the last time as head coach—March 31, 1975—following UCLA's tenth national championship. In truth, my learning continued even after that.

Nevertheless, coaching was not something I set out to do growing up. It's fair to say that my primary objective back on our family farm was to beat my older brother Maurice ("Cat") in a race around the barn or any other competition we thought up. Most of the time I lost, because my brother's nickname was accurate: Maurice was quick as a cat. Nevertheless, the two of us loved to compete, which meant we were no different from you and just about everybody else, then and now.

Americans, perhaps by nature, are most competitive. In sports, business, and almost all areas of life they not only ask *Who's number one?*, they want to be number one and constantly compare themselves against that standard: "Am I the biggest? The best? The fastest?"

However, for most of my life I have believed these are the wrong questions to ask oneself. This comes mostly from what I was taught by my dad back on the farm in Centerton, Indiana, population 49.

The principles and values I learned back there stuck with me and became the compass that I've followed—or tried to follow—for more than 90 years. My devotion to what he taught as well as my belief in its importance and practicality remains as strong today as ever. Stronger, in fact.

Whatever I accomplished as a leader came mainly from what he accomplished as a father and teacher.

## THE SECRET OF SUCCESS

My dad, Joshua Hugh Wooden, was a good man with strong convictions and gentle ways. Self-educated through reading, he passed his love of learning along to his four boys. He was very proud that all of us graduated from high school, even prouder when we received college degrees and became teachers—each one of us.

Although Dad suffered terrible setbacks and sorrows—deaths of two daughters, loss of his beloved farm, financial hardships during the Great Depression—he never complained, criticized, or compared himself to others who were better off. Through it all he made the best of what he had and was thankful for it. That is one of my strongest memories of him and something I tried so hard to copy as the years went by, both in my private life and as a teacher, coach, and leader.

Dad wasn't much for small talk or gossip and could play through a whole game of checkers or chess without saying a word. However, when he did say something it was always worth hearing. He possessed a simple wisdom, profound but extremely practical.

What he said about success—"winning the race"—was uncommon for his time and even more uncommon today. His words are at the core of my philosophy of leadership, perhaps the single most important concept I've learned and taught over the years. "Sons," he would tell my three brothers and me, "don't worry about whether you're better than somebody else, but never cease trying to be the best you can become. You have control over that; the other you don't."

Time spent comparing myself to others, he cautioned, was time wasted. This is a tough lesson to learn when you're young, even tougher when you grow up. "Johnny, work hard to get as good as you can get," he'd say. "Do that and you may call yourself a success. Do less and you've fallen short." I did my best to follow my dad's advice.

While it didn't happen overnight, the wisdom of his words eventually sunk in and became part of me. I gradually disciplined myself and later the teams I taught, coached, and led—the Dayton, Kentucky, Greendevils, the South Bend Central Bears, the Indiana State Sycamores, and the UCLA Bruins—to focus on and worry about only those things we controlled, namely, getting as good as we could get, striving to reach the ultimate of our capabilities both mentally and physically.

Whether that might, or did, result in outscoring our opponent—"winning the race"—was something I didn't lose much sleep over. I tried hard to teach those under my supervision to do the same, to understand that success was within their reach, regardless of the score, standings, or opinion of others (especially the opinion of others).

Make no mistake: We all want to win the race. Whether in basketball, business, or another competitive arena, victory can be glorious.

Losing is painful—at times, most harsh. I still hurt when I think back to a loss our Martinsville high school team suffered during the last seconds of the finals of an Indiana State Basketball Tournament. That was more than 75 years ago, and it still hurts when I recall it.

But ultimately, to my way of thinking, losing is not the end of the world, nor does victory put me on top of it—not even a national championship. There is something beyond, something even greater than winning the race.

Cervantes. "The road is better than the inn." Robt. Louis Stevenson. "To travel hopefully is better than to arrive."

For most of my life I have believed that success is found in the running of the race. How you run the race—your planning, preparation, practice, and performance—counts for everything. Winning or losing is a by-product, an aftereffect, of that effort. For me, it's the quality of your effort that counts most and offers the greatest and most long-lasting satisfaction.

Cervantes had it right: "The journey is better than the inn." Most people don't understand what he means, but thanks to my father I do. The joy is in the journey of pushing yourself to the outward limits of your ability and teaching your organization to do the same.

I believe most great competitors share this feeling. They recognize that the ultimate reward is in the competitive process itself rather than some subsequent gain or glory brought about by winning. Thus, in all my years of coaching I rarely, if ever, even uttered the word *win*, talked about "beating" an opponent, or exhorted a team to be number one, including those picked by experts to win national championships.

Instead, my words and actions always reflected Joshua Hugh Wooden's early advice—"Never cease trying to be the best you can become"—and were directed at helping those under my leadership achieve success as I came to define it.

And starting in the winter of 1934 as a first-year English teacher and coach at Kentucky's Dayton High School I defined it precisely like this: "Success is peace of mind which is a direct result of self-satisfaction in knowing you made the effort to become the best of which you are capable."

This definition hasn't changed since it was coined, nor do I think a change is required now. I've been teaching it to those under my leadership for my entire adult life, and it has proven effective. There is a standard higher than merely winning the race: Effort is the ultimate measure of your success.

> ## COMPETE ONLY AGAINST YOURSELF
>
> **R**emember my father's advice: Set your standards high; namely, do the absolute best of which you are capable. Focus on running the race rather than winning it. Do those things necessary to bring forth your personal best and don't lose sleep worrying about the competition. Let the competition lose sleep worrying about you. Teach your organization to do the same.

## HOLD YOUR HEAD HIGH

Before our team left the locker room and entered the arena, whether it was the first game of a high school season with boys named Rzeszewski, Kozoroski, and Smith or the last game of an NCAA championship season with young men named Walton, Wilkes, and Meyers, my final words were always about the same: "When it's over, I want your heads up. And there's only one way your heads can be up—that's to give it your best out there, everything you have."

This is all I ever asked of them because it was all they could ever give. And I required the same in every single practice I ever conducted, nothing less than their best effort. I gave the same.

Many cynics, then and now, dismiss what Dad taught me about success as being naïve or impractical. But I have yet to hear the cynics and skeptics describe what more you can give beyond your best.

To my way of thinking, when you give your total effort—everything you have—the score can never make you a loser. And when you do less, it can't somehow magically turn you into a winner.

When you truly accept this philosophy, it changes everything: your preparation and performance and your ability to withstand hard setbacks and defeats as well as the challenges imposed by victory. It redefines how you measure success and makes it achievable in every situation you and those in your organization face, whether good or bad.

I have also found that accepting this philosophy dramatically improves the probability of winning the race—the by-product all competitors seek. But first you must commit yourself—and your organization—to a goal beyond merely beating others. You must define success as making the complete effort to maximize your ability, skills, and potential in whatever circumstances—good or bad—may exist.

Sometimes the competition you and your organization face will be bigger or stronger, more experienced or better financed. Regardless of the situation you face as a leader, you must believe and teach those under your leadership that success is theirs when together you summon the will to put forth everything you have. Doing so is under your control. At least, it should be.

I recognize that incorporating my definition of success—my philosophy—into your own leadership methods may not be easy

## WINNING IS A BY-PRODUCT.
## FOCUS ON THE PRODUCT: EFFORT

We live in a society obsessed with winning and being number 1. Don't follow the pack. Rather, focus on the process instead of the prize. Even during the height of UCLA's best seasons, I never fixated on winning—didn't even mention it. Rather, I did everything I could to make sure that all our players gave everything they had to give, both in practice and in games. The score will take care of itself when you take care of the effort that precedes the score.

to accomplish because it runs contrary to almost everything we see and hear nowadays, especially in the sports and business sections of the newspapers. Believe it or not, it was no different when I was a young man. Then and now, all most people care to think about is, "Who won the race?" Nevertheless, I tell you with certainty that when you accomplish the formidable task of making the full, 100 percent effort to do your best and teach your organization to do the same, you may call yourself a success because you are one.

## ONLY YOU KNOW IF YOU SUCCEED

In 1959–1960, UCLA struggled to stay above .500, and, in fact, we had to win our last game of the season to finish with a record of 14–12. From a win-loss point of view, it was the worst year I'd ever had as head coach at UCLA. Some fans began to grumble about our "poor" results: "The program is mired down," some said, "Wooden can't win in the postseason"; "UCLA doesn't have a post-season." And there were other things said along that line. I had a different opinion.

The 1959–1960 season had been a success and pleased me a great deal, especially when I recalled a prediction made by Sam Balter, a well-known broadcaster and sports writer. In assessing UCLA's chances at the start of the year, he said, "I'll push a peanut with my nose down The Miracle Mile in Beverly Hills if UCLA isn't below .500 this year." I received no calls from anyone who disagreed with Sam's prediction—and for good reason.

The preceding year—1958–1959—UCLA had been third in our conference. Four of the five starters on that squad wouldn't be returning, including future Olympic gold medalist Rafer Johnson, Denny Crum (later to coach Louisville to two NCAA national championships), and Walt Torrence, perhaps the best player on the team.

I've often said that as a leader I'd rather have a lot of talent and little experience than a lot of experience and little talent. In 1959–1960 we didn't have much of either. And there was an additional handicap beyond our control.

A few years earlier, the football programs at UCLA and some other schools in the conference had been hit by scandal: Payments to athletes had exceeded the conference's strict limits. The football programs at the schools involved in the infractions had been placed on probation, and part of the penalty included a strict restriction on postseason play such as the Rose Bowl.

The penalty against UCLA applied not only to football but to all sports including basketball, even though we had played by the rules. Thus, for a time, UCLA basketball had been ineligible for any postseason tournament play. Some athletes with considerable basketball talent who might have attended our school no doubt stayed away. All this—lack of experience, limited outstanding talent, ineligibility, and more—impacted on our ability to outscore opponents.

Therefore when I reflected on the 1959–1960 season with its 14–12 record and the sizable obstacles we faced, I was of the opinion that our team might have gotten my best coaching up to that point in my career. And nobody knew it but me. That was fine.

I also believe those student-athletes under my leadership came as close to reaching 100 percent of their potential as some of the later UCLA teams with perfect 30–0 seasons. The 1959–1960 group just didn't have the extreme level of talent the championship teams possessed. However, I do not judge success based on championships; rather, I judge it on how close we came to realizing our potential.

Consequently, in looking back at all 27 years I coached the Bruins, I wouldn't put another season ahead of 1959–1960 for what we achieved in that regard. I have great pride in what we accomplished that season.

The team had come very close to achieving the formidable task of maximizing their abilities individually and as a unit. We stuck together, worked hard, ignored what was beyond our control, and perfected—or tried hard to—those things that were under our control. Our team achieved success.

And yet the critics were complaining. (Sam never got around to rolling that peanut down the street with his nose.) We were a success, but nobody understood it except us. But us is what mattered.

It's like character and reputation. Reputation is what others perceive you as being, and their opinion may be right or wrong. Character, however, is what you really are, and nobody truly knows that but you. But you are what matters most.

In 1959–1960 only we knew that success had been achieved. Four years later, in 1964, UCLA became one of the few teams in college basketball history to achieve a perfect season—30 straight victories—and, in the process, win our first NCAA national championship. The experts now declared that I had finally become a success. Once again the critics were wrong.

Although I was perhaps a smarter and more effective leader, I was no more successful during 1964's championship season than four years earlier when we had to win our final game to stay above .500. The critics didn't understand this, but their standard for measuring me—and the team—was one I had little use for.

My standard of success counted most to me. It was how I measured things. And it started with what my father taught us back on the farm. That, in turn, led to the definition of success I conceived and wrote down in 1934 at Dayton High School.

That is the standard I used to judge myself in all areas throughout my adult life, including my teaching, coaching, and leadership. It is also how I have always measured the success of those under my leadership.

UCLA   BASKETBALL

John Wooden, Head Coach

SUCCESS

Success in coaching or playing should not be based on the
number of games won or lost, but rather on the basis of
what each individual did in comparison with others when
taking into consideration individual abilities, the
facilities with which you had wo work, the caliber of your
opponents, the site of the contests, etc.

True success comes only to an individual by self-satisfaction
in knowing that you gave everything to become the very best
that you are capable of.  As George Moriarty once said,
"Giving all, it seems to me, is not so far from victory."
Therefore, in the final analysis, only the individual himself
can correctly determine his success.  You may be able to
fool others, but you can never fool yourself.

It is impossible to attain perfection, but that should be
the goal.  Less than 100% of your effort toward obtaining
your objective is not success, regardless of how many games
were won or lost.

Others may have far more ability than you have, they may be
larger, faster, quicker, able to jump better, etc., but no
one should be your superior in team spirit,  loyalty, enthusiasm,
cooperation, determination, industriousness, fight, and character.
Acquire and keep these traits and success should follow.

# RULES TO LEAD BY

### Before You Can Lead Others, You Must Be Able to Lead Yourself.

Define Success for those under your leadership as total commitment
and effort to the team's welfare. Then show it yourself with your own
effort and performance. Most of those you lead will do the same.
Those who don't should be encouraged to look for a new team.

### Don't Hastily Replace the Old Fashioned with the New Fangled.

There is no progress without change, but not all change is progress.
Those ideas that have stood the test of time should not be carelessly
discarded just for the sake of change. Over the years I made lots of
changes, but the basics of how I brought teams together in pursuit
of success didn't change much at all. They still work today.

**Learn to Master the Four P's.**

The Four P's are planning, preparation, practice, and performance. These are the keys to successful execution. Learn to live the Four P's yourself, always giving them the highest priority, above even winning. It is the responsibility of the leader to make sure the team puts the Four P's first.

**Write Down the Tasks, Initiatives, and Actions That Each Member of Your Team Needs to Do to Perform at His or Her Peak Level.**

Get as specific as possible for each of your direct reports. Don't make the mistake of overemphasizing results (for example, "increase sales by 15 percent"). Instead, focus on those actions that an individual needs to take in order to most effectively and productively execute his or her assignment (for example, spend 20 percent more time with customers, make five more calls per week, or take a course in presentation skills).

# 1

# THE PYRAMID OF SUCCESS

*"Ultimately, I wanted the Pyramid's 15 building blocks
to define me as a leader."*

CREATING A WRITTEN DEFINITION of success was a necessary exercise when I started out because many parents came to me to protest classroom grades or the roles I had assigned their sons on a Dayton baseball or basketball team (the bench, most often).

I was increasingly upset, disgusted at times, to hear parents howl about their child's grade or role on the team when I knew it was often the best the youngster could do. It was unfair to the child and, in fact, counterproductive. How would you feel having worked hard, studied diligently, and paid attention in class—done your best—only to be called a loser? Most individuals, young or old, would simply quit trying. I did not want those under my supervision to ever quit trying.

As a coach I also recognized that I'd be judged to be successful or not with a similar grading system—the percentage method—without regard to circumstance, situation, or anything else. This, as I have described, was exactly what happened in 1959–1960.

Had I helped those under my supervision come as close as possible to reaching their potential, doing their best? Had I done my

The Player who gives his best is sure of success, while the player who gives less than his best is a failure.

best? These questions were not asked, even though they are the most relevant.

The behavior of those parents in Dayton prompted me to define, declare, and write down a fair and productive measurement of success—a grading system for all that truly does produce the best of which individuals are capable.

## DIRECTIONS TO THE DESTINATION

Success—peace of mind which is a direct result of self-satisfaction in knowing you did the best of which you are capable—became the stated objective or destination for those I was teaching and coaching. A destination is meaningless, however, without directions on how to get there.

How do you achieve success? In 1933 I didn't have the answer. Moreover, I knew that just having the answer was insufficient. A method of instruction would be needed to help me teach the qualities I deemed necessary for success.

Consequently, I began searching for a teaching tool that was tangible—something you could see, study, and follow as clearly as a map. Those things we can see tend to be more meaningful and memorable than objects we just hear about.

Glenn Curtis, my high school basketball coach at Martinsville, Indiana, was an exceptional motivator who used everything from poetry to pep talks to stimulate his players. Occasionally, he would even produce an old cardboard poster on which he had drawn a ladder with five or six rungs.

Each rung represented some important tip he wanted members of the Martinsville High School basketball team, the Artesians, to keep in mind—footwork, for example, or hustle. At the top of his ladder, of course, was success as he and most others saw it, namely, beating another team.

Well, the ladder idea got me to thinking. It was a good start, but I wanted something more comprehensive and illustrative. And, of course, my definition of success differed greatly from Coach Curtis's.

I remembered reading about the Great Pyramid of Giza in Egypt while I was a student at Purdue. It was the last of the Seven Wonders of the Ancient World. Built with blocks of red granite and pure limestone, some weighing up to 60 tons, the Great Pyramid was constructed on a massive foundation whose huge cornerstones were the biggest and most important of the whole structure.

Additional blocks, each carved with a specific purpose and position in mind, were then painstakingly ramped and hoisted into place, creating successive tiers—each one supported by what had come before.

There was a center, or heart, to the Great Pyramid, which then rose to an apex that towered 481 feet over the sands of the desert. For 4,300 years it remained the tallest structure on Earth. And despite its size, the Great Pyramid was built with such precision that, when it was completed after decades of labor, you couldn't slide a single playing card between its huge blocks of granite and limestone. Even in the twenty-first century it is considered one of the sturdiest and best-planned structures ever built. And I am not alone in this thinking. The great management writer and analyst Peter Drucker, when asked who were the greatest managers of all time, answered, "The builders of the great Pyramids."

An Egyptian proverb says, "Man fears time, but time fears the Pyramids." The Great Pyramid of Giza was built to last—and it did. The symbolism of all this effort seemed very practical to me.

## THE REQUISITES OF SUCCESS

I soon adopted the pyramid structure as my teaching tool. At first, I didn't know how many "blocks" it would contain, what the blocks would consist of, or in what order they would be positioned. All I knew was that success would be found at the apex and that each block leading to the top would represent a personal quality necessary for getting there. The Pyramid's blocks and tiers would be my specific directions on how those under my supervision could achieve success by realizing their own potential, both individually and as part of a team.

Along the way, I came to see that it would also provide the directions for my own coaching—a leadership guidebook—offering a code of conduct for those given the privilege of leading others into the competitive arena.

However, first I faced the task of determining what individual characteristics were required to reach the top. I took this responsibility seriously, and during the winter of my first year as a teacher and coach began reflecting on what the answer was. What precisely did it take to become a success?

For many years afterward, I evaluated and then carefully selected the values necessary for success, as I defined it, as well as the location each would occupy in the structure. After much reflection, trial and error, and some soul searching, I chose 15 fundamental values as blocks for my Pyramid of Success. I believe they are prerequisites for a leader and an organization whose goal is to perform at the highest level of which they are capable.

I completed the Pyramid of Success shortly before leaving Indiana State Teachers College in Terre Haute for California and UCLA. Subsequently, as the new 37-year-old head basketball coach of the Bruins I began each season by introducing my definition of success and the Pyramid to arriving student-athletes— handing out mimeographed copies and reviewing it with them. A large poster of the Pyramid hung behind my desk in the office at Kerckhoff Hall.

## YOUR OWN EXAMPLE COUNTS MOST

Most of all I attempted to demonstrate in my *behavior*—on and off the court—those qualities I hold so dear, the values within the Pyramid.

I believe there is no more powerful leadership tool than your own personal example. In almost every way the team ultimately becomes a reflection of their leader. For me, I wanted that reflection to be mirrored in the Pyramid of Success. I attempted to teach it mainly by my own example.

Was my Pyramid the reason UCLA won championships? No, there were many reasons. However, I believe the Pyramid played a very important part, just as it played a role in that 1959–1960 season, when we achieved success while losing almost as many games as we won.

The ultimate role of the Pyramid was not to produce championships; championships were a by-product. Rather, it provided directions for reaching one's own ultimate level of excellence as a part of a team or as leader of the team. The Pyramid didn't guarantee that UCLA would outscore an opponent, only that our opponent would face individuals—united as a team—who were fully prepared to battle hard and compete at their highest level. The score would take care of itself.

In some years that produced the great "surprise" of a 14–12 record while in other years it produced a national championship. In all years, except 1973–1974, it produced UCLA teams that knew what was required to achieve success and then went out and did it. Beyond the *X*s and *O*s of basketball, I wanted the blocks of the Pyramid to define us as a team. I also hoped it would define me as a leader.

Let me share those 15 personal qualities I selected and carefully positioned in the Pyramid of Success. The blocks are not made of red granite or pure limestone but of material much stronger and more durable—material available to you and your team when you look hard enough within yourself and ask those with whom you work to do the same.

A structure is only as strong as its foundation; mine began with two cornerstones that were chosen early in my search. There is no success without them.

## INDUSTRIOUSNESS

I was raised on a small farm where a healthy mule was considered a modern convenience. So I discovered quickly that nothing gets done if you stay in bed. You must rise early and work late. It became one of the first lessons my brothers and I learned: There is no trick, no easy way to accomplish the difficult task, no substitute for old-fashioned work. Without it crops aren't planted, corn won't grow, hay isn't harvested. You perish.

> "The heights by great men reached and kept,
> Were not attained by sudden flight.
> But they, while their companions slept,
> Were toiling upward in the night."
> —Henry Wadsworth Longfellow

For the Wooden family, hard work was as common as dirt—and dirt is common on a farm. Thus, the first block I chose for the Pyramid of Success—a cornerstone of the foundation—was self-evident: hard work. I called it Industriousness, because "work" as performed by most people isn't real work; rather, it's going through the motions, putting in time, enduring boredom.

Many will complain about a hard day at the office when, in fact, they didn't lift a finger or think a thought. That's not work. I had something else in mind, the kind of work in which you are fully engaged, totally focused, and completely absorbed. There is no clock watching and no punching in and out. Industriousness, for me, means true work.

I also knew intuitively that for Industriousness to occur, an equally important quality is required.

## ENTHUSIASM

Work without joy is drudgery. Drudgery does not produce champions, nor does it produce great organizations. You will not reach the top—success—if you and those you lead are wearily trudging along, waiting for the workday to end so you can move on to something you'd rather do.

**"Joy makes the longest journey too short."**

As a leader, you must be filled with energy and eagerness, joy and love for what you do. If you lack Enthusiasm for your job, you cannot perform to the best of your ability. Success is unattainable without Enthusiasm.

> Enthusiasm - Comes from "your heart being in your work." You must be enthusiastic if you are to stimulate others. The enthusiastic man does not recognize defeat and in tough moments his love of the game and great desire to impart the same love to others will do much to carry him over the rough spots.

Enthusiasm was quickly chosen as the second cornerstone in the Pyramid's foundation because it transforms work into Industriousness and catapults you to most productive heights.

Your Enthusiasm does the same for those you lead. The energy and enjoyment, drive and dedication you exude stimulate the team. Enthusiasm must be real, not phony. False enthusiasm is common and easily detected. If you are faking it, posing and pretending, those under your supervision will spot it and do likewise.

Enthusiasm comes from within and is expressed in different ways. It is not necessarily jumping up and down and making a lot of noise. My high school coach, Glenn Curtis, was very demonstrative in expressing his Enthusiasm. Ward "Piggy" Lambert, my great coach at Purdue, had a very controlled, intense manner. Both men, however, had genuine enthusiasm, and those they supervised were the beneficiaries of this excitement for the game.

When they are joined together, Industriousness and Enthusiasm become the driving force, the engine that powers all subsequent blocks of the Pyramid. To my knowledge, the most effective leaders have these qualities in full measure. Take Jack Welch, for example, the former CEO of General Electric and the man declared "Manager of the Century" by *Fortune* magazine. Mr. Welch transformed the century-old corporation into one of the biggest and most valuable in the world. Importantly, Enthusiasm was at the center of the leadership assets he possessed. Jack Welch loved his job—not liked it, *loved* it. His Enthusiasm was infectious, and it ignited the spirit and Enthusiasm of those he worked with.

I tried to have the same effect on the people I led.

These two qualities, Industriousness and Enthusiasm, were selected soon after I had chosen the Pyramid structure as my teach-

## INDUSTRIOUSNESS AND ENTHUSIASM ARE THE TWIN CORNERSTONES OF SUCCESS

Each of the foundation's cornerstones, by itself, is a force of considerable magnitude. Combined, Industriousness and Enthusiasm create an irreplaceable component of great leadership. Hard work and enthusiasm are contagious. A leader who exhibits them will find the organization does too.

ing tool. While other blocks were selected and discarded or moved to other locations within the Pyramid over the next 14 years, I never considered changing the cornerstone locations for Industriousness and Enthusiasm.

You will perish without hard work, without Industriousness. Industriousness is not possible without Enthusiasm. Success is unattainable without both of them.

## COMPLETING THE LEADERSHIP FOUNDATION

Between the cornerstones of Industriousness and Enthusiasm I placed three blocks that involve working with others: Friendship, Loyalty, and Cooperation. Industriousness and Enthusiasm can be realized independently, alone, by yourself. But most of what we do in life, especially sports and business, involves others.

The three qualities I chose to place between the cornerstones to complete the Pyramid's foundation involve positive interaction with people—so necessary for successful leadership.

## FRIENDSHIP

You may question the role of friendship in the context of leadership. Is it wise for a leader to become friends with those under his supervision? Will Friendship hinder correct decision making when hard choices are called for?

**"To Make a Friend, Be a Friend."**

I believe there are various kinds and degrees of Friendship based on a wide range of appreciations. We may have an acquaintance with whom we are friendly because of a shared interest in politics or sports; another whose humor we enjoy; some may be golfing, bowling, or fishing buddies; perhaps we have an old friend from high school whom we haven't seen in 20 years. All are friends in different and good ways—but not in the way I mean Friendship.

The two qualities of Friendship so important for a leader to possess and instill in team members are respect and camaraderie. To me these are the most noteworthy characteristics of true Friendship as it pertains to leadership.

Camaraderie is a spirit of goodwill that exists between individuals and members of a group—comrades-in-arms. Think of how much you'll give when asked to do so by someone you respect and with whom you share camaraderie. You'll give plenty—everything you've got. Those under your leadership will do the same if you show them this part of yourself.

Contrast that situation with a leader who lacks camaraderie and respect for and from those in the organization. Which leader will get the most out of the team? The difference is immense.

Thus, I sought and valued these two particular qualities of Friendship in my relationship with individuals on the team. I did not seek their affection nor wish to be "buddies." Mutual respect and camaraderie strengthen your team. Affection, in fact, may weaken it by causing you to play favorites.

I tried extremely hard not to have favorites, even though there were many players over the years for whom I did have great affection. I did not want my personal feelings—liking a person or not—to be apparent, to give the appearance of favoring one over another. I was not always successful in my endeavor.

John Ecker, a player I liked perhaps as much as any I ever coached, told me years later he thought I disliked him while he was a member of our team. I was unhappy to hear this information; nevertheless, I took comfort in knowing that I'd not treated him as a favorite even though he was one.

Although I went overboard perhaps in attempting to avoid the

## BE A FRIEND AND STILL BE PROFESSIONAL

Camaraderie is commendable—even necessary—with your direct reports, but do not play favorites, and do not allow your preferences to cloud your judgment. Respect and the spirit of goodwill that it engenders further strengthen your bond with those you lead. Friendship, as I have defined it, does not preclude professionalism. First and foremost, you are their leader, not their buddy.

appearance of favoritism in his case, this is preferable to being perceived as a leader who gives special treatment to his buddies. Such a perception can be very destructive.

Leadership is an imperfect science, and I have my share of imperfections. Nevertheless, while mistakes made in the process of trying to do the right thing may hurt, they should cause no guilt or shame. Seeking to create a team that shares camaraderie and respect—Friendship—is the right thing to do. And where it exists you'll find a formidable organization. That's why I chose to place Friendship in the foundation of the Pyramid of Success.

## LOYALTY

Loyalty is part of human beings' higher nature. It is also part of the nature of great teams and those who lead them. The power of Loyalty is the reason I placed it in the center of the Pyramid's foundation.

It is impossible to be a good leader without Loyalty to your organization—your team—just as it impossible to be a good citizen without Loyalty to your country. You must, of course, have the courage to be loyal to those you lead. Doing so is not always easy.

It starts, however, with Loyalty to yourself—your standards, your system, your values.

"To thine own self be true," Polonius advised his son, Laertes, in *Hamlet*. I cannot improve on Shakespeare, but I will expand just slightly: "First, do not betray yourself. Second, do not betray those you lead. This is Loyalty."

> "There is a destiny that
> makes us brothers,
> None goes his way alone.
> All that we send out to others,
> Comes back into our own."
> —Edwin Markham

A leader who has Loyalty is the leader whose team I wish to be a part of. And so do others.

People do not arrive at your doorstep with Loyalty. It comes when those you lead see and experience that your concern for their interests and welfare goes beyond simply calculating what they can do for you—how you can use them to your advantage.

I believe most people, the overwhelming majority of us, wish to be in an organization whose leadership cares about them, provides fairness and respect, dignity and consideration.

Do so and you find Loyalty in abundance from those you lead. You will find yourself in charge of an organization that will not waffle in the wind. You will find a group of individuals who will stay committed even when things get tough.

## LOYALTY WILL NOT BE GAINED UNLESS FIRST GIVEN

To be effective, you must have real Loyalty from those you lead. First, be true to yourself and your core values. Then be true to those under your leadership. Remember: "All that we send out to others, comes back to us." Send out Loyalty and it will be returned in abundance.

In sports and business, the connection between the leader and members of the team can be deeply personal. It involves so many crucial aspects of life, including the mental, emotional, and financial. Outside of marriage itself, the professional team you lead can be the strongest connection in your life. For that to happen, you must be true to yourself and your team. You must have Loyalty. And when you have it, you will get it from your team.

## COOPERATION

As a leader you must be sincerely committed to *what's* right rather than *who's* right. For this to occur, the final block of the Pyramid's foundation must be present and active: Cooperation.

> "When the best leader's work is done the people say, 'We did it ourselves.'"
> —Lao-tse

It is often difficult for a strong-willed leader to incorporate Cooperation, because listening to others, evaluating—embracing—their opinions and creativity, may seem to suggest uncertainty and doubt about your own judgment and convictions. The ego gets in the way of your eyes and ears. It's easy to get lost in your own tunnel vision.

An effective leader understands that it is a sign of strength to welcome honest differences and new ways of thinking from those on your team as well as from others. Progress is difficult when you won't listen. Cooperation is impossible if we refuse to consider the merits of contrary opinions.

A dictator-style leader has all the answers and no questions. This kind of boss demands performance according to unbending and unchanging personal ideas. And, it can work. However, a leader who incorporates the productive ideas and creativity of others makes it work better. That's what we want, not just making something work but making it work better and better.

This occurs when Cooperation is present, when you are more concerned with "What's right" than "Who's right." For many years I've described one of the differences between a good leader and a prison guard as Cooperation. When you carry a rifle, it is unnecessary to listen and learn, change and grow—prerequisites for good leadership.

I note, however, there is one similarity between a prison guard and a leader: Both have the final word. When a decision is made, it must be accepted by those on your team, or they must be encouraged to find another team.

Cooperation—the sharing of ideas, information, creativity, responsibilities, and tasks—is a priority of good leadership. The only thing that is not shared is blame. A strong leader accepts blame and gives the credit. A weak leader gives blame and accepts the credit.

In basketball one of the undervalued acts that I valued most was the assist—helping a team member to score. The assist in basketball epitomizes Cooperation. The assist is valuable in all organizations, helping someone to do her or his job better. It makes producers out of everyone; it makes everyone feel, "We did it ourselves."

## RULES TO LEAD BY

### Leadership Success Begins with a Solid Foundation.
The Pyramid of Success starts with the powerful cornerstone of Industriousness. Success requires hard work. Absent the quality of Industriousness, you will fail as a leader. Commit to work hard and then stay committed until you are able to identify a single great leader who achieved success without it. (You will not find one.)

### There Is No Substitute for Enthusiasm.
A leader needs a fire-in-the-belly drive in order to ignite the team. Few will follow someone who seems to lack fervor for a challenging

job. To spark others to extraordinary performance levels, you need authentic Enthusiasm. It cannot be forced or faked. You must truly welcome—embrace—the trials and tribulations of competition.

**Friendship, Loyalty, and Cooperation Complete the Foundation for Leadership.**

The best leaders are more interested in finding what's right than in always being right. They understand how much more can be accomplished if no one cares who gets credit. The interpersonal characteristics of Friendship (camaraderie and respect), Loyalty, and Cooperation create the sincere and solid bond necessary between you and those you lead. These are qualities that must be nurtured in your organization. Put them in place, and you will have built a foundation that will eventually bring forth success.

# 2

# THE PYRAMID'S
# SECOND TIER

*"Discipline yourself and others won't need to."*

THE PREVIOUS CHAPTER FOCUSED on the foundation blocks of my Pyramid of Success—Industriousness, Enthusiasm, Friendship, Loyalty, and Cooperation. You may agree that this is a strong lineup for your starting five. I view these five personal qualities as being essentially values of the heart and spirit, less cognitive than those that make up the second tier, which is the focus of this chapter.

What follows is less about heart and more about the head; more specifically, how you put your head to use as an effective leader. I chose four traits for the Pyramid's second tier that primarily involve control and direction of your mental faculties. For many, the first block is the most challenging.

## SELF-CONTROL

Getting to the top, even once, is arduous. Staying there, many say, is even more difficult. My own experience is that both getting there and staying there present unique and formidable challenges. To do either requires great Self-Control.

*Control* of self is essential for consistency in leadership and team performance. I view consistency as a trademark of the true competitor and effective leader. *Self-Control* is

**"Control of your organization begins with control of yourself."**

necessary in *all* areas.

The choices you make in your personal life affect your professional life. They are not two separate entities, and leaders who act as if they are will likely bring difficulties upon themselves. To be a true leader requires credibility and consistency in one's actions, and this is hard to achieve when you lack Self-Control.

It starts with control of your emotions, but it also extends to having the resolve to resist the easy choice, the expedient solution, and, at times, temptation in its various and alluring forms.

> Self-Control - Must keep his emotions under complete control and think clearly at all times. He can do this and still be a fighter who lets his boys know that he is back of them. Discipline forcefully when necessary, but be fair and hold no grudges or he will lose respect. Keep your poise at all times.

Self-Control in little things leads to control of bigger things. For example, the reason I prohibited profanity—a small issue—during practices was because it was usually caused by frustration or anger. I felt that a player who couldn't control his language when he got upset during a scrimmage would be more likely to lose control in more damaging ways during the heat of a competition—fouling, fighting, or making other poor decisions that would almost always hurt the team.

Forcing a player to monitor and control his language was a useful device for teaching control of oneself. Our players were well disciplined over the years because I believed and taught that a team lacking Self-Control will get outplayed and, usually, outscored. The same is true for a leader who lacks Self-Control—whose personal discipline is weak.

How did I teach this block of the second tier—Self-Control? First, by stating clearly that I prized consistency and that Self-Control was necessary to achieve it. Second, I did not tolerate behavior that demonstrated lack of control on the part of any player. On those occasions when an individual violated this dictum, he quickly found there was a price to pay.

But, in large part I tried to teach it using the same method that worked well for my father: his own example. Dad had steely control of himself, and I sought the same in my leadership. He taught Self-Control by having it. (For example, in my 40 years of coaching you will not find a player who can honestly tell you that he heard me use profanity.)

It took me years to reach Dad's level, but Self-Control became a most valuable asset in my attempt to deliver consistent performance in my coaching. I demanded it of myself and taught the same to those under my leadership. In fact, as I watched a game unfold there would occasionally be an almost guilty pleasure in seeing our team exert enough pressure to cause the opponent to lose control. I never wanted to see the situation reversed.

I viewed Self-Control as a sixth Bruin out on the court. This gave us quite an advantage. It will give your organization a similar edge,

## SELF-CONTROL CREATES CONSISTENCY— A HALLMARK OF GREAT LEADERSHIP

It starts at the top with you, the leader, and must be taught by word and deed to your entire team. The team must understand that Self-Control is highly prized; loss of control will not be tolerated.

but only when the leader—you—possesses Self-Control. A team with good discipline is simply a reflection of a self-disciplined leader.

## ALERTNESS

While casual observers characterize UCLA's championship teams as having tall superstars, they are incorrect. In fact, UCLA's first championship team in 1964 is perhaps the shortest ever to win a NCAA Division I basketball title. It wasn't much different in 1965 when UCLA won its second championship.

**"It's what you learn after you know it all that counts."**

What all our teams had in common was not height, but quickness—physical quickness, of course, but also something of equal value: mental quickness, that is, Alertness.

Alertness, the ability to be constantly observing, absorbing, and learning from what's going on around you, is a critical component for the individual in charge, the leader who strives for continuous improvement. You must constantly be awake, alive, and alert in evaluating yourself as well as the strengths and weaknesses of your organization and your competitors. In sports today, we see instantaneous adjustments during play—film, photos, and spotters in the booths with binoculars providing immediate information to coaches and players during the game.

Should it be different with you and your organization? The same sense of urgent observation—Alertness—must exist in you and be taught to those under your supervision. A leader who is sluggish in recognizing what's going on may soon be out of a job.

Alertness - Be alert to observe weak spots in the opposition, in your own team, note fatigue, etc., and be quick to make the necessary corrections.

My father liked to remind me that most of what I'd learn would come from others. This can only happen if you're alert and aware—eyes wide open and paying attention. A driver who's asleep at the wheel will crash; the same happens to organizations whose leader does not exhibit Alertness. Their common refrain? "I didn't see it coming."

Make sure that you, the leader, see it coming. In fact, leaders who prevail in the competitive environment are most often those who see things coming when their counterparts aren't even looking. Alertness makes this possible, and it is a trait common to those who lead organizations that consistently stay ahead of the competition.

Basketball is played between the ears as much as between the lines. This is true for your organization. Alertness is a potent weapon for a leader—a great attribute. An alert leader creates an organization filled with people who pay attention, are open-minded, and strive always for improvement. This is true in sports, and it certainly is true in business.

## ALERTNESS IS A "HEADS UP" HABIT

Leaders who exercise this value of the Pyramid constantly monitor the competitive landscape and are quick to identify trends, changes, opportunities, and potential threats. They see things before others because they make it a habit to be on guard, alert for early signs and signals that necessitate adjustments along the way. Consequently, they see what others aren't even looking for. They are quick to see weaknesses in their organization and correct them and quick to see a weakness in the competition and take advantage of it.

## INITIATIVE

A basketball team that won't risk mistakes will not outscore opponents. The same is true for any organization. Fouls, errors, and mistakes are part of the competitive process in sports, business, and elsewhere. Don't live in fear of making a mistake. In fact, Coach Lambert at Purdue summed it up like this: "The team that makes the most mistakes usually wins."

> "Boldness has genius, power and magic within it; They can't be revealed until you begin it."
> —Goethe

He was talking about the next block of the Pyramid: Initiative. The kinds of mistakes he was referring to are not the result of carelessness or sloppiness but the result of assertive action based on proper assessment of risk. In sports, action often must be taken instantaneously to capitalize on opportunity. In every organization, time is of the essence when opportunity knocks.

Many leaders instinctively behave like a young college basketball player who picks up three quick fouls in the first half and becomes tentative and timid. A coach will sit this player on the bench before he can hurt the team.

The tentative business leader, however, stays in the contest, to the eventual detriment of the group. Hesitancy, indecisiveness, vacillation, and fear of failure are not characteristics I associate with good leadership. I told our team many times: "Be quick, but don't hurry." By that, I meant to make a decision, take action; decide what you're going to do and do it. Keep this word of caution in mind: "Failure to act is often the biggest failure of all."

Initiate quickly but not carelessly or in a hurried manner that makes a miscue more likely. I applied this same advice to my own actions.

Do not be afraid of mistakes, even of failure. Use good judgment based on all available information and then use Initiative. The leader who has a fear of failure, who is afraid to act, seldom will face success.

I also believe a smart leader teaches those in the organization the difference between mistakes of *commission* and those of *omission*. The former are calculated to make things happen; the latter, mistakes of omission, result too often from trepidation, fear of doing something wrong, just like the basketball player who picks up three quick fouls in the first half.

> I want a hustling, fighting team that never has time to crab or complain to anyone about anything.

I rarely, if ever, criticized a player who tried in an intelligent way to make things happen out on the court, even when he failed. The same standard applies to leadership. A leader must have Initiative—the courage to make decisions, to act, and the willingness and strength to risk failure and take a stand even when it goes against the opinion of others.

## THE MOST EFFECTIVE LEADERS UNDERSTAND THAT FAILURE IS A NECESSARY INGREDIENT OF SUCCESS

No one can win every time he gets on the court or enters the marketplace with a new product or service. Mistakes, even failure, can be permissible so long as they do not result from carelessness or poor preparation. Losing can provide learning, thus preventing future errors. Remember Coach Lambert's perspective: Mistakes are a part of winning. Make sure they're the right kind of mistakes.

You'll do well to remember this bit of verse by Philip Paul Bliss:

*Dare to be Daniel!*
*Dare to stand alone.*
*Dare to have purpose firm,*
*Dare to make it known.*

That poem could be entitled Initiative. Without this block of the Pyramid, you will soon be passed by the competition whose leader has the courage of his convictions and the will to act on them—a leader with Initiative.

## INTENTNESS

Intentness is as important as any single block in my Pyramid. Without it you will falter, fade, and quit. I chose the word *Intentness* to convey diligence and determination, fortitude and resolve—persistence. All these traits are present in great leaders.

> "The one who once most wisely said,
> 'Be sure you're right, then go ahead.'
> Might well have added this to it,
> 'Be sure you are wrong before you quit.'"
> —Anon.

And what is so remarkable is that when Intentness exists in you, it also exists in your organization. Unfortunately, the reverse is also true. A leader lacking Intentness will find himself or herself leading a team intent on giving up.

Intentness also implies a firm resolve to stay the course over the long term rather than meandering all over the place in bursts of short-lived activity. Intentness keeps you in the game even when others tell you the game is over. The game is over only when the leader declares it so.

Good things take time, usually lots of time. Achieving worthwhile goals requires Intentness. There are setbacks, losses, unexpected reversals, hardships, and bad luck. Does the fight continue? The team will look to you for the answer.

When thwarted, you go over, under, or around. Perhaps you do the same thing again—only better and harder. In the face of severe adversity, this conduct is only possible with Intentness, the willingness to persevere when hardship is forced upon you and those you lead.

I had Intentness for 28 years as a coach at the high school and college level—intent on doing my best to help others do their best. In my twenty-ninth year of coaching, something remarkable occurred: UCLA won a national championship. Intentness was required for this to happen.

Industriousness and Enthusiasm are a powerful combination, essential to Success. But the great force they produce must be constant, ongoing, relentless, and unremitting—Intentness.

Two tiers of the Pyramid are now in place. Think for just a moment about what each of the nine qualities I have described means to your leadership. When you have successfully incorporated them into your own leadership methodology, you've set yourself apart from the vast majority of your competitors. You're already in a select group of leaders.

But, it is my experience that there's more required to achieve leadership success. Before we continue the journey, try to put these plays into your own playbook.

## RULES TO LEAD BY

### Leadership Starts with Self-Control.

Remember, "control of your organization begins with control of yourself." When you lose control, you sanction the same behavior for those under your leadership—the team. There is never an excuse for violating this imperative, and when you do, your credibility and consistency as a leader diminish accordingly.

### Be a Heads-Up Leader.

Make Alertness a habit. Take the necessary steps to see what's coming. The most effective leaders think two or three steps ahead. They know the details of their business and constantly monitor their surroundings, the inner workings of their organizations, their competitors, and anything else likely to affect the performance of their team.

### Do Not Fear Failure or Punish Initiative.

Even well-reasoned actions can fail. Mistakes and failed action are part of progress. An effective leader understands this—accepts it—and strives to make sure those missteps are not caused by sloppiness, haste, or poor judgment. Furthermore, when you punish your people for making a mistake or falling short of a goal, you create an environment of extreme caution, even fearfulness. In sports it's similar to playing "not to lose"—a formula that often brings on defeat.

### Make Sure Your Team Does Not Come Up Short in the Long Run—Intentness.

Call it focus, persistence, determination, or relentlessness, all add up to the same thing: You, the leader, must make sure your team doesn't wander off the path of persistence. Losing focus, giving a half-hearted effort, or quitting before the task is complete are all hallmarks of those who aspire to, but never acquire, success. Few things are more important—especially in challenging times—than leadership that personifies Intentness, an unremitting determination to press on.

# 3

# THE HEART OF THE PYRAMID

*"In the end, the choice you make makes you."*

REPORTERS OFTEN ASKED ME: "Do you have a formula for teaching basketball, Coach Wooden, a system?" My answer was, and is, succinct: "Yes: condition, fundamentals, and unity." It was a formula I learned from Ward "Piggy" Lambert, the remarkable Purdue basketball leader whose influence on me as a person, player, and coach was so enduring. Coach Lambert's formula, in expanded form, became the heart of my Pyramid of Success.

Ward Lambert was a revolutionary who was, in part, responsible for changing the way the game of basketball was played. His influence is still felt today, first and foremost, in modern basketball's fast style of play. Coach Lambert loved speed. However, in his early days the basketball was bigger and the game slower, not far after the era in which a jump ball followed every single field goal. It was start and stop, scores were low, and shots few and far between. Coach Lambert was one who challenged and changed this old style of basketball.

He taught us to compete at a furious pace with no stalling, time-outs, or slowdowns: Get the ball; run the ball; shoot the ball. Then get the ball again and do it all over again. He made us do this over and over throughout every practice and game.

The media sometimes called it a "fire wagon" style because the running never ceased. Few teams were playing basketball at the speed Ward Lambert demanded, and I was his principal speedster. During the season while other players might go through two or three pair of tennis shoes, I wore out one pair of Chuck Taylor Converse tennis sneakers almost every week. (That's part of the reason why when I became a coach I was so adamant about players putting on their sweat socks correctly. Some laughed at me for doing this, but I understood from personal experience the absolute necessity of taking care of your feet—how folds, creases, and wrinkles could cause blisters that distract and then diminish performance.)

Coach Lambert's radical style of fast play had three primary requirements: condition, fundamentals, and unity. I adopted his style of basketball when I began coaching and kept to it for the 40 seasons that followed.

> Feeling that the ability to properly and quickly execute the fundamentals, being in excellent condition, and having a fine unselfish team spirit are the heart of any successful team, I have tried to permit those ideas to be the most influential at arriving at a satisfactory team offense and defense.

But I also realized these same three qualities transcended the game of basketball. Successfully applied, they had the potential to teach what it takes to achieve success off the court, in life and in leading any type of organization or team. Their importance is such that I placed them directly in the middle of my Pyramid of Success—at the center of the structure.

## CONDITION

Physical conditioning, of course, was Coach Lambert's first goal because he understood that players had to be strong to withstand the rigors of his demanding basketball style. However, in choosing

Condition as a quality for the center of my Pyramid, I went well beyond physical conditioning.

**"Ability may get you to the top, but it takes character to stay there."**

*Physical condition! - attained and maintained more by mental and moral conduct off the floor than by time on the floor.*

I believe that to achieve one's potential as a leader in any organization you need mental and moral strength. In fact, you cannot attain proper physical fitness unless it's preceded by mental and moral Condition. How does one attain moral Condition? Long lists of rules are the usual prescription, but I've offered a common-sense method for decades: Practice moderation and balance in all that you do. This advice, easy to remember, is also very effective.

Following a grueling basketball practice aimed, in part, at building up the players' physical strength, I would advise them of the following: "All we've worked so hard to accomplish on the court today can be torn down quickly, in a matter of minutes, if you make the wrong choices between now and our next practice."

I cautioned them that when moderation and balance are lacking in their choices and subsequent actions, the team can be damaged; dissipation is destructive. To help them understand what I meant—that accountability was their responsibility—I occasionally posted the following reminder on our bulletin board or recited it to individuals about whom I had special concerns:

*There is a choice you have to make,*
*in everything you do.*
*So keep in mind that in the end,*
*the choice you make, makes you.*
*—Anon.*

Of course, the choices made by the leader count most of all because they ultimately make, or break, the organization. This is as true in business as it is in sports.

The leader must set the example, not only in areas of right and wrong—character, of course—but elsewhere. Workaholics, for example, lack balance. Imbalance, in my opinion, is a weakness that sooner or later causes problems. The first problem is likely to be inconsistency in performance.

Thus, in my own life I tried hard to keep my job, coaching basketball and for many years teaching English, from taking over other areas of life such as family and friends. I strongly believe a good leader has the correct priorities and seeks good balance. Endlessly working 24 hours a day, seven days a week is an imbalanced set of priorities and eventually hurts your performance in all areas. When you hurt yourself, you hurt your team.

Being in good mental and moral Condition is crucial to strong leadership. It starts with good physical Condition, because a leader lacking it is less likely to summon the strength to stand up and fight for beliefs, ideals, and standards.

You may have observed how those who weaken themselves physically often fall prey to an assortment of lapses in the area of good judgment. Being in good physical, mental, and moral Condition

## PHYSICAL, MENTAL, AND MORAL CONDITION IS LEADERSHIP STRENGTH

Effective leaders seek balance in their personal and professional lives. Imbalance in one or the other creates vulnerability in both. Physical fitness is crucial. So is mental and moral fitness.

is essential to being a consistently effective and productive leader. That's why Condition is in the center of the Pyramid, so close to the heart of its structure.

## SKILL

Fundamentals for Coach Lambert meant having a comprehensive knowledge of the *X*s and *O*s and physical mechanics of basketball—where to go and when to go there, how to shoot correctly, and more.

**"When I am through learning, I am through."**

I felt this requirement was true, not only in basketball for both a coach and the players, but for any leader and organization. You've got to know what you're doing. Thus, Skill is at the heart of the Pyramid. You must know all facets of your job—not just parts of it—and be able to execute quickly and correctly. Being prepared to do all that your job requires will quickly separate you and your organization from much of the competition.

I saw many coaches who could teach offense but who were limited in their knowledge of defense. Similarly, I had players who were skilled shooters but couldn't get open. Others were skilled at getting open but couldn't shoot.

Whether in basketball or business, you must be able to perform *all* aspects of your job, not just part of it. You must be able to "get open" and "shoot." One without the other makes you a partial performer, someone who can be replaced because your skills are incomplete.

The range of skills necessary for leadership, of course, differs from job to job and organization to organization. Those skills required to manage a small business differ from those needed to lead a Fortune 500 company, just as skills needed for coaching basketball differ from those necessary for coaching baseball. But regardless of the specific skills required in a profession, you must master all of them.

## ENCOURAGE LEARNING THROUGHOUT YOUR ORGANIZATION

The best leaders understand that to successfully compete at any level requires continuous learning and improvement. Unless the leader communicates this up and down the line—and puts mechanisms in place to ensure it gets done—your team will not be at 100 percent in its performance level.

The best leaders are lifelong learners; they take measures to create organizations that foster and inspire learning throughout. The most effective leaders are those who realize it's what you learn after you know it all that counts most.

I recognized this fact quickly when I began my career as a basketball coach. While I understood the fundamentals necessary for playing the game, I had little understanding of the second part of my job, namely, the ability to teach the fundamentals of basketball. Once I recognized this, I set out on a journey to educate myself to become a better teacher. That, in turn, made me a better leader. I wanted to be able both to get open and to shoot. I wanted my skills to be as complete as possible.

## TEAM SPIRIT

In the process of learning to become a better leader, one of the most important things I learned was something that transcended the *X*s and *O*s on my chalkboard. That "something" became the final block in the center of my Pyramid.

"The star of the team is the team."

Coach Lambert called it *unity*, a good word, but I wanted a more expressive description of this valuable quality so directly linked to the success of an organization. *Teamwork* is an obvious choice of words, but it suggested to me a cold efficiency in performance, something akin to a well-oiled machine, everybody doing his or her job correctly. Of course, there is nothing wrong with everybody doing his or her job correctly, but I sought something more. I wanted a powerful and efficient machine, but one that also had heart and soul. The words I chose to describe the presence of this powerful block are *Team Spirit*.

Initially, I defined Team Spirit as "a willingness to sacrifice personal interest or glory for the welfare of all," but there was something in the definition that bothered me, something not quite right. Nevertheless, I left the description in place for several years. Then one morning at breakfast I read a newspaper story about a particular individual who repeatedly demonstrated an "*eagerness*" to do some activity that he was involved in. While I don't recall what the activity was, I recognized immediately what I had been unknowingly searching for.

When it came to Team Spirit, willingness was not enough; eagerness was the exact description of what I sought in myself and in those I coached. A willingness to be selfless suggests a begrudging aspect of doing what is required for the team. I wanted each player to be eager to sacrifice personal interests for the good of the group. To me, there is all the difference in the world between willingness and eagerness. Thus, I changed that single word in the definition.

Team Spirit—an eagerness to sacrifice personal interests or glory for the welfare of all—is a tangible driving force that transforms individuals who are "doing their jobs correctly" into an organization whose members are totally committed to working at their highest levels for the good of the group. Members of such an organization are unselfish, considerate, and put the goals of the organization above their own, even at the expense of their own personal desires. When this happens—and the leader is the one who makes it happen—the result is almost magical.

Just as Enthusiasm ignites Industriousness, Team Spirit is the cat-alyst for enhancing Condition, Skill, and all the supporting blocks of the Pyramid to extraordinary levels. It is so because it creates a deep desire on the part of each individual to do everything within his or her power to improve and strengthen the organization.

Team Spirit has the potential to increase the productivity of your organization exponentially: Your team becomes greater than the sum of its players; the organization greater than the number of em-ployees on its payroll. Each individual revels in the glory of the group rather than the glory of the individual. "What can I do to help our team today?" replaces "How can I get ahead?" (Of course, I believe the answer to the latter is found in the former.)

Team Spirit was difficult to teach when I was coaching, perhaps even more so today, although I doubt it. Television has made actors—stars—out of many players, coaches, officials, and refer-ees. In similar fashion, in recent years some CEOs have become media personalities whose own star, they seem to believe, shines brighter than the organizations they lead.

## HIRE AND REWARD THOSE EAGER TO PUT TEAM INTERESTS ABOVE THEIR OWN

If you only remember one thing from this book, the following point is perhaps it: The star of every successful team is the team. Individuals don't win games, teams do. Finding the right players who put the interests of the team ahead of their own involves probing for the qualities discussed in this and the pre-vious two chapters. It also requires finding mature individuals who understand that what helps the organization ultimately helps them.

There is only one star that counts: the team. Any organization whose leader seeks stardom at the expense of the team is one I would not want to join, regardless of the paycheck. That attitude goes against everything I believe about effective leadership and great teams. Similarly, a player who is more concerned with his or her own statistics rather than those of the team is a player I welcome on the opponent's side of the court. The presence of such an individual weakens the team and makes it vulnerable during competition to a disciplined group filled with Team Spirit.

Team Spirit is one of the most tangible "intangibles" I have ever encountered. It's difficult to see; you *feel* it. And it's a powerful feeling for an organization to have.

## GETTING TO THE TOP

The 12 Pyramid blocks I have so far described have been carefully chosen. Each has a unique purpose, and there is logic behind its position in the pyramid. Industriousness and Enthusiasm make up the foundation; they must be present at the outset, or nothing will be accomplished. They power all that follows.

To them we must add the qualities of the heart—Friendship, Loyalty, Cooperation—which allow you to create a powerful and honest bond with those in your organization. Have the courage to offer them, and they will, in turn, be offered back. Those few who don't reciprocate must be strongly encouraged to move on.

Upon this strong foundation—Industriousness, Enthusiasm, Friendship, Loyalty, and Cooperation—I placed a second tier, the disciplines of Self-Control, Alertness, Initiative, and Intentness. These four qualities are personal characteristics that, when combined with the Pyramid's foundation, create an increasing avalanche of productive, positive, and unrelenting leadership force.

Next comes the center of the Pyramid—Coach Ward Lambert's

essential threesome in greatly expanded form: Condition, Skill, and Team Spirit. Considered in isolation, this third tier of values constitutes a remarkable set of personal assets. However, as additions to your rising Pyramid of Success, they elevate you, the leader, propelling you very close to the top. Now, something quite powerful is about to occur.

**"As ye sow, so shall ye reap."**

Each of these 12 blocks is necessary, in my opinion, for leaders and organizations to excel, to become extraordinary. However, these qualities do not come easily. Great results come only with great effort. The Pyramid of Success is no exception.

However, when you have given your best to assemble these three tiers, they will, in turn, give something significant back to you: a rich and rewarding harvest, one that will take you and your organization the rest of the way.

## POISE

I define *poise* as being true to oneself, not getting rattled, thrown off, or unbalanced regardless of the circumstance or situation. This may sound easy, but Poise can be a most elusive quality in challenging times. Leaders lacking Poise panic under pressure.

**"If you can keep your head when all about you Are losing theirs and blaming it on you."**

**—R. Kipling**

Poise means holding fast to your beliefs and acting in accordance with them, regardless of how bad or good the situation may be. Poise means avoiding pose or pretense, comparing yourself to others, and acting like someone you're not. Poise means having a brave heart in all circumstances.

You'll know you possess Poise when you achieve what Rudyard Kipling described in his poem written a hundred years ago:

*If you can meet with Triumph and Disaster*
*And treat those two impostors just the same . . .*

That's Poise: not being thrown off stride in what you believe or how you behave because of outside events.

The competitive environment increasingly challenges your composure and equanimity as the stakes increase and the challenges to you and your organization mount. Few characteristics are more valuable to a leader than Poise, especially when she or he is under pressure. And that's what leaders are paid to do, perform under pressure.

When Poise is present, you'll perform at your own personal best because it precludes panic. You'll understand what you're supposed to do—and do it even when the odds are against you, even when everyone else says you'll fail. And even when they say you'll win.

How do you acquire Poise? In fact, you don't. Poise acquires you. It is part of the harvest you reap near the top of the Pyramid.

In spending many years thinking about the requirements necessary for success, I was eventually startled to see that when an individual acquires and implements the first 12 hard-won blocks of the Pyramid, a fourth tier arrives unexpectedly and without fanfare. Suddenly it is there, part of you and your leadership style and substance: Poise. In effect, Poise is a powerful gift from the Pyramid of Success. And, where you find Poise you will also find its valuable companion, which I placed next to it near the top of the Pyramid.

## CONFIDENCE

There is perhaps no stronger steel than well-founded self-belief: the knowledge that your preparation is complete, that you have done all things possible to ready yourself and your organization for the competition, whatever form it comes in.

Confidence cannot be grafted on artificially. Real abiding Confidence, like Poise, is earned only by tenaciously pursuing and attaining those assets that allow you to reach your own level of competency—the potential you have within. For me, those assets are contained and provided by the Pyramid of Success.

**"You must earn the right to be confident."**

Confidence must be monitored so that it does not spoil or rot and turn to arrogance. Arrogance, or elitism, is the feeling of superiority that fosters the assumption that past success will be repeated without the same hard effort that brought it about in the first place. Thus, I have never gone into a game assuming victory. All opponents have been respected, none feared. I taught those under my supervision to do the same. In fact, the quality of our opponent had nothing to do with my own Confidence.

The other team was not part of my equation. Rather, I drew strength, Confidence, from the sure knowledge that I had done all things possible to prepare myself and our team to perform at our highest level in competition. The opponent might perform at a higher level—or not. I didn't concern myself with the other team's preparation and potential; I just concentrated on ours.

Success requires Poise and Confidence. They come with proper preparation. Acquiring the personal characteristics and values of the Pyramid, I believe, constitutes proper preparation. When you have made the effort to prepare to the fullest extent of your ability—and do not underestimate the great challenge of proper and complete preparation—you will reap the crowning block of the Pyramid of Success.

## COMPETITIVE GREATNESS

For more than half a century I have defined Competitive Greatness as follows: "A real love for the hard battle, knowing it offers the opportunity to be at your best when your best is required."

**"A true competitor loves the battle."**

The great competitors I have played for, coached, and admired have shared a joy derived from the struggle itself—the journey, the contest. They have done so because only in that supreme effort is there an opportunity to summon your best, a personal greatness that cannot be diminished, dismissed, or derided because of a final score or bottom line.

Competitive Greatness is not defined by victory nor denied by defeat. It exists in the effort that precedes those two "impostors" as well as their accomplices: fame, fortune, and power—measurements of success I rejected long ago.

There is nothing tiresome or trite in the old adage, "When the going gets tough, the tough get going." I have tried hard to meet that criterion and teach it to others throughout my life. At the exact moment when the going gets tough, the thrill of competition gets going for a leader who has acquired Competitive Greatness.

I believe this is one of the most crucial concepts you can convey to those within the organization, namely, a love for the hard bat-

Game Competition

1. Have courage and do not worry. If you do your best, never lose your temper, and never be out-fought or out-hustled, you have nothing to worry about. Without faith and courage you are lost.

2. Have respect without fear for every opponent and confidence without cockiness in regard to yourself.

3. Think all of the time. Study your opponent and yourself all of the time for the purpose of increasing your effectiveness and diminishing his.

4. Never be a spectator while in the game. Be doing something at all times, even if it is only being a decoy.

5. Team work is essential. Unselfish team play and team spirit is one of the foremost essentials for success when any group are working together.

6. Be at your best when your best is needed. Enjoy the thrill from a tough battle.

tle, and the test it provides against a worthy opponent. The hard struggle is to be welcomed, never feared. In fact, when you define success this way, the only thing to fear is your own unwillingness to make the full, 100 percent effort to prepare and perform at the highest level of your ability. A leader who is a Great Competitor teaches the organization the same thing.

When you have achieved Competitive Greatness, you have arrived at the top, prepared to bring out your best in yourself and your team. You are ready for whatever the battle brings. Here is how the American sportswriter Grantland Rice describes it in his poem "The Great Competitor":

> *Beyond the winning and the goal,*
> *beyond the glory and the fame,*
> *He feels the flame within his soul,*
> *born of the spirit of the game.*
> *And where the barriers my wait,*
> *built up by the opposing Gods,*
> *He finds a thrill in bucking fate*
> *and riding down the endless odds.*
> *Where others wither in the fire*
> *or fall below some raw mishap,*
> *Where others lag behind or tire*
> *and break beneath the handicap.*
> *He finds a new and deeper thrill*
> *to take him on the uphill spin,*
> *Because the test is greater still,*
> *and something he can revel in.*

The struggle itself, the test, is what gives value to the prize and is something the competitive leader truly revels in. It is your responsibility to pass this on to those under your leadership.

Many years ago, when I had the great honor of leading others, I truly felt that if I had been a good teacher, I could sit in the stands during a game without witnessing any diminution in the quality of UCLA's performance—but only if I had done my job correctly; if I had taught Competitive Greatness to our team.

## FAITH AND PATIENCE

On the journey to Success, you will face frustration and fatigue, setbacks and serious obstacles; but a leader must remain undaunted. Thus, I added mortar at the top of the Pyramid in the form of Patience and Faith. At the apex they are symbolic and remind us that these two qualities must be present throughout the Pyramid, holding the blocks and tiers firmly in place. A leader must have Faith that things will work out as they should—a boundless belief in the future.

A wise leader also knows that accomplishing important things takes time. If difficult goals could be achieved quickly, more people would be achievers. But, most people, and many leaders, lack real Patience. Benjamin Franklin understood its value quite well: "Genius is nothing but a greater aptitude for patience."

Success is always attainable when defined correctly, that is, as making the effort to do the best of which you are capable. With that as your standard you will not fail. The 15 personal qualities, these durable blocks of the Pyramid, if embraced and acted upon, will elevate you and your organization to success.

My father's words described it well: "When you've done your best you may call yourself a success." You may also call yourself a Great Competitor—a leader who resides at the top.

## SUCCESS

As a teacher, coach, and leader, my goal was always to help those under my leadership reach the ultimate level of their competency,

"Success is peace of mind which is a direct result of self-satisfaction in knowing you made the effort to do the best of which you are capable."

both individually and as productive members of our team.

The 15 personal qualities of the Pyramid became a virtual leadership guidebook, a clear and concise method of illustrating what is required for achieving success as I have defined it. In precise words, it illustrates what I expected of those under my leadership and what they could expect from me: "As a teacher, the Pyramid is my textbook. Success is my subject matter."

Are you a Success? Only you can answer that question now and in the future.

Am I a Success? I believe I am, but not because of any final scores, titles, or championships.

## SEEK SATISFACTION IN THE EFFORT

When I'm asked, "Coach Wooden, how did you win those championships?" I reply, "Our team won championships, not

## TRUE SUCCESS—PERSONAL GREATNESS— SHOULD NOT BE DEFINED BY THE FINAL SCORE OR BOTTOM LINE

Recognition of this key truth—a central tenet of my philosophy—is essential to authentic leadership: Don't allow others, including your competitors, to define you or your organization. Instead, define yourself and those you lead by the qualities and characteristics of the Pyramid and its definition of Competitive Greatness and Success.

me. Furthermore, my success comes not from championships, but the knowledge that I did everything possible to be the best teacher, coach, and leader I was capable of being. The quality of that effort is where I found—and continue to find—success. Those championships were a "by-product."

While others will judge you strictly in relation to somebody or something else—the final score, the bottom line, or championship—this is neither the most demanding nor the most productive standard.

Throughout my career I did not allow others to make me adopt their standard, their definition of what constitutes success. The highest, purest, and most difficult standard of all, the one that ultimately produces one's finest performance—and the great treasure called "peace of mind"—is that which measures the quality of your personal effort to reach Competitive Greatness.

*Regarding pressure - largely self-imposed by every truly conscientious coach, no regrets if you can answer to yourself.*

That is the standard I have applied for most of my professional life, in preparing myself and others for competition, over many years of teaching, coaching, and leadership.

Did I succeed? Yes, but only because I can look at myself in the mirror and honestly say, "I did my best—near 100 percent—to become the best of which I was capable." I am proud of my effort and derive the greatest satisfaction from it. Today, when I look back over those decades, I can hold my head high just like I wanted our players to do when they walked off the court after a game or practice. I believe you can't separate who you are from your leadership. For me the foundation of my own leadership—who I am—is contained in the Pyramid of Success.

And it all started with the practical wisdom that my father taught my brothers and me back on our family farm in Indiana.

## RULES TO LEAD BY

**Condition Your Team to Love the Struggle.**
The teams that compete at the highest level love the thrill of the contest. They may have winning in their heads, but they have a love for the effort and struggle in their hearts. A strong leader inspires teams to relish the competition itself and view the outcome as a by-product—an important by-product, yes, but still a by-product.

**Remember That Success Can Take Months—or Years—to Achieve but Can Be Undone in Minutes.**
This is why conditioning—physical, mental, and moral—is so important. A leader must impress upon his or her team the paramount importance of ownership and personal accountability.

**Never Allow Anyone Else to Define Your Success.**
Only you, the leader can and should define the finish line—Success. Others will attempt to force their definition upon you. Don't allow them to do it. Define it properly, and Success along with Competitive Greatness will belong to you and your team.

**Organizations Succeed When They Become More Than the Sum of Their Players.**
That's one of the real tests of any leader, making the whole more than the sum of its parts. No team will consistently succeed unless the leader is able to achieve this critical goal.

1. You are in UCLA for an education. I wa[nt eve]ry boy to ea[rn]
and receive his degree. Keep that fir[st] in your thoughts
but place basketball second.

## PART 2

# LESSONS IN LEADERSHIP

UCLA   BASKETBALL

John Wooden, Head Coach

TEAM SPIRIT

[We] want no "one man" players, no "stars." We want a [team]
[made] up of five boys at a time, each of whom is a forward,
[guard] and center combined; in other words, each boy should
[be ab]le to score, out-jump or out-smart one apponent, [and] prev[en]t [an]
[an] opposing team from scoring, as the occassion dema[nd]s.

[A] chain is stronger than its weakest link, no team is stronge[r than]
[its] weakest boy. One boy attempting to "grandstand" can
[wreck] the best team ever organized. [We] must be "one for all" [and]
["all] for one" with every boy giving [his best] every secon[d]
[of th]e game. The team is first, individual [stars are] second.
[Ther]e is no place for selfishness, egotism, or envy [on] [our] sq[uad].

[We] want a squad of fighters afraid of no club, not cocky,
[conc]eited, a team that plays hard, plays fair, but plays to w[in]
[alway]s remembering that "a team that won't be beaten, can't be..."

# 4

# GOOD VALUES ATTRACT
# GOOD PEOPLE

*"The force of character is cumulative."*
*—Ralph Waldo Emerson*

WHEN I BEGAN COACHING I picked up a little extra money playing basketball on weekends with a semipro team in Indiana, the Kautskys, run by a good and decent man named Frank Kautsky, a grocer. My pay was $50 a game.

I was a good free throw shooter back then, and at one point over a period of many, many games sank 100 in a row. When I sank the one-hundredth free throw, Mr. Kautsky asked the officials to stop the game momentarily. Then he walked out onto the court and announced to the crowd that he was rewarding me for making 100 straight free throws with a brand new one hundred dollar bill. Of course, the crowd loved it and so did Nellie Wooden, who was soon holding the money for safekeeping.

Keep in mind that Mr. Kautsky had no obligation to pay me anything extra for making 100 or 1,000 straight free throws. It was not part of our agreement, nor did I expect even an extra penny for doing my job as best I could. He did it because that's the kind of man Frank Kautsky was.

A couple of years later I started the season playing for another team because it was based closer to home. The pay was the same—

$50 a game—but it was going to save me a lot of travel, which meant I could spend more time with Nellie and our youngsters, Nancy Anne and Jim.

Early in the season we were scheduled to play in Cleveland, and at the last minute I decided to drive there with a teammate who needed a ride. Unfortunately, we got caught in a blizzard along the way and were slowed down to about 10 miles an hour on a narrow highway caked with ice and snow. After a few hours of torturous driving I stopped at a filling station to call our team owner in Cleveland to explain our predicament and let him know that we might be late for the game. He said, "I hope you have better luck than those other two folks who tried to drive through this storm." I asked, "What happened to them?" The owner replied, "They're in the morgue."

My friend and I pressed on anyway and got to the auditorium at halftime with our team trailing by several points. We both suited up quickly, and when the game resumed I was on the court, played well, and helped our team come out on top.

Afterward, I showered and went in to collect my pay from the owner, who, thanks to the victory, was wearing a big smile on his face. As he congratulated me on my performance—"Nice going, Johnny. We needed you in the game to win."—he handed me an envelope with my pay in it. As he continued talking, I opened it and saw that it contained $25, half what had been agreed upon.

"Where's the rest of my pay?" I asked. He looked at me and said, "Wooden, you missed the entire first half of the game because you were late getting here. I'm paying you for the half you played—25 bucks."

Right there he revealed his true colors. My friend and I had risked our lives driving through that snowstorm for him, and I had then helped his team secure victory. But, as I learned when he handed me the money, all this meant very little to him; it meant a lot to me. His values were not my values.

We had one more game scheduled that weekend, so I told him I wanted the rest of my pay for the game we had just played plus $50 in advance for the next day's game. Otherwise, I was heading home.

There was some hesitation, but he realized that he needed me on court the following day because they expected a full house and a boisterous crowd. The owner paid up even though it was clear to me he did it grudgingly.

The next afternoon I played the entire game and we outscored them without much trouble, but that was it for me; I couldn't play for such a person. After the game I resigned and signed up again with the Kautskys, a team run by a leader with a decent set of values, someone I respected and who respected me and what I was willing to give to his team, namely, everything I had.

What happened in Cleveland taught me a good lesson. I saw how character—doing the right thing—is fundamental to successful leadership. It became more and more apparent over the years of my own coaching, including for UCLA.

> "Most anyone can withstand adversity, but to test a man's character, give him power."
> —Lincoln

## SHARED VALUES

Whether Kareem Abdul-Jabbar is the greatest college basketball player of all time is a question better left for others to decide. He was, however, in my opinion, the most valuable player in the history of the college game. As a professional, he continued to perform at extraordinary levels with the Milwaukee Bucks and the Los Angeles Lakers, and became the NBA's all-time leading scorer, a record he holds to this day.

Kareem was known as Lewis Alcindor, Jr., when he played for UCLA. During his three years on the varsity team, the Bruins won three consecutive NCAA championships and 88 of the 90 games on our schedule. Had he been allowed to play basketball his first year at school—freshmen were ineligible back then—I believe UCLA might have won another NCAA championship. My reason is simple: In a preseason game, Lewis's freshman team easily defeated our varsity squad 75–60. The varsity Bruins had won the NCAA championship several months earlier. Onlookers couldn't believe what had happened to the defending national champions.

In fact, the score would have been even more lopsided if Gary Cunningham, coach of the freshman squad, hadn't pulled the starters, Lewis included, from the floor in the last minutes of play. Nevertheless, he scored 31 points, with 21 rebounds against the NCAA national basketball champions. (Some reporters thought that I'd be upset about the loss, but I took comfort in the fact that in 12 months Lewis would be wearing a UCLA varsity uniform.)

His presence obviously had a profound, positive, and lasting impact on our program. But before it did, something had a profound impact on Lewis. That "something" was values. I believe Lewis's story—like my lesson in Cleveland—has meaning for any organization; specifically, that good values attract good people.

## BASKETBALL IS ABOUT MORE THAN BASKETBALL

When Lewis Alcindor, Jr., was a student-athlete at New York's Power Memorial High School, he was gaining national fame for his great physical skills and ability to play the game of basketball. He was also an outstanding student who came from a good home. Colleges and universities nationwide courted him with such abandon, lavishing praise and promises on the gifted seven-foot two-inch student-athlete, that, at times, it perhaps bordered on the embarrassing. (However, Abe Lemons, the great Oklahoma basketball coach, told me later he would never have Lewis on his team after what the young man said to him when offered a scholarship. I asked, "Abe, what was it Lewis told you that was so offensive?" Coach Lemons replied, "He told me, 'No.' ")

While nearly every college basketball coach in America wanted Lewis to choose their school and many contacted him directly about doing so, I would not initiate a meeting. Throughout my career I had a policy of doing virtually no off-campus recruiting of student-athletes. In those rare instances when I did visit a young man and his family at their home—perhaps 10 or 12 over a period of 29 years as a college coach—it had to be preceded by an inquiry directly from them or someone speaking on their behalf. I would not make the first move to meet a prospective student, and Lewis was no exception. My reason was simple: I didn't think I should have to talk a young man into attending UCLA and playing basketball for the Bruins. If he wasn't eager to join us, then perhaps it was best he attended another school.

I believe my policy, in effect, helped keep things in perspective for the young man. Also, it may have had the added benefit of weeding out individuals who were simply shopping around for the best offer, waiting for me, and others, to come and "sell" them on our school. If any selling was going to be done, I preferred to have the young athletes try and sell me something; let them take the initiative, reach out and contact us. That would serve as a good indication they had a strong desire to come to UCLA and be a part of our team.

My policy of not contacting players had its downside, of course, but one with which I was willing to live. Prior to Lewis's emergence

> ## SEEK THOSE WITH A FIRE-IN-THE-BELLY ENTHUSIASM FOR YOUR ORGANIZATION
>
> **I** always felt that my nonrecruiting policy for players was the right thing to do—a productive part of the screening process. Before I talked to an individual about joining us, I first wanted to see evidence of his desire to be a part of the Bruins. The last thing you want is people in your organization who had to be talked into being there, who needed convincing that your team was worthy of them. When hiring, be diligent in discerning what the individual's motives are; be alert for those who express a sincere desire to join and contribute to your team and show some understanding of who and what your organization is all about. Recruiting should be a two-way street.

as a high school basketball star, two other talented and tall young men had gained prominence—Wilt Chamberlain, at Philadelphia's Overbrook High School, and Bill Russell, at McClymonds High School in Oakland.

While I would have been interested in having either, or both, of them join us at UCLA, I was not contacted by them or by anyone speaking on their behalf. Subsequently, Wilt attended Kansas, and Bill went to the University of San Francisco, where he led the team to victory against us in the 1956 NCAA regionals on their way to a second consecutive national championship.

## VALUES COME FIRST

My meeting with Lewis came about only because his high school coach, Jack Donahue, called me from New York and said that he and Lewis had watched UCLA outscore Duke in the national championship game a few days earlier. Coach Donahue went on to say that his young student-athlete had narrowed the list of colleges he was considering down to five. UCLA was on his short list. He suggested we talk further at an upcoming coaches' clinic the two of us would be attending at Valley Forge, Pennsylvania. I agreed.

At the clinic, Coach Donahue asked a few questions about our program at UCLA and told me about Lewis—his family, academic achievements, attitude, work ethic, ability to get along with team members, and more. Coach Donahue indicated that Lewis wished to visit UCLA and meet me at a later date.

I had a single request: Could UCLA be the last on the list of schools that Lewis visited? Coach Donahue said he would pass my request along to Lewis and his family. During his trip to our campus—even though it rained the whole time—Lewis realized that we had much to offer, including a new sports facility, Pauley Pavilion. It would replace the old Men's Gym and be ready for use by the time Lewis arrived.

Nevertheless, other schools had good basketball programs and excellent facilities. Additionally, all of them offered something very important that UCLA lacked, namely, they were much closer to Lewis's friends and family in New York. In other words, he had a number of alternatives—many fine schools and opportunities—when it came to making a decision on his future.

Why did Cora, Lewis's mother, and Lewis Alcindor, Sr.—and their son—choose UCLA? There were several reasons, but four in particular resonated with the young man and his parents. All four reasons had to do with their values. And those they found at UCLA:

*Evidence of equality:* One evening while Lewis and his parents were watching the old *Ed Sullivan Show*, Ed Sullivan went out of his way to introduce Rafer Johnson, a former UCLA basketball player I had coached and later an Olympic gold medalist. Rafer's introduction included his athletic credits, but it concluded by saying that he was in New York representing the entire UCLA student body. He was its president. UCLA students, predominantly white, had elected a black student to represent them. There were other schools with the same ideals, of course, but on that night, Ed Sullivan provided visible evidence to the Alcindors of what UCLA stood for.

*Scholastic merit:* UCLA's academic standards were high. Student-athletes who attended our school received a good education. And they graduated.

*Credible, heartfelt testimonials:* Lewis had also received a letter from a former UCLA basketball player who vouched for the ideals and standards of our school. It came from the winner of the Nobel Peace Prize, Dr. Ralph Bunche, who had written on his own initiative. Dr. Bunche was black. Jackie Robinson, the first black professional baseball player in the major leagues, had also written a letter expressing similar sentiments.

*Blind to color:* Willie Naulls, a member of the New York Knicks who had been an All-American at UCLA, informed Lewis that John Wooden was color-blind when it came to race.

Values and standards, ideals and principles mattered to Lewis and his parents, Cora and Lewis, Sr. They also mattered at UCLA and to me. Good values are like a magnet—they attract good people.

<u>Your Education</u>

1.  You are in UCLA for an <u>education</u>. I want every boy to earn and receive his degree. Keep that <u>first</u> in your thoughts, but place <u>basketball</u> <u>second</u>.

2.  Do not cut classes and do be on time.

3.  Do not fall behind and do get your work in on time.

4.  Have regular study hours and keep them.

5.  Arrange with your profs <u>in</u> <u>advance</u> when you must be absent.

6.  Do not expect favors. Do your part.

7.  Boys on grant-in-aid should arrange for tutoring through the Athletic Department at the first indication of need.

8.  Work for a high grade point average. Do not be satisfied by merely meeting the eligibility requirements.

9.  Those on campus jobs for grant-in-aid must arrange to get in the required hours. Do your assignment without comparing it with that of another boy.

10. Earn the respect of everyone, especially of yourself.

# VALUES CREATE AN ENVIRONMENT OF INTEGRITY

Leadership is about more than just forcing people to do what you say. A prison guard does that. A good leader creates belief—in the leader's philosophy, in the organization, in the mission. Creating belief is difficult to do where a vacuum of values exists, where the only thing that matters is the end result, whether it's beating the competition on the court or increasing the profit margins in the books.

Let me be clear: Results matter. They matter a great deal. But if this is an organization's singular purpose, then the people who sign on are often doing it for the wrong reasons. Individuals of this type are perhaps more interested in winning the race than in running the race, which means they are less inclined to put in the hard work that "winning" requires. This is the kind of person who is quick to quit in tough times, eager to leave when offered a better chance of winning or making more money elsewhere. That type of person's allegiance, loyalty, and commitment are paper thin, and it is difficult to build an ongoing and successful team when fidelity is no deeper than a dollar bill.

A person who values winning above anything will do anything to win. And such people are threats to their organizations. We don't have to look further than the daily newspaper headlines to see how true this is.

```
Never stoop to playing dirty -- play hard and don't com-
plain.
```

Character counts, and without it even the most talented individual is hamstrung—a potential danger to the team. This holds true whether it's the owner, the leader, the coach, or any other member of the group.

I wanted to run the race with those with whom I shared a code of conduct, those who subscribed to the same set of values that mattered to me. This outcome didn't always happen; after all, people are human. But one of the primary ways to ensure it occurs is to make your values visible, to let the outside world—potential employees and others—know what you stand for and who you are. In doing so, you will attract those who share similar principles and standards—your code of conduct for competition. The opposite is also true, of course, as the owner in Cleveland discovered when he revealed that $25 meant more to him than my commitment and loyalty to his team.

For me, of course, the Pyramid of Success defined the code of conduct and characteristics that I valued, both on and off the court. I also prized the simple rules of behavior in my father's "two sets of three": two lists, each with three admonitions, that he taught to my brothers and me: "Never lie; never cheat; never steal. Don't whine; don't complain; don't make excuses."

> **"Never lie; never cheat; never steal. Don't whine; don't complain; don't make excuses."**

They are pretty easy to remember, but not so easy to do. Nevertheless, it was behavior I expected, and taught, to all I coached.

## ADVERTISE YOUR IDENTITY

In order to make sure that your values are on full display, you may need to do some "advertising" of various kinds. Deeds count more than words, but words count too. You may have to take steps to ensure that people know what you stand for. I handed out copies of the Pyramid of Success at the start of each season and had a big drawing of it hanging in the office. Find the means and methods that work for you, depending upon your industry and organization. What is your version of the *Ed Sullivan Show* and the testimonial letter of Dr. Ralph Bunche?

## CHARACTER IS WHAT YOU DO

Here is a small example of how I tried to offer some guidance to players in the area of values and character. You may think it's triv-

ial, but I believe the lesson that was taught had application far beyond the specific issue.

Basketball players would often take home their cotton UCLA
practice T-shirts as souvenirs to wear around campus and elsewhere. For some reason, those T-shirts were very popular. I don't
think it was even viewed as theft by the student-athletes who took
them, any more than employees view as theft the taking of office
supplies such as paper and pens to their homes. I viewed it differently. Taking equipment that doesn't belong to you is wrong. "If
you want a T-shirt," I'd say to them, "just come in and ask me for
one. I'll give you a T-shirt, but don't just take it; it's not yours."

This mattered to me because it went to the kind of person I
wanted on our team. It made me feel bad to look the other way
while individuals I cared about were doing something wrong. And
taking what isn't yours is wrong—even if it's just a cotton T-shirt
used in practice. I thought it mattered, and I still do. I'm sure some
T-shirts were subsequently taken without asking, but at least I had
let them know it was wrong. I also have no doubt that others
changed their behavior for the good because of my words. Furthermore, knowing I would take a stand on this issue gave players
an insight into my value system and what I stood for. Aristotle said:
"We are what we repeatedly do." He was referring to character—
the values and habits of our daily behavior that reveal who and
what we are. I wanted to create good habits in those under my leadership, not only in the mechanics of playing basketball, but also in
the fundamentals of being a good person. Thus, a small issue such
as putting towels in the towel basket where they belonged was
something I viewed as big, something that connected to my overall principles and beliefs—values—that went beyond just picking
up after yourself.

A student-athlete who feels so privileged that he can throw
things on the floor while a student manager follows behind clean-

ing up the mess has a bad habit, one that contributes to selfishness, sloppiness, and disrespect—three character traits I particularly dislike. By requiring each student-athlete to pick up after himself, I may have encouraged a positive habit, good behavior, and a way of thinking that carried over to the court and our team. (It was my hope that some of my teaching might even carry over to what the players did in their lives after basketball.)

## THE POWER OF A GOOD EXAMPLE

I sought character in players rather than players who were characters. For me, a good explanation of character is simple: respect for yourself, respect for others, respect for the game, whether it's basketball, business, or anything else. Character starts with little things

```
Attitude and Conduct


1.  Be a gentleman and do nothing that will bring discredit
    to you or your school -- on or off the floor when at home
    or away.

2.  Develop great personal pride in all phases of your play --
    offensively and defensively as an individual and as a team
    man.

3.  The player who has done his best has done everything,
    while the player who has done less than his best is a
    failure.

4.  Be a keen student of the game.  Basketball is a mental
    game:  perhaps, 50% fight and 50% knowing how.

5.  Truly believe that you are better than your opponent
    in knowledge of the game, in condition, and in fighting
    spirit and you will be mighty difficult to defeat.
```

like picking up after oneself, and it ends with big things like not cheating to win.

A leader with character attracts talent with the same. Think of the quality of human resources on your team when they adhere to your high ideals and standards. Then consider what happens when they don't—when you bring an individual on board for whom character doesn't count for much. You've placed a rotting apple into a barrel of good ones. This is a terrible mistake for a leader to make.

Thus, I believe who you are inside—what you believe—is important, but what you do means more, much more. Actions trump words, and your values must be visible if they are to have an impact on those you lead or hope to attract as part of your team. War-ren Bennis, a professor of business administration at USC and founding chairman of the Leadership Institute, says it like this: "Successful leadership is not about being tough or soft, sensitive or assertive, but about a set of attributes. First and foremost is character."

> "Successful leadership is not about being tough or soft, sensitive or assertive, but about a set of attributes. First and foremost is character."

When it comes to character and values, you don't need to become a preacher, just an effective teacher who understands the power of setting a good example, especially when it comes to standards and values. In part, this is why Lewis Alcindor, Jr. was attracted to UCLA. From a variety of sources he learned that his values were our values.

I once interviewed a very talented young man who wanted to attend UCLA on a basketball scholarship. I was even prepared to offer him a scholarship during our meeting. His mother was there, and at one point she politely asked me a question. Her son immediately looked over at her and snapped, "How can you be so ignorant? Just keep your mouth shut and listen to what the coach says." I assured her the question was fine and answered it.

The young man, however, had revealed an aspect of himself that wasn't fine. In fact, it was unacceptable to me: disrespect for his mother. If he couldn't respect her, how could he possibly respect me when things got tough? I politely ended the meeting and excused myself. The scholarship was never offered.

The individual who had been so rude to his mother went on to play for another school and did very well. In fact, he helped his team defeat UCLA on more than one occasion. In spite of that, I was delighted that I had discovered something so important before it was too late, before allowing him to contaminate our team with his "values."

Your behavior as leader—what you do—creates the environment in which the team functions. For some leaders it's anything goes. For me, what goes is defined by the Pyramid of Success, my dad's two sets of three, and plain good sense and decency. I believe this is one of the reasons Vince Lombardi became very uncomfortable when a writer quoted him as saying, "Winning isn't everything, it's the only thing." It suggested Coach Lombardi sanctioned winning at any cost. What he sanctioned—as I understand his beliefs—was giving all you have to the contest rather than doing "whatever it takes" to win.

There's a difference—a big difference. Coach Lombardi believed in the power of good values, and so do I. If you don't care what kind of person you have on your team so long as they help the team win, I question whether you'll attain consistent and long-term success. I'll go further than that: If you don't care about the code of conduct held by those you lead, you're not a good leader.

Character counts and values matter. And you, the leader, set the standard for both in your organization. Let me offer these additional thoughts that may help you lead by example in creating a winning organization.

## RULES TO LEAD BY

### It's Tough to Coach Character.

When parents asked, "Coach Wooden, will you be able to teach my son character?" I told them no. If they didn't have it, I couldn't give it to them. While you, the leader, can teach many things, character is not taught easily to adults who arrive at your desk lacking it. Be cautious about taking on "reclamation projects" regardless of the talent they may possess. Have the courage to make character count among the qualities you seek in others.

### Character Starts with Little Things.

Remember the T-shirts. Every leader should create his or her agenda of things that make a difference. It could be everything from being punctual to completing projects on deadline. But it could also be something a bit subtler, such as how a manager talks to an employee or administrative assistant. The important thing is to let people know what you expect of them and to inform individuals when they violate your code, values, or standards.

### Character Is More Than Honesty.

An individual can be honest as the day is long and still be short on character. How? He or she can be honest but selfish, honest but undisciplined, honest but unfair, honest but disrespectful, or honest but lazy. Honesty is a good place to start, but it doesn't stop there. There's more to character than just telling the truth—for both leaders and those on the team.

### Beware Those Who'll Do Whatever It Takes to Win.

Winning at any cost can be very costly—fatal, in fact. A good set of values is part of successful leadership and great organizations. Be wary of those who will do anything to win. This is not the attitude of a great competitor, but rather of a competitor who is greatly flawed. Find those who love the battle and play by the rules.

# ON WOODEN

**Kareem Abdul-Jabbar:** UCLA Varsity, 1967–1969;
three national championships

## COACH WOODEN'S FIELD OF DREAMS

You may have seen the Kevin Costner movie, *Field of Dreams*—
"Build it and they will come." Coach Wooden did that. He
built his basketball program a certain way—athletically, ethi-
cally, morally—because he believed it would attract a certain
type of person; the kind of individual he wanted on the team.

And if he didn't have success that way, it was all right
with him because he felt his program made sense; in every
way it made sense to him. So he was going to do it that way.
Coach was almost a mystic in knowing what would happen.
And, he was right—when he built it, they came. I was one of
them.

I chose UCLA in large part because of what I saw and
heard regarding those values. Dr. Ralph Bunche and Jackie
Robinson wrote to me saying UCLA was a great place for an
education and athletics. Willie Naulls told me that race
wasn't an issue with Coach Wooden.

And one of the most important things in my decision was
seeing Rafer Johnson on the *Ed Sullivan Show*. I knew he was
a world-class athlete, but he was on the show as president of
the student body at UCLA. That told me the school appreciated him for more than just being a jock. It told me a whole
lot about what UCLA was about.

With his hair parted in the middle, Coach looked like he
fell off a box of Pepperidge Farm cookies. That was mislead-

ing. In the gym he was a very, very tough man, extremely demanding. He wanted it done a certain way, and he would get out there and demonstrate what that way was.

Coach was about 57 years old when I arrived at UCLA—almost 40 years older than the rest of us. But he would never ask his players to do what he wouldn't do. You appreciate that, when the leader is willing to get right out there and work alongside you. You're not just hearing stuff from somebody who hasn't been there and done it. He knew what he was talking about, so he had that credibility. He got respect.

Winning was never mentioned by him. For Coach Wooden it was, "Fellas, we've got to play at our best. Let's do that." That's a lot different from saying, "Fellas, we've got to win." A lot different.

Race? Religion? They didn't matter. What mattered was the effort you made on the court and in the classroom. What mattered was your behavior, your conduct, your values. Of course, that included a strong work ethic.

He wanted our best effort. If that wasn't good enough, he accepted the results. Coach Wooden figured maybe that's the way it's supposed to be. But he wanted our best effort before he'd be willing to say, "That's the way it's supposed to be."

By the second week of practice at UCLA I was just totally hooked on how he did things—the progression of skills he had us work on and then putting it all together as a team.

When they outlawed the dunk, he told me, "Lewis, everybody will be playing under the same rules no matter what they are. This game isn't about the dunk shot. So just go on and play; it's the same for everybody." Very matter of fact. Mentally, I got past the rule change outlawing the dunk shot very quickly.

One of his strongest assets as a leader was his patience. A lot of players were skeptical about various things, and it would take a while to win them over. Coach would let them try it their way and fail. He was good at that. It's the best way to teach. Because after they failed they wanted to know how to do it right. They wanted to learn how to do it right more than they wanted to prove Coach wrong.

So, here's this 57-year-old guy, and he gets out there and shows them how to do it right.

He knew how to do it right—in all departments.

# 5

# USE THE MOST POWERFUL
# FOUR-LETTER WORD

*"I will not like you all the same, but I will love you all the same."*

A T SOME POINT, LATER than I'd care to admit, it became clear to me that the most productive model for good leadership is a good parent. A coach, teacher, and leader, in my view, are all basic variations of being a parent. And while parenting is the most important job in the world, leadership isn't far behind. I revere the opportunity and obligation it confers, namely, the power to change lives and make a difference. For me, leadership is a sacred trust.

A leader in sports, business, or any other field of endeavor should possess and provide the same qualities inherent in a good parent: character, consistency, dependability, accountability, knowledge, good judgment, selflessness, respect, courage, discipline, fairness, and structure.

And while all these will make you a good leader, they will not make you a great leader. For that, one additional quality—perhaps the most important of all—is necessary. Although it may sound out of place in the rough-and-tumble context of sports or corporate competition, I believe you must have love in your heart for the people under your leadership. I did.

For a parent, the family counts most of all; for a good leader, the team is nothing less than extended family. Those you lead are not just a random collection of people who show up at your doorstep, put in time, and collect a paycheck. At least, they shouldn't be.

For me the members of our teams were never plug-in parts, "jocks" whose individual value was in direct proportion to the number of points they could score. Never. In fact, next to my own flesh and blood they were the ones closest to me. Those I led were my extended family. And love is present in every good family. You must truly care about the lives and welfare of your team members, and demonstrate it with concern and support within a disciplined environment. However, it took me a while to figure out what this really means and how to apply it in my own way.

## SOME MORE; SOME LESS

In my early days back at Dayton, Kentucky, and South Bend, Indiana, I told players at the start of a new season that I would like them all the same. Of course, this turned out to be false. There were some whom I could barely stand. This troubled me because it seemed that a coach should have affection for—and be friends with—those under his supervision. I wanted to like all the players on our team.

That had been my own experience as an athlete. Coach Ward Lambert at Purdue seemed to like all of us on the team equally, and I considered him a friend. My teammates, I assumed, felt the same. This had also been true when I played basketball in high school at Martinsville.

As a coach, I found this same kind of relationship simply did not exist with certain members of my team, and I was very concerned about it; it didn't seem right. But then I read a statement by Amos Alonzo Stagg, Chicago's legendary football coach, which helped in my understanding of the relationship between a leader and the organization. Coach Stagg said: "I loved all my players the same, I just didn't like them all the same." He had love in his heart for everyone on the team, but not necessarily "like."

> "I will not like you all the same, but I will love you all the same. And whether I like you or not, my feelings will not interfere with my judgment of your effort and performance. You will be treated fairly. That's a promise."

By the time I got to UCLA, my message at the start of each season had changed to reflect Coach Stagg's sentiments. Making friends was not the responsibility or the goal of leadership, and I cautioned the team of this.

This is no different than a parent who may not like one child as much as another on any particular day or week, but whose love for each child is constant.

## TEAM MEMBERS WHO DIDN'T LIKE ME

I also recognized over time that members of the team wouldn't all like me the same—and that was fine. Andy Hill, a reserve player on three national championship teams, wouldn't speak to me for 27 years after he graduated from UCLA because he didn't agree with my decisions. What decisions? First and foremost, he didn't like that I would not make him a starter. Andy had been a good player in high school, and it was difficult for him to accept the fact that he was not in the starting lineup at UCLA. He was extremely upset—perhaps bitter—with my decision to sit him down.

Your children might hate you for doing what's best, but eventually, like Andy, they may come around. After 27 years he decided that what his old coach had been doing made sense. He even called me up to say so—that I had been right, after all.

Of course, "what's right" is often the most difficult decision a leader is forced to make, and a strong leader must expect some in the organization to resist and even be angered by your judgment and decisions. That's just one of the many things that makes leadership, at times, a solitary profession. You are the person charged with making the final, tough choices, while everybody else has the option of sitting on the sidelines, complaining about it.

Hard feelings occur even within the best of families. But a strong family survives when love is present. A team—your organization—is a family. Love must be the glue that holds it together, and love must start with the leader.

When Andy called after 27 years I was happy to hear from him—just like a father welcoming the return of a son who's been gone a long time. When I picked up my telephone, a voice on the other end said, "Coach Wooden, this is Andy Hill. Remember me?" I said, "Andy, where have you been?"

## NOBODY CARES HOW MUCH YOU KNOW (UNTIL THEY KNOW HOW MUCH YOU CARE)

Love may not conquer all, but it conquers much, and a leader who has it in his heart is much better equipped to handle the natural challenges, differences, and difficulties created by those in your organization.

Could you be a great parent without love? Probably not. And the same answer is true in leading your organization. The players on our UCLA teams, and those I coached at Indiana State Teachers College, South Bend Central, and Dayton High School—hundreds of individuals over the decades—became true members of my extended family.

While I never violated a recruiting rule while I was coaching, I did ignore a few rules after players arrived at UCLA, but only in extending a kindness—love and concern—to those under my leadership. At UCLA during holidays such as Thanksgiving or Christmas, my wife, Nell, and I would invite them for dinner when they could not make it home to be with their immediate families. We knew this was a violation of NCAA rules; however, it was a rule I was willing to ignore. A young person should be with family on an important day.

I bailed players out of jail for minor traffic violations on occasion even though, again, it violated rules. There was just no sense in letting a young man spend a weekend in jail for something like that. It was no different than what I would do for my own children.

<u>Coaching</u> - Coach and player relationship

1. Keep a close personal player relationship, but keep their respect. Be sincerely interested in their personal problems and easy to approach.

2. Maintain discipline without being dictatorial. Be fair and lead rather than drive.

3. Study and respect the individuality of each player and handle them accordingly. Treat each man as he deserves to be treated.

4. Try to develop the same sense of responsibility in all.

5. Analyze yourself as well as your players and be governed accordingly.

6. Approval is a great motivator. Use the "pat on the back", especially after severe criticism.

7. If you teach loyalty, honesty, and respect for the rights of others, you will be taking a big step toward a cooperative team with proper team spirit. Jealousy, egotism, envy, criticism and razzing of each other can ruin this.

8. Consider the team first, but don't sacrifice a boy just to prove a point.

Before a game in 1950 I found out that the wife of our captain, Eddie Sheldrake, was ill—not a life-threatening illness, but very sick. As a true team player he felt it would be disloyal to the Bruins to stay home and skip an upcoming road trip. I valued his loyalty but understood that his place was at home with his wife. Eddie was relieved when I told him he couldn't go on the trip.

These acts of concern on my part were very small things, but I mention them because they were a direct result of the feelings—the love—I had in my heart for those I coached. It's important to let those you lead know you care.

A coach, just like the leader of any organization, has a deeply personal relationship with those on the team—mental, educational, emotional, and more. For a leader in business, it also includes financial ties.

Outside of your immediate family—marriage and children—how much closer can it get? My players are family. Their accomplishments have made me proud, both while they played basketball and after they moved on to other things.

## IF YOU DON'T THINK OF YOUR TEAM AS A FAMILY, WHY SHOULD THE TEAM THINK OF YOU AS HEAD OF THE FAMILY?

It took me a while to learn this lesson, but it is true. You must have love and respect for those under your leadership if your team is going to fire on all cylinders. We live in a cynical age. Don't let cynicism preclude love or lead you to believe those under your leadership are simply interchangeable parts to be used and discarded.

## APARTNESS IS A PART OF THE JOB

Over the years my thinking had also evolved to understand that while a quality leader has love and genuine concern for the people within the organization, there is an "apartness" necessary in leadership. The aim is not to make new friends but to do what is best for the team without carelessly damaging its members in the process. When I understood that objectivity—"apartness"—could exist in the context of love, it made my decision making much easier as head coach at UCLA, especially those decisions that would cause hard feelings and resentment.

At one point in my career, I also told players I would treat them all the same way. This is what I told my own two children. I thought treating everyone the same was being fair and impartial. Gradually I began to suspect that it was neither fair nor impartial. In fact, it was just the opposite. That's when I began announcing that team members wouldn't be treated the same or alike; rather, each one would receive the treatment they earned and deserved. This practice may sound discriminatory or suggest partiality, but it is neither.

A player who is working hard and productively for the group shouldn't receive the same treatment as someone who is offering less. And while each and every person on your team fills a role and performs a function, some of those roles and functions are filled by people much harder to replace than others.

It would be naïve to suggest that a superstar in your organization—a top producer—won't receive some accommodations not afforded others. This is not a double standard but rather a fact of life. Those *small* accommodations, however, must not apply in areas of your basic principles and values or they will soon be replaced by the perception that favoritism and special treatment are the norm.

One of my players joked that when he wanted to break curfew, he did it with an All-American. That way, if *they* got caught, he'd escape any disciplinary action. This was not true, but did reflect that those under my supervision were not all treated the same.

The All-American he was referring to may have been Bill Walton, who consistently tested the limits of what was acceptable behavior. One afternoon before a rather important conference game at USC (University of Southern California), Bill arrived at the team bus looking unkempt.

Over the years my rule on dress and hygiene for traveling to away games had changed from requiring a coat, tie, slacks, and short hair to a more general rule: "a clean and neat appearance."

## FIRM AND FLEXIBLE

On this particular day, as Bill prepared to step onto our team bus, he did not look "clean and neat"—keep in mind, this was during the hippie era. I would not allow him on the bus and sent him home. He had violated a rule I viewed as important, one that connected to a bigger picture.

To have ignored his appearance would have sent a bad message to his teammates: Bill Walton gets special treatment because he's so important. "Bill can break the rules, but you guys can't." This perception not only creates dissension, in my opinion, but it soon leads to others breaking any rule they want. Ultimately, no rules matter, and everyone does whatever he or she wants.

On the other hand, when Bill became a vegetarian he requested that he not be required to eat the team meals we served at our training table, which, of course, included steak. Even though I put a great deal of thought into what was consumed by players before a game and spelled it out right down to the size of the steak and how it was cooked, I granted Bill's special request.

To have allowed him to board the bus having violated my dress and hygiene rule would have had ramifications beyond Bill and could hurt the team. Allowing him to skip steak and eat beans and yogurt was, in my opinion, acceptable even though some viewed it as favoritism. Had you been in my position you may have come to the opposite conclusions, but they made sense to me. These issues may seem trivial; however, I think they have great bearing on a leader's effectiveness.

I tried hard to avoid giving special treatment, or the appearance of it, on important matters while remaining flexible on lesser issues. If others wanted to skip the steak, I would have evaluated each request individually. If others had arrived at the team bus looking unkempt, they would have received *exactly* the same treatment that Bill got.

Unlike my earlier years, I had gotten smarter when it came to creating and enforcing rules—just like a good parent who loves his children. When to be flexible? When to be firm? There's the challenge.

Over and over in my years of coaching I found the complicated questions and answers of raising a family much the same as those presented in leadership. Success is much more likely when love is present in your heart for the people who make your organization a *real* team, that is, a family.

Love is so important because it moves you to do the right things in all areas of life, including leadership. As a former English teacher, I pay particular attention to the meaning of words. What is love? Let me offer the following definition:

"Love is patient; love is kind. It is not jealous; it is not pompous; it is not inflated; it is not rude; it does not seek its own interests; it is not quick-tempered; it does not brood over injury; it does not rejoice over wrongdoing but rejoices with the truth. Love bears all things, believes all things, hopes all things, and endures all things."

A leader filled with this kind of love is a powerful force and has the potential for creating a forceful organization. As you may have noted, I draw inspiration and direction from a wide array of sources, including my father, Coach Ward Lambert, Abraham Lincoln, and the Great Pyramid of Giza. This particular bit of wisdom about love and what it is comes from the Good Book.

A leader who tries to lead without love will turn around one day and find there is nobody following. The family will have disappeared. Love is essential—for the competitive struggle itself, for the people on your team, and for the journey you and they are taking.

Consider the following important suggestions in striving to build an even stronger organization, one that is connected like family.

## SUGGESTIONS TO LEAD BY

### Lead with Love.

Great organizations are marked by an extraordinary bond within. For me, that bond included genuine love, and I didn't feel awkward about it. I put my heart into my work and those with whom I worked. Teams with a sense of family have uncommon strength and resiliency. A good family—whether in life, sports, or business—involves love. (A reminder: It also involves good structure, sensible discipline, and personal sacrifice.)

### You Don't Have to Treat Everyone Alike or Like Everyone the Same.

You may have favorites within your organization, but never replace fairness with favoritism. To be impartial, give each individual the treatment he or she earns and deserves.

### Seek Out Opportunities to Show You Care.

The small considerations often mean the most—a genuine expression of interest or concern, a helpful hand, individual recognition. I didn't place a wall between my professional and personal life, and at appropriate times I invited players and coaches to our home. I knew about their families and their challenges away from basketball. Oftentimes, it really is the thought that counts most.

**Know What Time It Is.**

With regard to policy, effective leadership recognizes that there is a time to be flexible and a time to be firm. Recognize the difference between rules that can be waived occasionally and those that go to the core of your philosophy. For example, my dress code had repercussions beyond the individual; replacing steak with beans and yogurt didn't. Knowing the difference is often most challenging. However, a good leader knows what time it is: Time to be flexible? Time to be firm?

# ON WOODEN

**Jim Powers:** South Bend Central High School Varsity, 1941–1943; Indiana State Teachers College Varsity, 1947–1948

---

## NOBODY IN THE FAMILY GETS LEFT BEHIND

When I got back from World War II I went to Indiana State Teachers College, because that's where Coach Wooden had been hired. A lot of his former South Bend High School players followed him there because we wanted to get back to that family he created in basketball.

However, during the war I had been shot down in a B-24 raid on some oil fields in Italy, and came very close to getting killed. I didn't want to fly for a long time after that, including when I was at Indiana State. When the Indiana State Sycamores were supposed to fly to New York for a game at Madison Square Garden, I told Coach, "There's no way I'm getting on a plane. You can go without me, but I'm not flying."

Coach refused to leave me behind—got station wagons and we *drove* out to New York. It was family; nobody got left behind.

In 1947 we got invited to a big national tournament. One problem: They prohibited blacks from playing. One of our teammates, Clarence Walker, was black. Coach Wooden turned down the invitation. He wouldn't leave Clarence behind.

It happened again the next year. We got the same invitation. Again, Coach turned it down. This time the tournament backed off. They changed the rules. Only after that would Coach accept the invitation. The Sycamores got to the finals before losing to Louisville.

Our whole team went; everybody played, including Clarence. You don't leave somebody in the family behind. At least, Coach Wooden didn't. His concern for us went way beyond basketball. We were part of a family.

# 6

# CALL YOURSELF A TEACHER

*"No written word nor spoken plea can teach your team
what it should be."*

THE OUTSIDE WORLD KNOWS your profession, what you do, by
the title on your business card: sales manager, CEO, production
supervisor, or something else. However, your business card informs
someone even more important about what you do professionally,
namely, you. Don't be misled by what it says.

In the eyes of most observers, my title is "Coach" Wooden, but
this is not what I would list first on my résumé or business card.
From my earliest years I have viewed my primary job as one of ed-
ucating others: I am a teacher.

I believe effective leaders are, first and foremost, good teachers.
We are in the education business. Whether in class or on the court,
my job was the same: to effectively teach those under my supervision how they could perform to the best of their ability in ways that
best served the goals of our team. I believe the same is true for productive leaders in any organization.

Among experienced coaches in sports, there is little difference in
their technical knowledge of the game. All leaders basically evaluate the same information, draw from the same talent pool, and are
constrained by similar financial considerations. Not always, but

most of the time. The difference usually comes down to the ability of a leader to be an effective teacher of what it takes to "move the ball" in the process of creating a winning organization.

What is your title? Call yourself a teacher. Put that on your business card and remember it well. However, I will confess that just calling yourself a teacher is not enough. You must also know how to teach.

In 1933, when I moved with Nellie to Kentucky to begin my career, I arrived with great confidence, especially when it came to basketball. I had been a three-time, all-consensus, All-American guard with the Purdue Boilermakers—national champions just months earlier. In fact, I had been the captain of the team during my junior year. Before that, our high school team, the Martinsville Artesians, played in the finals of the Indiana State High School basketball tournament three straight times and won it in 1927. My basketball skills even produced an offer of $5,000 to turn professional and tour with the old Boston Celtics.

With all that experience and know-how as a player, I thought I understood basketball pretty well—and I did. Unfortunately, I didn't know beans from apple butter about teaching it.

> The coach must never forget that he is, first of all, a teacher. He must come (be present), see (diagnose), and conquer (correct). He must continuously be exploring for ways to improve himself in order that he may improve others and welcome every person and everything that maybe helpful to him. As has been said, he must remember, "Others, too, have brains."

I still recall my first day on the court as a basketball coach at Dayton. I was a leader who couldn't teach but didn't know it. A leader who can't teach isn't going to have much of a team in basketball—or anything else. And we didn't.

I began my career as a coach with a losing season in spite of all my experience, awards, and accumulated knowledge in the subject of basketball. In fact, one of the games we lost was to my alma mater, Martinsville High School, led by my former coach, Glenn Curtis. While I may have known as much about the game as Coach Curtis, the difference was this: He knew how to teach it and I didn't. It was pretty much as simple as that.

As you might imagine, the leadership graveyard is full of failed teams whose leaders, like me at the outset, were very well informed but could not teach to save their soul. This is true in basketball, business, and most other organizations.

Of course, knowledge is absolutely essential. I put it smack dab in the heart of the Pyramid and called it Skill. But knowledge is not enough. You must be able to effectively transfer what you know to those you manage—not just the nuts-and-bolts material, but your standards, values, ideals, beliefs, as well as your way of doing things.

Most of all, you must teach those under your leadership how to become a real team rather than a group of individuals who simply work at the same place for the same boss. All this is possible only if you know how to teach.

If there is a single reason the UCLA Bruins enjoyed success in basketball while I was head coach, it is because I learned how to be a better and better teacher. The following is what I learned.

## KNOWLEDGE IS NOT ENOUGH

Effective teaching is intrinsic to effective leadership, the kind that can build and maintain a successful team. I am unaware of any great team builders who were not also great team teachers.

## PRAY FOR PATIENCE

Initially, my athletic experience and knowledge of basketball worked against me as a teacher and leader. As an athlete, I was a quick learner. When my high school or college coach told me to do something in a specific way, I was able to do it almost immediately. Things had come very easy for me on the court. I concluded, incorrectly, that's how things were taught; specifically, tell somebody to do it and he will do it, immediately, just as I had in high school and college. For the most part, that's exactly how teaching is not done.

Most often the leader is required to do more than just "tell." Many leaders don't fully appreciate the fact that before telling someone *what* to do you must teach him *how* to do it. And this process requires patience. It is also important to note that this applies not only to an individual's execution of a specific task but also to his or her adoption of your organization's philosophy, its culture of expectations, norms of behavior, and more. Imparting all this knowledge requires good teaching.

As an impatient first-year coach, I lacked these skills and became quickly frustrated at the slow learning curve exhibited by the basketball players on the Dayton Greendevils team. In fact, I'm not sure I understood there was such a thing as a learning curve. I pushed harder and talked louder. Harder and louder were my teaching techniques. When that didn't work, I started complaining to others about the players' problems, lack of progress, and inability to learn what I was teaching.

But the problem was with me rather than the athletes. My impatience precluded good teaching. I am embarrassed to say that during my second week of practice as Dayton's football coach, I got involved in a fracas with one of the players, a fight, because my teaching skills were so green and my fuse—my patience—so short.

I'm a believer in the laws of learning: explanation, demonstration, imitation, correction when necessary (and it usually is), then repetition. The laws of teaching, of course, are the same as learning, and both take time; both require great patience.

Some of those under your supervision will catch on quickly, others not. Understanding that patience is an integral part of good teaching and effective leadership allowed me to accept the varying speeds at which people learn and to accommodate, within reason, those differences. Patience became an asset for me rather than a liability. I came to understand that good things take time.

> You must have patience and expect more mistakes, but drill and drill to reduce them to a minimum. A hard-working, fast-breaking team will often make more mistakes then their opponents because they attempt more and perhaps accomplish more.

## GET A GOOD HAT RACK

An effective teacher must have a good hat rack, one with plenty of hooks. In the course of a day's work, I eventually became adept at wearing many different hats: teacher, of course, but also disciplinarian, demonstrator, counselor, role model, psychologist, motivator, timekeeper, quality control expert, talent judge, referee, organizer, and more.

In fact, when I first arrived at UCLA, I also wore the custodian's hat and washed the court before practice. My assistant coach, Eddie Powell, would walk behind me with a mop as I dipped my hand into a bucket of hot water and sprinkled it on the court behind me like I was feeding chickens back on the farm. It was just one more hat I wore.

A good leader knows how and when to delegate, of course, but in addition to the delegation of duties, an effective leader assumes many roles and wears many hats. I also understood that there was one hat I didn't wear; namely, I was not a player. In 40 years of coaching, I never scored a point or blocked a shot. My job was to teach others how to do it.

Whatever the context of your leadership—sports, business, or otherwise—your team scores the points. You, as leader, are responsible for teaching the team how to accomplish that. In the process you'll wear many hats, and they must all fit. Unfortunately, when I began my career I had one whistle and one hat. While that's enough whistles, it's not enough hats.

## THE SECOND LAW

Demonstration is what we call the second law of learning in sports—demonstrating how to throw the ball, catch the ball, and so forth. Words are powerful, but demonstration is more powerful, and it applies to more than throwing a basketball. What you do counts more than what you say.

The things you hope to teach those under you are best taught by your own behavior—demonstration—whether it's the act of showing respect for others, being on time, shooting a free throw, or exercising self-control. Action speaks louder than words.

I am fond of a little verse that I have kept in mind over all these years. I've changed it slightly, but the sentiment is the same:

*No written word nor spoken plea,*
*Can teach your team what they should be,*
*Nor all the books on all the shelves,*
*It's what the leader is himself.*

I used to smoke cigarettes as a young high school coach at South Bend. I would quit during the basketball season to set a good example, but then I realized I was also setting an example in the off-season by smoking—a bad example. So I quit. That little verse was one of the reasons. My example, I felt, meant more than my words.

I taught the Pyramid of Success primarily by my own example—demonstration. Of course, I handed out mimeographed copies of the Pyramid to players and discussed it at the beginning of our season. But handouts and discussions were meaningless unless team members could see lots of evidence of the Pyramid in my own behavior as a leader and coach.

Just talking about a goal—living the laws of the Pyramid—meant very little without the second law of learning: demonstration. Your own personal example is one of the most powerful leadership tools you possess. Put it to good use: Be what you want your team to become.

*5. Some essentials for the coach - industriousness, enthusiasm, sympathy, patience, self-control, attentiveness to detail, impartiality, appearance, vision, an optimistic disposition*

## DON'T CAUSE INDIGESTION

By the time I arrived at UCLA, I had accumulated an extensive body of instructions, rules, and regulations—perhaps even some wisdom. It covered practice drills, plays, academic requirements, specifics of shooting, passing, guarding opponents, balance, rebounding, attitude, dress codes, and very many other specifics.

All this was printed out and put together in a big blue UCLA handbook that I issued to each Bruin at the start of the year. It was a great feast of information. However, I eventually came to see that I had overwhelmed the players with all the material I had given them. It was just too much at once. Instead, I began cutting it up into bite-size pieces that were easily consumed, understood, and utilized, rather than serving it up in one big feast.

My assistant coaches and I doled out the most relevant material judiciously as the season progressed. I had come to understand that my big blue UCLA handbooks with all that information caused indigestion.

> "The greatest holiday feast is eaten one bite at a time. Gulp it down all at once and you get indigestion. I discovered the same is true in teaching. To be effective, a leader must dispense information in bite-size, digestible amounts."

```
Coaching Methods

1.  Be a teacher. Follow the laws of learning -- explanation
    and demonstration, imitation, criticism of the imitation,
    repetition until habit is formed.

2.  Use lectures, photographs, movies, diagrams, mimeographed
    material, etc., to supplement your daily practices.

3.  Insist on punctuality and proper dress for practice.

4.  Insist on strict attention.

5.  Permit no "horse play". Practice is preparation.

6.  Show patience.

7.  Give new things early in the practice period and then repeat
    daily until learned.

8.  Avoid harsh, public criticism. Use praise as well as censure.

9.  Encourage teamwork and unselfishness.

10. Do considerable individual coaching of individuals.

11. Use small, carefully organized groups.

12. Have a definite practice plan -- and follow it.
```

## IT'S WHAT YOU LEARN *AFTER* YOU KNOW IT ALL THAT COUNTS

I was fortunate to be taught basketball by true masters of the game: Coach Piggy Lambert at Purdue and Coach Curtis at Martinsville High School. Without realizing it, I accumulated a body of knowledge that was comprehensive—perhaps equivalent to earning a doctorate in the skills of playing basketball.

When I began coaching, even though my skills as a teacher were lacking, I truly understood the game's physical mechanics and more. Regardless of the profession, a leader who lacks full knowledge will soon be exposed. It's difficult to get people to follow you if you don't know what you're doing. While I was hardly a good teacher at the onset, there was no question that I knew plenty about playing basketball.

I owed my knowledge to the great mentors I had along the way. I was lucky to have found them in basketball—men who were ahead of their time and loved teaching the game. Mentors are available at all stages of your leadership life—early, middle, and late. Seek them out and listen; absorb their knowledge and use it.

Of course, knowledge is never static or complete. A leader who is through learning is through. You must never become satisfied with your ability or level of knowledge. Subsequently, after each season I picked one particular aspect of basketball to study intensively. For example, I might select the fast break and begin compiling information from books, newspapers, and magazines. I would closely examine the way various experts—other coaches—executed and taught the fast break. I greatly admired the expertise that Coach Hubert Brown's teams demonstrated in executing it against opponents. At Ohio State, Coach Fred Taylor ran a great sideline fast break—a specialty within a specialty. I called these coaches and others such as Kentucky's Adolph Rupp to discuss whatever topic it was that I had chosen to study. Sometimes it led to change, other times not. But it was part of an ongoing desire to increase my knowledge of what I was being paid to teach: basketball.

It is very easy to get comfortable in a position of leadership, to believe that you've got all the answers, especially when you begin to enjoy some success. People start telling you that you're the smartest one around. But if you believe them, you're just the dumbest one around. That's one of the reasons it's extremely difficult to stay at the top—because once you get there, it is so easy to stop listening and learning.

When success comes your way, you must work even harder and avoid the great temptation of believing that previous achievements will occur in the future without even greater effort than was required in the past. As a leader, you must never become satisfied, never content that what you know is all you need to know. This is especially true when it comes to understanding human nature. No two people are alike. Each individual under your management is unique. There is no formula that applies to all. Some need a push; others you lead. Recognizing the difference requires a good understanding of human nature, which, in turn, helps us know how to get the most out of those we work with, promotes rapport, and strengthens team play.

I was asked, "Coach Wooden, how can I learn about human nature?" I replied, "Get old." Of course, I was referring to the value of experience, the knowledge gained from doing something for years. There's a quicker way to gain the information experience provides, namely, ask somebody who already has it.

This is what I was doing in reaching out to other coaches throughout my career. Some were mentors; others were teachers. All had experience and knowledge that I could draw on and benefit from. I paid attention to what they said because it made me a better teacher. I was shy as a teenager, but I was bold as an adult when it came to seeking ideas, opinions, and knowledge.

I believe that all effective leaders not only are great teachers but also have a genuine love for teaching. In fact, for me teaching is what I miss most of all since I left the game of basketball. And I like to believe that over the years I got pretty good at it.

Here are a few reminders that will help keep you progressing and improving along the way (at least they did for me).

## SUGGESTIONS TO LEAD BY

### Do Not Equate Professional Expertise with Your Ability to Teach It.

There's a big difference between knowing what you're doing and knowing how to teach what you want done—in *all* areas. A great basketball player may be unable to teach others how to play great basketball, just as an outstanding salesperson may be inept at teaching others how to sell. In your ongoing efforts to increase your knowledge within the profession, don't overlook improving your ability to be a better teacher.

### When You Start Having All the Right Answers, You Will Stop Asking All the Right Questions.

The path to success lies in the realization that there is always more to learn. Strive to create an environment where individuals continually seek knowledge that will benefit their team, where you and those in the organization aren't afraid to ask questions—to admit, "I don't know." Remember, the best CEOs are often those credited with developing "learning institutions." Take meaningful steps to make this a reality. Invite managers from other companies to speak to your people on a key topic. Encourage others to take relevant courses and, most of all, lead by example; specifically, let those you lead see their leader continually learning.

Kentucky's legendary basketball coach, Adolph Rupp, winner of four NCAA championships, defeated UCLA each of the two times we met. All the more reason for me to call him and discuss basketball. And I did. Coach Rupp, in turn, had studied the game under the legendary University of Kansas coach, "Phog" Allen. Good leaders recognize that other productive leaders are a valuable resource.

**Remember That a Good Demonstration Tops a Great Description.**

This adage is most apparent in sports, but it applies equally elsewhere. Memos, discussions, and verbal instructions have merit. Demonstration, however, is often the most effective tool for change.

# ON WOODEN

**Denny Crum:** UCLA Varsity, 1958–1959; Assistant Coach, 1969–1971; three national championships

## KEEP TEACHING; KEEP LISTENING, KEEP LEARNING

Coach Wooden's teaching was so effective because he was so well organized with his details. Everything was written out on the 3 × 5 cards and in notebooks: What was happening from 3:07 to 3:11; what we'd do from 3:11 to 3:17; who was doing what when. Nothing was left to chance, every minute was accounted for—every single minute.

And he was extremely disciplined in keeping to the schedule. I saw that when I was his assistant coach, and I saw it when I arrived at UCLA as a player. He taught details.

On my first day of practice, Coach Wooden sat us down and told the players to take off our sneakers and socks. He did the same. Then he went through his careful demonstration showing us how to eliminate wrinkles, creases, and folds in our sweat socks. We'd usually wear two pair of socks, and he showed how to smooth them out one pair at a time; tuck 'em in from the toe on down, kind of squeeze out the wrinkles and folds. Very precise. He wanted those socks to be smoothed out all the way up the calves.

There were some funny looks around me, but Coach was not willing to take any chances on details he deemed important to performance. So he taught us how to do it right.

That attention to detail was in *everything* he did—the way he planned practice, ran practice, evaluated practice and games. It applied to details of travel, equipment, and food. Absolutely everything that could affect performance got taken care of.

Here's something else that set him apart from 99 percent of the other coaches: Coach Wooden never thought he knew everything. In spite of the fact that he'd been winning championships every year—four or five of them when I got there as an assistant coach—he wanted to keeping learning, improving as a coach and leader.

I had spent a few years coaching at the junior college level when I joined him as an assistant in 1968. I brought with me some experience and my own ideas—which he welcomed. Those he liked we put in during practice. If they worked, fine. If not, we took it out.

He never thought his way was the only way. He continued like that right up to his final game. We used to have disagreements, really argue over things, and people would ask him about it. Coach would say, "I don't need 'yes men.' If they're going to yes everything I do, I don't need them around."

When I came up with an idea, he would never tell me, "Well, this is the way we've always done it and we're winning championships. So, no, I'm not changing." He was open to change.

His approach was to listen; if he thought it made sense, try it. If it works, great. If not, move on. He was always searching for ways to improve.

In the daily coaches' meetings there was never an interruption from outside. We would have out our notebooks, evaluate the previous day's practice—what worked, what needed more work, what to do that was new. Adjustments and refinements.

Then we started formatting the practice minute to minute: a change-of-pace drill; change-of-direction drill; defensive sliding drill; reverse pivot on the dribble drill—on and on and on. We'd put it down in notebooks and on cards.

But through it all there was a wide-open flow of ideas and opinions. He was open to suggestion and contrary thoughts, but he was tough. You had to know your stuff to convince him to change. He never did something on a whim. You had to have your reasons in place, but he'd let you have your say.

Then, when everyone had their say, he made the decision. And that was it.

Coach Wooden never talked about the winning or the losing. It was never part of the conversation like you would think is normal. He wouldn't come in before a game and say, "This team is tied with us in the conference so we've got to step it up tonight. Let's win this one."

He just wasn't concerned about the opponents and what they might be up to—didn't even scout most of them. His philosophy was to do what was necessary to make UCLA a

better team. Teach it; practice it. The details and the fundamentals were his main concern.

He just was completely absorbed in improvement for our
team without trying to always be adjusting to what another
team might be up to. "Let them adjust to us," he said.

Fundamentals, condition, play together as a team. That's
all he did—simple as that. So simple.

# 7

# EMOTION IS YOUR ENEMY

*"Intensity makes you stronger. Emotionalism makes you weaker."*

THE SWISS ALPS HAVE majestic peaks and scenic valleys. Peaks and valleys belong in the Alps, not in the temperament—the emotions—of a leader.

I prize intensity and fear emotionalism. Consistency in high performance and production is a trademark of effective and successful organizations and those who lead them. Emotionalism destroys consistency. A leader who is ruled by emotions, whose temperament is mercurial, produces a team whose trademark is the roller coaster—ups and downs in performance; unpredictability and undependability in effort and concentration; one day good, the next day bad.

This is a pattern I sought to avoid at all costs. I would not accept inconsistency—the pitfalls of repeated highs and lows. I wanted the individuals on our team to play the same way, game to game, that is, with the greatest intensity while executing at the highest performance level of which they were capable. Emotional ups and downs preclude this. Consequently, I never gave rah-rah speeches or contrived pep talks. There was no ranting or raving, histrionics or theatrics before, during, or after practice and games. For every artificial emotional peak they might create, a subsequent valley, a letdown, is produced.

Instead, absolute intensity—intelligently directed and applied—was my objective. I achieved that goal with increasing regularity as I matured as a teacher, leader, and coach. I never wanted to seem out of control. I worked hard to avoid ever looking riled up or dejected. I consciously paid attention to my posture and wanted it to be the same in a preseason game as in a national championship game. And following either, I wanted to conduct myself in a manner that would not reveal to an observer whether UCLA had outscored an opponent or not. Even my dear wife, Nellie, said she usually couldn't tell from my expression.

I wanted those under my leadership to see me always on an even keel—intense, of course, but even. How could I ask others to control themselves if I couldn't do it? And emotional control is a primary component of consistency, which, in turn, is a primary component of success.

I demanded intensive effort—"positive aggression," I called it—with the goal of producing ongoing improvement rather than trying to get everybody excited and fired up about some arbitrary peak in performance. I wanted to see fervor during UCLA basketball practice and games, intensity that didn't boil up and over into emotionalism.

Good judgment, common sense, and reason all fly out the window when emotions kick down your door. Unfortunately, this usually happens in times of turmoil or crisis when you and your organization can least afford it. Thus, I explained to our players, managers, trainer, and assistant coaches that there was to be no excessive exuberance when we scored against an opponent at an important juncture nor excessive dejection when an opponent scored against UCLA. I expected this same emotional discipline following a game—win or lose.

Obviously, you should feel good—even exuberant—when you are victorious. Likewise, it is normal to feel dejected when the opposite occurs. It is excessive emotion that I deplore.

I am very leery of excess in most things—language, dress, haircuts, and much else. But I especially dislike emotional excess because it produces inconsistency. You may have observed that championship games are often somewhat disappointing because neither team seems to be at its best. This is because championship games produce great emotion not only in fans but also in players. That emotionalism is often what brings down the quality of the game itself.

My performance goal for our team was one of steady and tangible progress. If you drew it on a graph, the line would be rising every day each week through the season until the players were theoretically at their finest on the final day of the season. There would be no sharp spikes or peaks; no sudden drop-offs or letdowns. To achieve this goal requires control of emotions. It starts with the leader.

## CULTIVATE CONSISTENCY

The hallmark of successful leadership is consistently maximum performance. Emotionalism opens a leader to inconsistency. Seek intensity coupled with emotional discipline. Display those behaviors and then demand them from those you lead. A leader with a volatile temperament is vulnerable. And so is the team he or she leads.

## EMOTIONALISM CAN CAUSE DAMAGE

Early in my career I let emotions spill over and affect my judgment in ways that I am still ashamed of. At South Bend Central High School, an incident occurred that involved one of our basketball players whose father was on the school board. Although the boy hadn't qualified for a letter, the athletic awards committee allowed coaches discretionary power to make exceptions if the situation warranted it.

This particular young man had worked hard with a good positive attitude throughout the season, and though he lacked adequate playing time, I was strongly considering recommending him for a letter in basketball. In those days, a coach's recommendation was never turned down by the athletic awards committee. However, a few days before I had written out my final list of lettermen, the boy's father suddenly appeared in my office. Without even a hello, he demanded to know if I was going to put his son's name on the list. "I haven't made my final decision yet," I answered. "I may include him, but technically your son doesn't qualify."

The man poked his finger in my chest and threatened, "Wooden, he'd better get a letter or I'll have your job."

That really got to me. I shot back that he could do whatever he wanted with my job, and furthermore, "It's fine with me if you want to take our discussion outside and settle things there." I challenged him to a fight. Emotion had taken over for common sense. Fortunately, the boy's father just turned and stormed out of my office, but not before he repeated his demand and the threat against my coaching job.

I didn't recognize it at the time, but the real damage was still ahead. Because I was so filled with anger—emotionalism—I decided not to recommend his son for a letter even though moments before I was 99 percent sure the boy would be on my final list. It was an awful thing for me to do. In fact, after turning in the list of student-athletes who were going to get letters, I came to my senses, cooled off, and tried to get the boy's name added. But it was too late.

The young player was badly hurt because I let emotions take over my thinking and interfere with good judgment. Seventy years later I still regret what I did. What I don't regret is that it provided a powerful lesson in the dangers of being ruled by emotions.

## CHANGE COMES SLOWLY

That incident was not the only time I let my feelings spill over. Following a game with one of South Bend Central's archrivals, I trotted across the court to offer my condolences to the losing coach. Little did I know that he was extremely upset and in no mood to listen to somebody whose players had just beaten his team for the second straight time that year. This hadn't happened to them in 13 seasons.

As I approached him, he let out a string of expletives I didn't hear again until I joined the Navy—called me every name you could imagine right there in front of the players, fans, and officials. He even suggested that I had bribed the referees to get good calls.

I immediately saw red and, without thinking, knocked him down to the court as players and fans rushed in to stop us. His actions were unacceptable; mine, inexcusable. Both of us had demonstrated how losing control of oneself can be destructive.

Over the years I got very good at preventing my emotions from getting out of hand. It didn't happen overnight, but the process was accelerated by the incidents I've detailed above.

Some observers later described me as being "a cold fish," as if I was no more than a detached spectator during UCLA basketball games. In fact, at one point a play-by-play announcer said, "Coach Wooden just raised his eyebrow. His must be very upset about something." He was exaggerating, but his point was close to the mark. I had become very good at controlling myself. Now you know why. For me, being called a "cold fish" was a compliment—especially if it occurred under pressure. I had learned some hard lessons when it came to letting my emotions take over back in my days as a high school coach.

## THE LEADER'S EXAMPLE

Emotionalism—ups and downs in moods, displays of temperament—is almost always counterproductive, and at times disastrous. I came to understand that if my own behavior was filled with emotionalism, I was sanctioning it for others. As leader, my behavior set the bounds of acceptability. And letting emotions spill over onto the court was simply unacceptable.

The impact my example had on those under my leadership was another compelling reason to become vigilant in controlling my feelings and behavior. The message I sent to the team was simple: "If you let your emotions take over, you'll be outplayed."

Of course, when you're outplayed, you'll be outscored. For them to fully comprehend this lesson about emotional restraint, however, I had to be vigilant in controlling my own feelings and behavior. Some evidence of my success in this area may be that I can recall only one technical foul ever being called against me during my coaching career.

**"If you let your emotions take over, you'll be outplayed."**

UCLA basketball teams under my leadership played in 10 games to determine a national champion. In those games where victory was in hand with minutes to go, I reminded our players during a final timeout: "Don't make fools of yourself when this is over." I asked them to behave in a manner that didn't bring discredit upon us.

I demanded the same emotional constraint if we came up on the losing end. And most of all, I desired emotional control in their performance before the final score was known, that is, during the contest itself. I insisted on that same control and intensity during practice—*especially* practice. On those occasions where I didn't see it in a player or the team, I would end the practice—or threaten to. That was usually enough to get them back on track.

My teaching stressed that "losing your temper will get us outplayed because you'll make unnecessary errors; your judgment will be impaired." I didn't mind an occasional mistake unless it was caused by loss of self-control.

Consequently, I never second-guessed myself when a decision didn't work out so long as I made it without emotion becoming involved. It wasn't a mistake if I used good judgment and the available information. It became an error, however, when the decision was made because I lost control of my feelings, as I did back at South Bend when I was threatened by a player's father. That was a very big error.

I worked hard to eliminate errors in my behavior as the years progressed. The errors decreased only because of my strong belief that consistency, steadiness, and dependability are necessary for high-performance results and for Competitive Greatness. And emotionalism destroys all of this.

A volatile leader is like a bottle of nitroglycerine: The slightest knock and it blows up. Those around nitroglycerine or a temperamental boss spend all their time carefully tiptoeing back and forth rather than doing their jobs. It is not an environment, in my opinion, conducive to a winning organization.

Strive to provide a leadership model that is dependable and reliable and productive in the area of emotions.

Here are some reminders you may consider adding to your own playbook.

# RULES TO LEAD BY

### Control Emotion or Emotion Will Control You.

Intensity, correctly applied and directed, produces consistent and positive improvement and results. Uncontrolled emotion or mercurial displays of temperament erode a leader's stature, lessen respect from others, and will undermine your team's efforts. The leader who does not know the difference between intensity and emotionalism may succeed on occasion, but the success will usually not be repeatable, reliable, or ongoing.

### Avoid Excess. Shoot for Moderation.

In my opinion, effective leaders understand that moderation and balance are linked to long-term success. Excess in just about anything has the potential to create erratic performance. Communicate this fact throughout the ranks, and, of course, don't forget that your own example is frequently the very best method of communication.

### Instill Emotional Discipline.

Much of the overwrought behavior we see in sports today is the result of insufficient discipline. For example, a football player putting on a big show of celebration after making a tackle when his team is losing 27 to 3 late in the fourth quarter is demonstrating poor judgment, bad perspective, and lack of emotional discipline—characteristics I do not associate with success. It is up to you, the leader, to insist that those in the organization demonstrate the same great emotional control that you have. Do you have it?

# ON WOODEN

**Fred Slaughter:** UCLA Varsity, 1962–1964;
three national championships

## A COOL LEADER PREVENTS OVERHEATING

I think there were four or five games in my career at UCLA when we started out behind something like 18–2—just getting killed. I'd look over at Coach Wooden, and there he'd sit on the bench with his program rolled up in his hand—totally unaffected, almost like we were ahead. And I'd think to myself, "Hey, if he's not worried why should I be worried? Let's just do what the guy told us to do."

And you know what? We won all those games except one, and even that was close. It's the doggonest experience to see that. He was cool when it counted; his confidence and strength became ours. In my three years on the UCLA varsity team I never once saw him rattled.

Coach Wooden dealt in the positive. He would not spend time on the negative—he was always focusing on moving forward with what we had to learn to make us better.

He could sense when we might be thinking negatively, getting down on ourselves. Then he'd come in all positive: "This is what you guys are supposed to do. Follow this and we'll be fine." No browbeating or yelling. And after a while we'd look back and, doggone, we were fine. Coach Wooden had his system, and he believed in it, and he taught us to believe in it.

He'd keep telling us, "Focus on what I'm teaching. Don't focus on the score. Just do what you're supposed to do and things will work out fine. Just play as a team and we'll be fine." He was always supportive, even when he was correcting something wrong.

Most of all he taught us unity and oneness of purpose in what we were doing, namely, working to be the very best we could be—to perform our best out there on the court.

And he understood how to get you to listen. When I arrived at UCLA, I was shooting a fade-away jump shot and it was good. I used it in high school to become the number-one high school player in Kansas. But Coach Wooden didn't like it. He told me, "Fred, you know what I want is when you're finished with the shot to be around the basket. We need you to rebound. Now, if you fade away, you remove yourself from rebounding."

But I loved that shot. I wouldn't give it up until I heard him say very calmly, "Fred, you can do it the way I am teaching you or you can watch the game next Saturday sitting next to me on the bench. Your replacement knows how to shoot the jump shot correctly."

Oh my goodness, I've got to tell you, you don't understand the impact of that statement. And he didn't have to throw a chair across the floor to get his point across to me.

We lost to Cincinnati in the semifinals of the national championship because of a bad charging call on us during the last minute of the game. It was a phantom call, and it cost UCLA the game and maybe the national championship. Coach's reaction in the locker room was the same as if we'd won—cool. No complaining; he told us to keep our heads up: "Adversity makes us stronger." And then he said, "Remember, you've still got one another."

But he should have added, "and you've still got me." He was part of us. He was out on the court with us even when he was sitting on the bench. And, he was right about adversity. It made us stronger. Two years later, UCLA won its first NCAA national championship.

# 8

# IT TAKES 10 HANDS TO SCORE A BASKET

*"For the strength of the pack is the wolf;
and the strength of the wolf is the pack."*
—*Rudyard Kipling*

WHEN THE USA BASKETBALL team failed to win the gold medal at the 2004 Olympics in Athens, Greece, many asked, "How could this happen? How could the USA team—every player an NBA All-Star—lose to Argentina, Lithuania, and Puerto Rico?"

It was a reasonable question. Many observers felt that the foreign teams had at very best only two or three players talented enough to make it in the NBA. Every single USA player was already in the NBA—in fact, they were some of the best in the league. How could the other countries beat us?

The answer is simple: We sent great players. They sent great teams. This is not to lay any blame on Larry Brown, coach of the USA Olympic Basketball team. As head coach, he guided the 2004 Detroit Pistons to victory in the finals over Los Angeles and its superstar lineup that included Shaquille O'Neal, Kobe Bryant, and Karl Malone. Detroit, without a single superstar, was taught fine team play by Coach Brown.

The Detroit Pistons were not superstars, but they became a super team. In the Olympics, Coach Brown had very little time to teach the talented USA players that "we" is more important than "me" and may have done very well to have secured a bronze medal.

The nature of professional basketball today is rarely about team play; rather, it features spectacular *individual* performance—the 360-degree dunk, driving the ball the length of the court with great speed, dazzling dribbling, and more. It's all very entertaining to watch, but has little to do with creating the most effective, productive, and successful team.

Entertainment itself was of little importance to me in coaching. Piggy Lambert, my coach at Purdue, however, did explain the one advantage of having a team that fans found entertaining to watch: If you're not winning many games, they'll keep you around a little longer than a coach whose losing teams are dull. Nevertheless, entertainment for the sake of entertainment was not a priority for me.

## UNDERSTAND THE BIG PICTURE

On the first day of each new season—October 15—15 players along with assistant coaches, our manager, trainer Ducky Drake, and I would gather together for our official team picture. The photograph was a study in equality. No individual on the team got special treatment or more space in the picture because of talent, seniority, past contributions, press clippings, race, or religion. You couldn't tell an All-American player from the player who occupied the far end of the bench. The head coach took up no more space than a student-manager in charge of handing out towels.

In our official photograph, *the star of the team is the team*. And that's exactly what I wanted the players to remember when the

Develop the same sense of responsibility in every player regardless of the amount of time they may get to play. The varsity squad is one team, not regulars and substitutes.

photographer was gone and the ball was in play. However, attaining this goal is most difficult for a leader to accomplish.

Managing egos—the over- and underinflated, the forceful and the fragile—is one of the great challenges facing any leader. It is a crucial task, however, if a group is going to have a fighting chance to succeed, to become a true team rather than a collection of individuals—lone wolves—each looking out for him- or herself rather than the "pack." Leadership must get those individuals thinking in terms of we rather than me. This is possible only if the leader himself thinks this way.

> **"A leader must accomplish the difficult task of getting those on the team to believe that 'we' supersedes 'me.' "**

## FEW WANT TO SHARE THE BALL

Teaching those under your leadership to put the team's welfare ahead of their own personal desires is hard because it runs counter to human nature—the natural instinct to watch out for yourself first, to take rather than to give, to withhold rather than to share.

In basketball, it is the ball itself that must be shared, quickly and efficiently, in order for the team to achieve success. A guard who spots his teammate cutting to the open basket must control his own urge to score and instead, give up—share—the ball for the benefit of the team. A player who does that consistently has made the often-difficult transition from me to we and become a true team player, the kind of individual who brings great value to the group.

In business and other organizations, the "ball" that must be shared is knowledge, experience, information, contacts, new ideas, and much more. All these things must be freely exchanged with others throughout the organization if it is going to succeed—prevail—in these extremely competitive times.

<u>TEAM SPIRIT</u>

We want no "one man" players, no "stars." We want a team made up of five boys at a time, each of whom is a forward, guard and center combined; in other words, each boy should be able to score, out-jump or out-smart one opponent, or prevent the opposing team from scoring, as the occassion demands.

No chain is stronger than its weakest link, no team is stronger than its weakest boy. One boy attempting to "grandstand" can wreck the best team ever organized. We must be "one for all" and "all for one" with every boy giving his very best every second of the game. <u>The team is first, individual credit is second.</u> There is no place for selfishness, egotism, or envy on our squad.

We want a squad of fighters afraid of no club, not cocky, not conceited, a team that plays hard, plays fair, but plays to win - always remembering that "a team that won't be beaten, can't be beaten." We want our boys to believe that "a winner never quits and a quitter never wins." Make up your mind before the game that you won't lose, that you can out-smart and out-fight the opposing team; in other words, if you have confidence in your team's ability to win, you will be plenty tough to whip.

Others may be faster than you are, larger than you are, and have far more ability than you have - but <u>no one</u> should ever be your superior in team spirit, fight, determination, ambition, and character.

A "me-first" person puts the team second, places personal gain before group success, and withholds rather than shares the "ball." This attitude is simply not acceptable and one I would not tolerate.

Getting your people to think "Team First" is vital. It starts when you teach each member of the group how she or he contributes to the organization, when you make each one feel connected to the team's efforts, productivity, and ultimate success.

Some individuals are more difficult to replace than others, but every person contributes—or should—to overall organizational success. Each individual must feel valued, from the secretary to the superstar salesperson and the senior manager. And, above all, each person must comprehend precisely how his or her own job performance is linked to the team's welfare and survival. When this is accomplished, you have made each one feel a part of something much bigger than her or his individual job. You have expanded that person's perception of the connection between his or her role in the organization and the organization itself.

## DON'T LET THE WHEELS FALL OFF

I often used the analogy of a race car team at the Indianapolis 500. The driver gets all the attention and credit as if he alone wins the race. The driver is much like a top scorer in basketball—Keith Wilkes or Dave Meyers or Bill Walton, or perhaps similar to a top producer in your organization, the one with the so-called hot hand.

However, the driver going around the track at 200 miles per hour is helpless without the rest of the team filling their "lesser" roles. One man is solely responsible for putting fuel in the car during the pit stop; another is responsible for removing and replacing lug nuts; another takes off the worn tire; another puts on a new tire. The man responsible for putting fuel into the race car must do it without making a mistake or another team member—the one doing "nothing" but holding the fire extinguisher—will be called on to prevent total disaster.

The team's success—even the driver's life—depends on each member of the group performing his or her job correctly and expeditiously regardless of how big or small the task may seem in relation to the man or woman behind the wheel. Likewise, the person who answers the telephone at your company plays a role in your success (or lack thereof). Do this person and the others who perform the tasks that make your organization really "hum" understand their connection and contribution? Do you let these individuals know, for example, how important that first contact with a potential customer or client is? Or do you let them operate in a vacuum, unconnected to everything around them?

The telephone operator and all others who may perform less "important" tasks will not feel important unless you, the leader, teach that them they are valued and explain how their contribution helps the company as a whole. Individuals who feel they don't matter will perform their jobs as if they don't count. The driver of that car race doesn't want the fellow responsible for putting the lug nuts on correctly thinking that his job doesn't really count.

Each member of the team is there for a reason, a reason that in some way contributes to the team's success. If not, why on Earth are they on your team in the first place?

I used the racing car comparison to teach our players that all roles were vital to our success, that everyone is connected to the mission in some important way. The man sitting at the far end of the bench and the person who tightens the lug nuts both can make great con-

## EXPLAIN TO EACH TEAM MEMBER PRECISELY HOW HIS OR HER CONTRIBUTIONS CONNECT TO THE WELFARE AND SUCCESS OF THE ENTIRE ORGANIZATION

Many managers and coaches take for granted that people who work with them know how their efforts help the organization. This is often not the case, especially for those in lesser roles. Go out of your way to make them feel included rather than excluded from the productivity you seek. Thank them for their efforts—if deserved—and explain why their work matters and how it contributes to the welfare of the group. You will be surprised by how quickly this raises morale and performance and creates a team sensibility.

tributions to their team's success. If the lug nuts come off, the race car crashes. I did not want UCLA to crash because people weren't doing their jobs because they felt their contributions didn't count much.

## ACKNOWLEDGE THE UNACKNOWLEDGED

I was conscientious about making those with less significant roles feel valued and appreciated. I singled out individuals who seldom saw the limelight—the player who made an assist on an important basket, a pivotal defensive play, or a free throw at a crucial moment in the game.

I also was careful to give recognition to those who did not get much playing time—the players who worked hard in practice to improve not only themselves but also their teammates who were receiving more game time. Their contributions were important and sparked the play of the stars, All-Americans such as Bill Walton and Lewis Alcindor, Jr. (Kareem Abdul-Jabbar), and others.

Regardless of my emphasis on the "quiet" contributors, reporters only wanted to ask about the stars: "Coach Wooden, what did you think of Bill Walton's great performance tonight?" I would deflect the question and call attention to the contributions—crucial contributions—that other players made. The superstars get enough attention—too much attention, in my opinion.

Whether in business or in basketball, no superstar or top performer, regardless of his or her level of God-given talent and productivity, does it alone. Every basket Bill Walton ever made utilized "10 hands." In truth, it involved many more than 10—the hands, heads, and hearts of nonstarters, the assistant coaches, the trainer, the managers, and, of course, the coach.

Here's a more dramatic description: Without teamwork in basketball, the slam dunk would become extinct. Without teamwork in business, your organization may become extinct.

Ultimately, every member of the UCLA Bruins basketball team was involved to one degree or another in every point scored and every shot blocked. And while I didn't always succeed, I tried hard to make that fact understood and appreciated by all those I allowed to join our group. I say more on this subject in Chapter 12, "Make Greatness Attainable by All."

"Ten hands" was one of the most important concepts— principles—that a player or employee can be taught. It was also one that frequently required some diligent teaching on my part. It began with my own firm belief that a player who made the team great is better than a great player.

*Selecting players – quickness over size, spirit over temperament; team contribution over individual.*

It was important that those who help the superstar *become* a superstar share in the accolades felt important and strongly connected to the team's welfare and success. Otherwise, jealousy, envy, backbiting, and backsliding are inevitable. All members of your organization need to feel their jobs make a difference, that they are connected to the success of their team.

If there are those under your leadership who do little or nothing for your organization, then you must ask yourself some uncomfortable, but necessary, questions:

Why is that person in our organization if he or she is not contributing?

What is the impact of a negligible producer on other team members?

What can we do to enhance that person's contribution?

Do we move him to another "position," restructure his current job, or make other fundamental changes that would amplify that person's contributions?

Should that person be removed from our team?

The marginal producer who may elicit these questions, however, is usually the exception to the rule. For the majority of others, those who labor hard in near anonymity, I was conscientious in recognizing them both in public and during practice.

My policy of making sure that players who didn't receive much attention were consistently recognized—made to feel valued—was actually tabulated during an independent study done many years ago that measured the amount of praise I gave out during practice. It showed that individuals in lesser roles received compliments, support, and acknowledgment—praise—at a much higher rate than so-called superstars. That was exactly my intention.

The results raised some eyebrows, however, because they suggested I was ignoring the contributions and impact of the top performers, almost overlooking their efforts. This was not true. What the study failed to record, because it wasn't evident on the court during practice, was the ample praise I gave to our top performers privately, away from the other players.

There was no way I was going to let a Lewis Alcindor, Jr. feel unappreciated or neglected. I simply felt it counterproductive to add to the praise heaped on him by others. Consequently, my compliments and supporting comments were offered most often in private.

Of course, with Alcindor and Walton, to name just two, I was fortunate to have individuals who believed in a team first philosophy. For example, Alcindor could have been the greatest scorer in college basketball history, but he was willing to forgo that personal glory to do what best served our team. Walton was the same. These were two superstars who genuinely viewed their own press clippings as secondary to those of the team. When your top producers behave in this manner, it makes a leader's job much easier and your organization much stronger. Of course, the opposite is also true. Effectiveness and productivity are most likely diminished when you are plagued with individuals who view your team as secondary to their own interests.

## PRIVATE AND PUBLIC PRAISE

Acknowledging top producers does not always have to be done publicly. It is often more effective for a leader to praise their outstanding performance when others are not around. It gives the "superstar" deserved recognition without creating envy or resentment. Conversely, praise for those in lesser roles is often maximized by doing it in a more public manner.

## COAX THOSE WHO NEED IT

Of course, talented individuals often require a little coaching—that is, coaxing—to really *get it* when it comes to selfless team play. For example, a future All-American such as Sidney Wicks initially kept too close an eye on his personal statistics. The statistics I was noting, however, showed that regardless of the various combinations of players with whom Sidney scrimmaged, his personal numbers stayed high while those of the others tended to drop off. He was focused on his own welfare—statistics—above that of the team. Despite the fact that he was more talented than those who played ahead of him, I kept him out of the starting rotation as an incentive for Sidney to become a complete team player.

When he came to understand and accept my philosophy, that the best players don't necessarily make for the best teams and that personal statistics matter only to the degree to which they enhance overall team performance, Sidney changed dramatically for the better. During his second season on the UCLA varsity, he emerged as the best college forward in America—a wonderful team player who embraced the philosophy that it takes 10 hands to make a basket.

One last word for the record: As much as Sidney wanted to be a starter his first year, he did not become embittered when I ruled otherwise. In part, this was because I enforced my decision without personal attacks, ridicule, or animosity. My directives and discipline were delivered in a businesslike and professional manner.

Sidney, in fact, also had a great sense of humor and never lost it during his, at times, trying first season on the UCLA varsity. One day he arrived at practice with a gift that was all wrapped up. As he handed it to me, Sidney said, "Coach, this for Mrs. Wooden. I think she'll want to put it up in your living room." I was touched by his thoughtfulness. That night when Nell opened Sidney's gift at the dinner table, we both chuckled. It was a big picture of one of the leading counterculture revolutionaries of the time.

Sidney was an exceptional individual, but like most of us he had his own peculiarities. I am pleased that in the course of a difficult transition for him, from "me first" to "Team First," I was able to keep the process on track and productive. It would have been a shame to lose Sidney because I lacked the skills necessary to teach my philosophy and methodology to a very talented young man. This is true for leadership in any context.

## THE WOLF AND THE PACK

I sought only to put the best possible *team* together, the group of individuals who worked best—selflessly—as a unit. I didn't see black players or white players. I didn't care about their politics or religion.

"All for one and one for all" is not an empty slogan for me. I don't need scientific proof to know that Rudyard Kipling was correct: "For the strength of the pack is the wolf; and the strength of the wolf is the pack." That describes the relationship between the individual and the organization—the player and the team. In basketball, a field goal is usually scored only after several hands have touched the ball. No shot is blocked, no play is run, no game is won, unless everyone is doing his job—serving the team to the best of his ability. No one player should take credit for the effort of all the others.

That is the primary reason I strongly discouraged individuality—showboating or flamboyance—in the context of team play. Showing off or doing something contrived to gain attention for oneself not only demeans that individual, it is dismissive of the effort made by all the other team members.

A player who is thumping his chest after he makes a basket is acknowledging the wrong person. Thus, I insisted the player who scores give a nod or "thumb's up" to the teammate who helped—the one who provided the assist. That way it was more likely to happen again.

I taught our players to think as one, a unit, and not just a collection of independent operators in which every person was out for himself. By insisting that the scorer acknowledge others, I was strengthening the connection those "others" felt to the production process.

Sharing credit is a surefire way of improving the performance results for any organization. Everyone starts helping everyone. To confirm that this was happening at UCLA, I would periodically check the statistics and look for balance in our attack to ensure that no one position or player had a disproportionate role. For example, I once added up the numbers and found that in the preceding 20 seasons our scoring was distributed as follows: Out of 39,135 baskets scored, guards had made 16,131 of them; forwards had made 15,355; centers had made 7,649. This meant that during a typical season our guards had taken just 1½ fewer shots per game than the forwards. This was exactly my goal, balanced scoring, which meant that no opponent could stop us by defending against just one player. And the only way to ensure balance in scoring was to involve everyone in the production process. This occurs when you are able to get those under your leadership to think "Team First" rather than "me first."

An organization that has all members focused first and foremost on doing what benefits the group is a force to be reckoned with. I know personally what can happen when everyone truly believes it takes 10 hands to make a basket. It happened most dramatically during my sixteenth season as head coach at UCLA.

## A KEEN EYE FOR TEAM SPIRIT

In 1964, for the first time ever, UCLA advanced to the finals of the NCAA national basketball tournament. Despite the fact that we were undefeated going into the championship game, most critics discounted our chances and predicted we would lose. Duke was taller and had great talent, but the Bruins had a significant asset. A visiting foreign coach who had been analyzing the teams for several weeks recognized it.

On the morning of the championship game that coach, Aleksandar Nikolic from Yugoslavia, boldly announced to reporters that UCLA would beat Duke. "Why?" the journalists asked with great surprise. Coach Nikolic held up his right hand with five fingers outstretched. Then he curled them into a tight fist: "UCLA is team! UCLA is team!" he announced confidently.

The UCLA players that faced Duke in the finals later that night were a team—a *real* team, a group of individuals who understood it takes 10 hands to score a basket. Because of it, UCLA surprised the experts and won its first-ever national championship in basketball.

What we did then in basketball is no different than what any organization can do when leadership creates a true spirit of sharing and selflessness directed at what most benefits the group. When those you lead believe their best interests are served when they place the team first, the results will often be first place for the team.

## RULES TO LEAD BY

**The Star of the Team Is the Team.**
As leader, you must be consistent and persistent in delivering your Team First message. Top performers and producers must fully comprehend that others in the organization "assist"—make possible—their success. Individual awards and accolades are fine, but they must never overshadow the organization and its primacy. Remember Walton and Alcindor: As talented as they were—All-Americans—they put the team's welfare first.

**Insist that Members of Your Team Share the "Ball"—Information, Ideas, and More.**
The most effective leaders understand the importance of making sure that no member of the team hoards data, information, ideas, and the like. In business, it is the sharing of ideas and putting them to work that leads to a "best practice" mindset.

**Go Out of Your Way to Praise Those "Quiet" Performers Who Make Things Happen.**
In every organization there are those vital individuals who seem to get things done with little effort and less notice. In more cases than not, however, these key players work very hard to achieve what they do. Often their efforts are not visible to the group. These are the people that make the trains run on time, and they deserve your attention.

**Seek Players Who Will Make the Best Team Rather Than the Best Players.**

Astute leadership understands the chemistry of teams and organizations. Often the most talented individuals will not be a good fit for your group. Be alert to overall impact—chemistry. Remember future All-American Sidney Wicks, who achieved personal greatness soon after he began putting the team first.

---

# ON WOODEN

**Gail Goodrich:** UCLA Varsity; 1963–1965;
two national championships

---

## SHARE THE BALL; THINK BEYOND YOURSELF

I came out of high school—LA Poly—as a guard who always thought in terms of having the ball. That's how a guard thinks: "Give me the ball so I can shoot."

Coach Wooden wanted me to think beyond just having the ball because he had decided to install the Press—a full-court defense. Of course, when you play defense you don't have the ball. He was having a little trouble getting me to change my thinking until one day Coach said, "Gail, the game is 40 minutes long. The opponent has the ball approximately half the time. That leaves us 20 minutes with the basketball.

"We have five players. In my system balance is important, so each player should handle the ball about the same amount of time. That means you will have the basketball for approximately four minutes per game. Gail, what are you going to do for the team during those *other* 35 minutes when you do not have the ball?"

It only took him about 15 seconds, but he dramatically broadened my understanding of the role I needed to play on the team. Coach used a variety of ways to teach what he wanted you to learn. Sometimes during practice he would have the guards switch positions with the forwards—have us do the other guy's job. He wanted everybody to understand the requirements of the player in the other positions. Coach Wooden wanted the guard to appreciate the challenges a forward faced and the forward to appreciate what a guard had to deal with.

He worked very hard to figure out ways to have us think like a team, to work as a unit, not every man out for himself.

I chose UCLA because of how he conducted practices (I had watched the Bruins at the Men's Gym while I was in high school). I was so impressed by his control of the practice, totally in charge.

He had his 3 × 5 cards and notes and was always looking at the clock to stay on time. He went from one drill to another and then another and another—complete organization; no fooling around, no lulls. He was a master of using time efficiently. Coach could tell you exactly what he had done in practice on that same day 10 years earlier at 4:35 p.m.

He believed that winning is a result of process, and he was a master of the process, of getting us to focus on what we were doing rather than the final score. One drill he had was to run a play over and over at full speed, but he wouldn't let us shoot the ball. He made us concentrate on what happened before the shot was taken, what happened to make it possible. He made us focus on execution. He built teams that knew how to execute.

You knew you were in trouble when you heard him say, "Goodness gracious, sakes alive!" Big trouble. You knew the hammer was heading your way when you heard that. The hammer was the bench, or worse, the shower. Many times he wouldn't exactly tell you what you couldn't do, but he worked things so that it was hard to do them.

Every year during football season there was a Cal Weekend up at Berkeley when the Bruins played the Bears. Coach didn't want his players going up there because it was a big party weekend. But instead of telling us we couldn't go, he just moved practice on Friday back to 6 p.m. Then he kept us late and worked us so hard that nobody had the time or energy to drive all night to get there.

But one year John Galbraith and I decided to fly up for Cal Weekend. I was a Beta Theta Pi and had a couple of beers at the fraternity party on Saturday night after the game. Somehow, Coach Wooden found out not only that I went up to Berkeley but that I'd had a few beers.

Monday morning I got a call that he wanted to see me in his office. "Did you have fun this weekend?" he asked. I nodded. "You know, Gail, if I ever see you drinking, you're gone." I nodded, but I was in shock. "How does he know? How did he find out?" I was thinking.

"Now, you've got a very good year coming up. You don't want to jeopardize that, do you? You don't want to hurt the team, do you?" I answered, "No, Coach. I don't want to hurt the team."

"Good. I'll see you at practice."

The thing was, he wouldn't try and catch you doing something wrong like having a beer. That wasn't his style. He wanted you to assume responsibility for your actions, to have self-control. The whole point of that conversation on Monday was to make me think about what choices I was making. And I did.

He always talked about balance: body balance, scoring balance, team balance, and most of all, mental and emotional balance. Your feet have to be in balance. Your body has to be in balance over your feet. Your head needs to be in balance with your body and your arms. He said if you're not in balance, you'll eventually fall over, and he meant it in more ways than one.

I came to see balance as one of the keys to success not only in basketball, but in life. When things get out of balance, it's generally not good. Everything needs balance. That one word he kept drilling at us—balance—has stuck with me, became important in how I try to do things.

He never talked about winning, even in the locker room just before the first national championship game against Duke. He calmly went through our game plan and said if we played a good 94-foot game, meaning execution of the Press at one end of the court and good play making at the other end, we'd be able to come back in the locker room afterward with our heads held high. Never mentioned winning a championship or winning the game.

But then, just before we went out on the court, he asked us, "Does anybody here remember who was the runner-up in last year's national championship?"

Nobody raised his hand. That's as close as he ever got to a pep talk.

# 9

# LITTLE THINGS MAKE BIG THINGS HAPPEN

*"Think small. Work hard. Get Good."*

Hᴵɢʜ ᴘᴇʀꜰᴏʀᴍᴀɴᴄᴇ ᴀɴᴅ ᴘʀᴏᴅᴜᴄᴛɪᴏɴ are achieved only through the identification and perfection of small but relevant details—little things done well. Sloppiness in tending to details is common in sports as well as other types of organizations. When it occurs, blame rests with you, the leader, not with your team. Those under your leadership must be taught that little things make the big things happen. In fact, they must first learn there are no big things, only a logical accumulation of little things done at a very high standard of performance.

I derived great satisfaction from identifying and perfecting those "trivial" and often troublesome details, because I knew, without doubt, that each one brought UCLA a bit closer to our goal: competitive greatness. If you collect enough pennies you'll eventually be rich. Each relevant and perfected detail was another penny in our bank.

Often we place such emphasis on distant goals (annual sales targets in business; a national title or championship in sports) that inadequate attention is given to what it takes to get there—the day-by-day particulars of how you conduct business. At UCLA I sought

> Attentiveness to Detail – Leave nothing to chance. The difference
> in the championship and merely good team is often the perfection of
> minor details.

to ensure that in the course of conducting our business, basketball, we maintained very lofty standards in the detail department. My norm was abnormally high.

Many onlookers thought the hundreds of specifics I selected and refined were laughable, but I wasn't laughing. I knew very well that those relevant details, done right, were the foundation for UCLA's success. It's the same for your organization. Little things make all the difference in the world.

## WEAR THE OPPONENT'S JERSEY

When it came to perfecting details I worked "feet first," from the ground up. Socks? During our first team meeting I personally

### HER PERSPECTIVE IS CORRECT

Mother Teresa once said: "There are no big things. Only little things done with love." That sums it up very well. When you derive pleasure and pride in perfecting seemingly "minor" details—and teach those you lead to do the same—big things eventually start falling into place. This is what separates achievers from the also-rans, the great from the good, the doers from the dreamers. (Of course, you may have noticed that many exceptional achievers are *both* doers and dreamers. It's a good combination, so long as you make sure to do those little things "with love.")

showed players how to put them on correctly. Shoes? We didn't ask players what size they wore. I insisted our trainer measure each student-athlete's foot—right *and* left—to ensure that newly issued sneakers fit properly. I wanted no slippage. Shoestrings? I sat down and showed players how to lace and then tie their sneakers correctly to avoid having them come undone during practice or a game.

Attention to these items—socks, shoes, and shoestrings—could prevent problems during performance. I applied this same meticulous attention to details in many other areas. For example, the only real concession I made to preparing for a specific upcoming opponent was to buy inexpensive cloth vests that were the same color as the opposing team's uniform. For Stanford, red vests; for Cal (University of California, Berkeley), blue vests; for the Washington Huskies, purple vests.

In practices before the game, our starting players scrimmaged against teammates who were wearing vests with the color of our next opponent's uniform. Did this detail of vests make a difference? Did wearing the opponent's "uniform" help prepare our starting team for what it would see on the court during the next game? I thought it might make a difference. That's all the convincing I needed.

Additionally, I insisted that jerseys always be tucked in, because I felt it helped create a sense of self-identity and unity. It was a detail that helped teach our players that sloppiness was not tolerated—in anything. Eliminating sloppiness and creating unity were very important to me and were effectively instilled by attending to such details.

When I arrived at UCLA, practice uniforms were in poor shape and players often brought T-shirts from home and wore sneakers of their own choosing. I stopped that immediately by ordering new practice uniforms and sneakers. I didn't want to look out on the court during practice and a see a rag-tag collection of outfits. Nor did I want players to look at one another and see sloppiness in the appearance of their teammates. New practice uniforms, good shoes, jerseys tucked in—these things make a difference.

From the minute a UCLA Bruin put on a UCLA uniform— even a practice uniform—I wanted him to recognize that he was now part of something special, an organization, a team, a group that did things differently. And it did things the right way all the time, starting from the ground up.

For much the same reason, I wanted the players to look "professional" when we traveled as a group—shirt and tie, coat, and slacks. Not only were they representing the university, but their wearing that attire also signaled to the players themselves that being a Bruin was something special and that they should conduct themselves accordingly.

## NOT A PERFECTIONIST

Nevertheless, while I strove for perfection, "'perfectionist" is not the description I would choose for myself. Perfection, as I understand it, is not attainable by mortal man. Striving for it, however, is very attainable. And I strove for it ceaselessly.

I don't think it's being a perfectionist to identify those things that would improve team performance. If something occurred to me that might help us, I implemented it. It was as simple as that— common sense. Do it enough times in enough ways, and good things will happen.

> Different drills are devised to teach each man the specific fundamentals required for his position, and then additional drills are added which have two positions working together, then three, then four, and finally the entire five man unit.

For example, I stopped providing bits of chocolate to players during halftime because I determined that it left phlegm in their windpipes. I decided that orange slices provided the same energy boost without creating phlegm. Phlegm, like shoestrings that come undone, can cause distraction, which leads to errors that can get you outplayed.

I also insisted that players deposit the rinds from those orange slices in a wastebasket and not just toss them carelessly on the floor *near* the wastebasket. Carelessness, like sloppiness, is not a characteristic seen in successful organizations; tolerating either is the mark of an ineffective leader.

I believed, and still do, that teaching a player not to be careless and sloppy starts with such things as putting orange rinds in the wastebasket. Nevertheless, I know that this logic will strike some as humorous. For me, it was not humorous; I was dead serious.

And there was much more. At team meals, water was served at room temperature without ice to avoid the possibility of stomach cramps. It was just another potential problem that was easily headed off. All this eventually starts to add up and make a difference: socks and shoestrings, ice and oranges, neatness and uniformity. These are little things that are neither unimportant nor incidental. And when I identified a detail that seemed relevant, I took care of it, because our team would benefit. To me, this is less about being a perfectionist and more about having a determination to be seeking improvement constantly, to always be looking for a better way of doing things.

The exact nature of "relevant details" differs from sport to sport and organization to organization. And, of course, some adjustments come simply because times change. But the basics of success in leadership, in my opinion, don't change much, especially when it comes to the connection between the identification and perfection of little things and achievement of those big things we strive for.

An effective leader develops the ability to correctly identify the *pertinent* detail or details—incidentals in a market, industry, or sport, for example, that might create an incremental advantage. While the specifics may be small, it is no small task. Success, not the devil, is in the details.

A word of caution: Balance is very important when it comes to allocating time to these issues. To maintain balance, a leader must be very well organized, establish productive priorities, and allocate the appropriate amount of time and attention to each of the many details that is deemed relevant.

Of course, judicious delegation is necessary, but ultimately the leader is the one delegated with responsibility for the welfare of the team. Balance is crucial in this regard. Losing it can be fatal. For example, some years back there was a prominent basketball coach who decided that the free throw—making it—was the single most important factor when it came to winning or losing games. Consequently, he set out to have his players master every detail required for shooting a free throw. The team practiced free throws in a manner that was disproportionate to other important aspects of the game.

## PERFECTION OF DETAILS MUST NOT COME AT THE EXPENSE OF EQUILIBRIUM

Balance and moderation are most essential to your organization's strength and survival. The most effective leaders focus on the right details in a balanced way. If you are engaged in a complex business, enlist the help of others to ensure that details are executed properly. (Of course, always remember this detail: Just because you've delegated something doesn't mean it got done.)

Of course, they became very proficient when it came time to make a free throw. By season's end his players were perhaps the finest free throw shooters in America. Unfortunately, they had trouble winning basketball games. In the process of perfecting free throws, balance was lost in other important areas: the details of playing defense, shooting, fast breaks, and so much else. Everything but free throw shooting had suffered.

When balance is lost, an organization grows weaker and is made vulnerable. This particular coach had pursued perfection of a single detail at the expense of most everything else. Details are vitally important, but so is balance. Like a man walking on ice, balance is most difficult to regain once it starts to slip away.

## THE RIVET AND THE WING

I consider each detail like a rivet on the wing of an airplane. Remove one rivet from the wing, and it remains intact; remove enough of them, however, and the wing falls off.

I didn't want anything to fall off when it came to the quality of performance of the UCLA Bruins basketball team. Whether in practice or in a game, I made sure every relevant "rivet" was in place and tightened up. In my coaching, it started with feet (socks, shoes, and shoestrings), but I addressed other parts of the anatomy as well. Beards and long hair were forbidden, because I knew that during competition they become soaked with sweat. A player who touches his beard or runs his hand across his hair will have slippery hands and fingers. Slick fingers lead to poor ball handling, and poor ball handling leads to turnovers and other costly errors. Thus, to reduce the chance of a

> "Minor details—like pennies—add up. A good banker isn't careless with pennies; a good leader isn't sloppy about details."

turnover caused by perspiration, the solution was simple: short hair, no beards, and not even muttonchops (long sideburns).

Now, before you conclude that I was concerned with everything *except* how to actually play basketball—long hair, phlegm, and all the rest—let me assure you that my attention to details extended even more deeply, meticulously, and forcefully into the physical mechanics and execution of the game itself. For me and the assistant coaches, socks were just a starting point.

> ~~~, environs, ream, ~~~
> Ball handling- close to body, chest high, finger pressure only, quickness with accuracy, no ball fakes.
> 16. Shooting - "touch" finger pressure, close to body, head follow.
> 17. Receiving - target - open hand away from danger, block and tuck
> 18. Dribbling - quickness of bounce, elbow in contact with body
> 19. Stop and turn - inside turn only.
> 20. Eyes - on offense - always on ball when some one else has the ball. on defense - always know the location of the ball, as you look "through" your man or at the midpoint between your man and the ball.

## SEEKING THE RIGHT WAY ALWAYS

Just as there is a correct way to tie your sneakers, there is a correct way of executing virtually everything in the game of basketball. You may have discovered it's much the same with your own organization. Consequently, for me, there isn't an "approximate" way to shoot a jump shot; there is a precise method for doing it—one that affords the optimum chance for making a basket and scoring points.

I was not trying to create robots who simply did as they were told, but rather individuals who were *extremely* well grounded in the correct fundamentals, who had good performance habits. From there, players could, and would, make adjustments based on whatever pressures and obstacles the competition imposed upon them. An individual grounded in the fundamentals has, I believe, a much higher likelihood of success when sudden change is forced upon him.

Before making the change or the adjustments, I wanted each player to know how to do things the right way. After that, I had some flexibility when it came to allowing exceptions where results were, or could be, significantly above the average. For example, Keith Wilkes shot free throws from behind his head; that is, as he lined up to shoot, his head was between the basket and the basketball. You could hardly make it any more difficult on yourself unless you were blindfolded.

> *"Over-coaching" can be more harmful than "under-coaching." Don't give them too much and don't take away their initiative.*

When it came to free throws, I was willing to wait until the shooters started missing free throws before I taught them how to shoot correctly. Once they started missing, it was easy to get them to change. However, Keith never started missing. In fact, during my 27 years as head coach of the UCLA Bruins, Keith had a stellar single season record for making free throws: 87.2 percent. During that particular season, he had 94 free throw attempts, made 88 of them, and missed only 12. I've coached players who missed more than 12 free throws before the season was two weeks old.

Occasionally, I found it best to let those I coached do it their own way, when it was productive. In those instances, their own way worked best and I didn't change it. This was the case with the unorthodox style of Keith Wilkes.

An effective leader allows exceptions to the rule for exceptional results or when circumstance demands. On those occasions when it happened—and didn't adversely impact on the behavior or attitude of the rest of the group—I allowed for variations, alternative methods, and individual creativity. Otherwise, I taught and insisted on a very precise way of doing things.

This applied to all aspects of the game: passing, pivoting, preparing for a rebound, in-bounding, body balance, faking, feinting, guarding, shooting, running patterns, and much more. The small details of performing these tasks were, of course, those I deemed extremely relevant to our improvement and ultimate success.

Rebounding, for example, included the following specifics:

1. Assume every shot will be missed and produce a subsequent opportunity to get a rebound.
2. Immediately get your hands shoulder-high, *not* above your head. While many coaches instructed players to put both hands above the head, I didn't because this position ignores the fact that the ball often bounces off the backboard or basket at a lower angle. I wanted our players ready for either a higher or a lower rebound. A small thing, perhaps, but over the years I observed it made a difference in performance results. UCLA players often were able to out-rebound taller opponents.
3. After steps 1 and 2, *go get the ball.*

There was much more to it than that—for example, how to pivot and block out an opposing player near the basket—but those three directives perhaps illuminate the approach I took to identifying and perfecting some of the physical mechanics of rebounding. I took the same approach to all aspects of execution.

Everything was connected to everything; all details connected to other details as part of the whole. For example, sweat socks, put on correctly, reduce the chance of blisters, which, in turn, ensures that

## ALLOW EXCEPTIONS FOR
## EXCEPTIONAL RESULTS

**I**f you have a performer in your organization who makes great things happen in an unconventional way, be tolerant so long as the path she or he chooses is ethical and does not impact negatively on the behavior and attitude of others. A leader needs good judgment in these situations. In sports we see coaches constantly evaluating the risk and reward of bringing players onto the team who have extreme talent but who march to their own drummer in style, substance, and personal morality. It is easy to be blind-sided by talent.

a player can rebound—or shoot free throws or play defense—free from pain and distraction. Likewise, the possibility of executing a successful fast break is more likely if a shoestring doesn't come untied.

My dedication to identifying and perfecting relevant details in all areas was intended to set the tone both in style and in substance for how the UCLA Bruins conducted business during games. Our standards were very high when it came to the execution of fundamentals. And fundamentals, done well, are the foundation upon which effective leaders build highly productive teams and very competitive organizations.

## MAKE EXCELLENCE A HABIT

My details are not your details. Nevertheless, identifying and perfecting those that apply to our own situation is a duty entrusted to those in leadership. Being negligent in this area breaks the trust.

"Little things make big things happen" is the phrase I used in pointing out the importance of correct selection and perfection of details. Of course, I recognize that a team also needs talent to make big things happen, but talent alone won't get the job done. Talent must be nourished in an environment that demands the correct execution of relevant details.

Although we never achieved perfection in basketball at UCLA, we were ceaseless in our effort to attain that level of performance. Only then is there some chance of approaching it—not attaining it, but approaching it.

UCLA had four so-called perfect seasons (30–0) during my years as head coach, and yet we never played a perfect game. However, we never ceased striving for the perfect play, the perfect pass, the perfect game. And it all started, in my view, with teaching those under my leadership how to put on their sweat socks "perfectly."

## DEFINE AVERAGE AS ABOVE AVERAGE

There was no single big thing that made our UCLA basketball teams effective, not the press or the fast break, not size, not condition—no single *big* thing. Instead, it was hundreds of small things done the right way, and done consistently.

A leader must identify each of the many details that are most pivotal to team success and then establish, and teach, a high standard of behavior or performance in executing those details. How you—the leader—define "average" is how your team will define it. Some leaders define average as average; some define average as being significantly above average.

It is easy to be lazy when it comes to details. Laziness is a euphemism for sloppiness, and sloppiness precludes any organization from achieving competitive greatness and success. Your ability as leader to set and achieve high standards in the domain of details—

to insist that average will be well above average—is one of the accurate predictors of how effective you will be as a leader, and how productive those under your supervision will be as a team.

Once you recognize the connection between sweat socks and success, you have acquired one of the most valuable assets for effective leadership, namely, that little things, done well, make big things happen for you and your organization.

## RULES TO LEAD BY

### It All Starts with the Socks.
Success begins from the ground up. It never bothered me to be chided over my commitment to doing the little thing right. Make sure that you and your team put their "socks" on in the correct manner.

### The Right Rivets Are Essential.
There are no big things, only an accumulation of many little things. Remove enough rivets and the wing falls off. However, it is up to you, the leader, to identify the correct rivets and determine how much attention each will be given. Do this correctly and your organization will survive flying through even the most turbulent competitive storm.

### Nourish Talent in an Environment of Perfected Details.
Only then will your team achieve consistent success. Remember that talent alone will not suffice. Each year in sports and business we see talented teams—and individuals—fail because of neglected details.

### Sloppiness Breeds Sloppiness.
From the first moment of the first day of UCLA's season, I insisted we do things right—not almost right, but completely right. It's an atti-

tude, a way of conducting business. A casual approach to executing the details of a job ensures that the job will be done poorly. And then another job will be done poorly. It grows.

# ON WOODEN
**Lynn Shackleford:** UCLA Varsity, 1967–1969;
three national championships

### DETAILS ON THE FIRST DAY

The very first team meeting I ever attended at UCLA was a shock. Sitting next to me was another freshman—the guy who had been the most coveted high school player in America, Kareem Abdul-Jabbar (Lewis Alcindor, Jr.).

Scattered around us were our freshman teammates—some of the best in the country—as well as the returning members of UCLA's varsity team that had won the NCAA national championship several months earlier—Edgar Lacey, Kenny Washington, Doug McIntosh, Fred Goss, Mike Lynn, and others.

There was a lot of energy and talent in that room waiting for the arrival of Coach Wooden and his words of wisdom. Pretty soon he walked in and went directly to the front of the classroom in which we had gathered. Finally, the big moment had arrived, my first experience as a member of a UCLA team—reigning national champions!—coached by the famous John Wooden.

He looked at us for a moment and began his remarks. And that's what was shocking: "Gentlemen," he said, "Welcome. Let's get down to business. I want to remind each one of you of a few important rules we have here at UCLA. Number one: Keep your fingernails trimmed. Number two: Keep your hair short. Number three: Keep your jersey tucked into your trunks at all times." He looked around the room for a moment and then added solemnly: "Am I clear?"

I wondered, "Is he making a joke?" But there was no laughter, not even smiles, from any of the varsity players. They knew better. Nevertheless, I couldn't understand why he was wasting his time on stuff like that.

As the months—eventually years (and three more national championships)—went by, I came to recognize that "stuff like that" was part of the genius in his leadership. There was logic to every move. Details of fingernails, hair, and jerseys led to details for running plays, handling the ball, and everything else—hundreds of small things done right.

Everything was related to everything else; nothing was left to chance; it all had to be done well. Sloppiness was not allowed in anything; not in passing, shooting, or trimming your fingernails and tucking in a jersey.

Coach Wooden taught that great things can only be accomplished by doing the little things right. Doing things right became a habit with us.

He kept it simple. What's more simple than short hair? What's more simple than squaring up for a shot? All these simple little things added up—one at a time—to an enormous amount of information that he presented in a plain and direct way, bit by bit. Ultimately, he and the team put it all together in practice and then in games.

To accomplish this, he thought out his lesson plan for each day's practice with great precision. He knew what he wanted to accomplish and how to do it. Part of his effectiveness may have come from the fact that he has a master's degree in English. He could say in one short sentence what it took others a long time to get out. He could communicate so much so fast—no wasted words, no beating around the bush.

Coach Wooden's practices were very businesslike and his presence very strong. There were times when he got to a level of sternness mixed with some anger that was nothing to fool with. There was never any screaming or yelling, but his intensity was something else. Especially when he thought we weren't giving it our best effort—watch out then.

During a game against Cal (University of California, Berkeley), we went to the locker room at halftime with a lead, but he was very unhappy. The score didn't matter. He felt that we weren't playing with intensity. And he gave us a tongue lashing that I still remember well. And he did so without screaming or shouting.

The fact that we were ahead was incidental. What mattered to him was that we weren't playing to our potential. And, it worked the other way too. If the score was going against us, but we were giving it our best effort, he wouldn't get upset. Instead, Coach would very calmly instruct us on changes that should be made.

In 1968, number-one ranked UCLA played number-two ranked Houston in the Astrodome. It was called the Game of the Century. The Cougars were undefeated on the year and UCLA had a 47-game winning streak going.

It was the first regular-season game ever seen on national television, the first ever played in the Astrodome, and the first to have attendance of over 50,000. It was a big deal. Nobody had ever seen anything like it before in college basketball.

UCLA lost in the final seconds, 71–69, and our 47-game winning streak came to an end. After the game, in the locker room, all the Bruins were very interested to see Coach Wooden's reaction. As UCLA players we had never seen him lose a single game. Suddenly, he had lost, and it was a big game. How would he react?

When Coach walked into the locker room after losing the Game of the Century, he was very even keeled. There was even a slight smile on his face. He told us, "It's not the end of the world. We'll do better next time." He was pleased with our effort. The score was secondary; having our winning streak snapped was not his concern. Our effort on the court had been total. That made him happy.

In 1967, UCLA played in the finals of the NCAA tournament in Louisville. We hadn't lost a game all season. Just before we went on the court to play Dayton for the national championship, the whole team sat in the locker room for Coach Wooden's pregame talk. Four of the starters were first-year varsity players who were about to face their first national championship game in a few minutes—Kareem, Lucius Allen, Kenny Heitz, and me.

Coach Wooden walked up to the chalkboard and began to diagram something, maybe a new play or defensive tactic. But it wasn't. Coach was diagramming where we should stand during the national anthem! He then spoke about our conduct following the game. The day before, players on another team had gotten rowdy, and he cautioned us about behaving badly. He never mentioned anything about the opponent we were going to play for the national championship; no plays, no specifics of the game. None of that.

What this was about, of course, was his belief that by game time his teaching was complete; if he hadn't taught us what we needed to know by then, it was too late.

Of course, he *had* taught us what we needed to know. And it started on the very first day when he walked to the front of the class and said to the freshman and returning varsity players, "Gentlemen, let's get right down to business." And then he told us about fingernails, short hair, and tucking in jerseys. It's still a little shocking when I think about it.

# 10

# MAKE EACH DAY YOUR MASTERPIECE

*"Activity—to produce real results—must be organized and executed meticulously. Otherwise, it's no different from children running around the playground at recess."*

I N A COMPETITIVE ENVIRONMENT, there is never enough time. As such, a leader must be skillful—a master—in using time productively and teaching others to do the same. Your skill in doing this directly impacts on the ability of your organization to compete—even survive.

Time, used correctly, is among your most potent assets. For many leaders, however, it seems otherwise. The months, weeks, and minutes are ill defined and almost intangible in their minds, evaporating without leaving a trace of achievement behind.

In the mind of those leaders whose organizations get things done, time is tangible, a commodity as touchable as gold. They also understand that unlike gold, time cannot be recovered once lost or squandered. A good leader understands that without time you are left with virtually nothing.

My own understanding and appreciation of this fact goes back to one of my father's favorite refrains: "Make each day your masterpiece." This axiom was his way of reminding me to always use time prudently—each day, each hour, each minute.

He wanted me to understand the value and great potential that time offers; he wanted me to use it wisely, not wastefully. Of course, Dad was talking about more than time spent at work. He was referring to how I should live each day of my life, to use whatever time the Good Lord grants in a fruitful and positive manner. I tried to apply his advice in all areas, including, most particularly, my profession.

Only when you fully comprehend the magnitude of the potential that exists in every *individual* minute will you begin to treat time with the grave respect it deserves. Over the decades I've observed that most effective leaders do not disrespect time, not a minute. They understand that when it comes to success—real achievement—time is of the essence. And the essence of success is time.

As I evolved as a coach and leader, my appreciation for time increased along with my skill in using it more and more effectively. Although perfection is not possible, I tried hard at UCLA to make every minute of my teaching as good as it could be—each meeting a masterpiece, each practice a pursuit of perfection. There was a sense of urgency in everything we did; not haste, not hurry, but hustle.

## FAILING TO PREPARE IS PREPARING TO FAIL

This came from my sure knowledge that how you practice is how you play—in sports and in everything else. I was motivated, in part, by knowing how little time was available to do my job, namely, getting the most out of what we had as a team.

UCLA practices, on average, were two hours in length; each practice week had five days; the regular basketball season was 21 weeks long. The multiplication was simple and the tallies clarifying. On average, I had 210 hours of practice time to accomplish my teaching goals (105 practices, each two hours long). Or, as journalists, fans, and alumni might have declared, "John Wooden has 210 hours to win a national championship." That comes down to 12,600 minutes of actual practice time during the regular season. Those minutes can go by quickly—evaporate—if you're careless with them. Carelessness is not something I've been accused of with any frequency.

I placed great significance in every *single* one of those minutes—each an opportunity to teach our team what they needed to know to improve, what they needed to do to achieve competitive greatness and, hopefully, outscore opponents. Each hour offered the potential for helping us get better and better, closer and closer. Wasting even one minute was painful for me—like throwing a gold coin into the sea, never to be recovered.

## YOU CAN'T GIVE 110 PERCENT

"Give me 100 percent. You can't make up for a poor effort today by giving 110 percent tomorrow. You don't have 110 percent. You only have 100 percent, and that's what I want from you right now."

I taught our players, assistant coaches, and everyone connected to our team to think the same way. To meet my expectations, they were asked to offer all they had all the time.

Consequently, one of the very few rules I did not alter from my first day of coaching at Dayton, Kentucky, until my last day at

Never think of your bruises or fatigue. If you are tired, think of how "all in" your opponent may be.

It is the hard work you do in practice after you are "all in" that improves your condition. Force yourself when you are tired.

UCLA was as follows: Be on time. Period. Players—even assistant coaches—who broke this rule faced consequences.

Being late showed disrespect for me, disrespect for the members of our team, and perhaps worst of all, disrespect for time itself. I wouldn't allow a casual attitude about this most valuable commodity. One of the ways I could signal my reverence for it was to insist on punctuality and give no quarter when someone violated this simple directive. It was a rule I would not allow anyone under my leadership to trifle with.

Of course, I understood that each coach in the country had the same amount of time to teach his team how to win. In some ways it was like the 100-yard dash—each runner has exactly the same distance to cover; each step is of great consequence, and one misstep can cost you everything.

As a leader, it is important to acknowledge that you and your rivals are essentially the same in this regard. Therefore, the contest comes down to who uses their allotted time to best advantage—who has the fewest missteps when it comes to building productivity into each moment of time.

"Failure to prepare is preparing to fail."
"Don't mistake activity for achievement."

Is it you? Or is it the leader of one of your competitors? Even if you work 24 hours a day, seven days a week, your competition can do the same. Thus, what happens during that time—how effectively it is used—becomes a determining factor in who prevails in the contest.

> ## GOOD CLOCK MANAGEMENT IS AS IMPORTANT IN BUSINESS AS IN SPORTS
>
> Time is finite; its potential, infinite. The quality of your allocation and execution of time determines the level of your success. America's great poet Carl Sandburg understood this well: "Time is the coin of your life. It is the only coin you have, and only you determine how it will be spent." Effective leaders spend it most wisely.

I believe effective organization—time management—was one of my key assets as a coach. In fact, organization was perhaps my greatest strength. I understood how to use time to its most productive ends. Gradually, I learned how to get the most out of every minute.

## RUNNING PRACTICE

My skills in the area of running practice—clock management, you might call it—may have begun when I was participating in practices conducted by my college coach, Ward Lambert. His sessions were highly organized and extremely efficient. He seemed to move at 70 miles an hour. Coach Lambert delivered instructions, information, and advice on the run during scrimmages and rarely stopped practice to address the group as a whole. Instead, he would take a player aside briefly for instruction while the rest of us continued working; not a moment was wasted. Everybody was doing something productive during every minute of Coach Lambert's practices at Purdue.

Never did we stand around shooting the breeze. The only breeze came from Purdue Boilermakers racing up and down the court—

and Coach Lambert racing right alongside us barking out instructions on what we needed to do to improve our performance.

I also had the privilege of watching Notre Dame's legendary football coach Frank Leahy conduct practices while I was a high school coach at South Bend, Indiana, near Notre Dame. Although he allowed very few outsiders into his practices, I was fortunate enough to be invited. What I saw was a leader who had become a master at organizing time efficiently. He also, of course, paid attention to details—lots of attention to pertinent details. Coach Leahy, like Coach Lambert, didn't waste a single second, and it made a very strong and lasting impression on me.

Both these coaches created winning organizations that won national championships. It was very clear that one of the primary reasons they succeeded was their highly efficient use of time. I saw a very direct connection between success—achievement—and the intelligent use of time.

For many years, I also was forced to improve my "clock management" skills by teaching English classes. I vividly remember the challenge of trying to teach grammar, Shakespeare, spelling, poetry, and more in the short hour of each day's class during the semester. To be effective, I had to go into the classroom with a carefully crafted plan each day—one that was a microcosm of a longer and equally precise curriculum. I learned a great deal about using time effectively when given the challenge of teaching *Hamlet* to high school students. My skills in managing in class carried over directly to the court, as I incorporated the ideas and style of coaches Leahy, Lambert, and others I observed over the years.

## DON'T MISTAKE ACTIVITY FOR ACHIEVEMENT

To help me reach the same high level of efficiency—productivity—in teaching basketball that I had in the classroom, I began using small index cards containing a detailed schedule of each day's practice. In fact, I was called "The 3 × 5 Man" at UCLA, because the note cards were always with me. I used them to write down the exact minute-to-minute timetable for that day's practice: who, what, when, and where (including, for example, how many basketballs should be at a particular location on the court at specific times during practice).

Some time after practice I would generally throw away my 3 × 5 cards after transferring their information into my private notebook for later reference. In Part III of this book, you'll see examples of how each and every minute was accounted for in my practices at UCLA.

Although I no longer have the 3 × 5 cards or notebooks from my years at South Bend Central, the system for organizing time during my high school practices was the same. I didn't use 3 × 5 cards in my English classes, but the strict budgeting of minutes within the hour was similar. In fact, as I mentioned, the written formatting for teaching the English curriculum served as my prototype for basketball practice.

I had a fetish about using time efficiently—not wasting it. Bustling bodies making noise can be deceptive. It doesn't mean that anything is actually being accomplished. Activity must be organized with a productive purpose or goal in mind; otherwise it's no different from what you'd see on a school's playground—kids running around, lots of movement but little achievement.

I've observed hundreds of practices by other coaches over the years. I got so I could tell in minutes whether or not that coach knew how to handle time. There's a tautness in how things are run—no slackness, sloppiness, or standing around. It's like sailing a ship whose sails are tight in the wind rather than fluttering in the breeze. It is the effective leader who creates that tautness in an organization.

The assistant coaches also carried my 3 × 5 cards that contained the same detailed information. We made sure to hold to our precise timetable as if our futures depended on it. (They did.) Each one of us knew what we were supposed to be doing and exactly when we were going to do it. Those instructions and directions dictated virtually everything that happened during a UCLA Bruins practice. There were neither wasted minutes nor unintentionally frivolous moments. There was no "downtime" as players waited for the coaches—their leaders—to figure out what was going to happen next.

Before the first whistle of the day blew—in fact, hours before the first player laced up his sneakers—I had meticulously detailed with my assistant coaches what we would accomplish and how we would accomplish it. The specifics in my notes changed daily, but once I had written down the afternoon's plan, it ran very much like a well-run railroad. And the players will tell you even today that it was a railroad that ran very fast—and on time.

The morning of each practice I would meet with my assistants to discuss our plans for the day. During the meeting there were absolutely no outside distractions or intrusions—no telephone calls, messages, visitors, or anything else that might disrupt our plan-

## PLAN EVERY MEETING AS IF YOUR FUTURE DEPENDS ON IT (BECAUSE IT DOES)

Each meeting with your managers and employees offers a unique opportunity: a chance for you and your team to get better at something, share vital information, boost team spirit, and the like. Don't waste a moment of it; carefully plan every minute.

ning. During this time, we reviewed the previous day's practice and made decisions about the work to be done that afternoon—what we would run, what we would accomplish. We wanted to pack as much as possible into the 120 minutes of teaching time available on that particular day.

## HOW NOT TO WASTE TIME

How much of a detail person was I? Prior to the daily coaches' meeting, I would privately review my notebook from the previous year's practice for that exact day, looking for clues as to what had been effective and what did not work as well. In fact, I regularly reviewed notes from two or three years back—sometimes even more. Those notes provided me with a precise record of ways not to waste time. In fact, eventually I could go back 10, 15, and 25 years to see exactly what we'd done in practice.

I would use those detailed records to make comparisons and note where a certain drill had worked well for the previous group or an individual member of the team. Other drills might be marked as needing to be altered or eliminated. I collected this information from both my 3 × 5 cards and notebooks where I kept records of my observations from each day's practice, each game's statistics, and each season's results. My record keeping was comprehensive but really no different from that of a banker who accounts for every penny and can show you the records of transactions going back years and years.

I kept track of minutes like a banker keeps track of money. And if I had to do it all over again, I would do it exactly the same (hopefully, with fewer mistakes).

## EXPANDING TIME

All this was a result of the great respect I had—and still have—for time. I fully understood that the success of my leadership was directly linked to using time wisely. Intelligent and effective teachers, leaders, and coaches understand this better than their counterparts who stand back and wonder how the competition gets so much done in so little time.

You "expand" time with proper organization and execution—an hour becomes longer than 60 minutes. A well-organized leader can get more done in two hours than a poorly organized coach gets done in two days.

Over the course of weeks and months, this effort becomes the difference between those who achieve great things and leaders who merely dream about doing so. I was never the greatest *Xs* and *Os* coach around, but I was among the best when it came to respecting and utilizing time. Respect time, and it will respect you.

# RULES TO LEAD BY

### Remember That a Great Quarter in Basketball or Business Starts with a Great Minute.

A well-organized leader has finished his fourth cup of coffee before a poorly organized leader has located the coffeepot. Your first minutes working with a team or on a vital project can determine your ultimate success. Lead with the certain knowledge that you don't have a moment to lose.

### Set the Proper Tone with Meticulous Time Management Technique.

A leader who is careless about time sanctions the same attitude throughout the organization. Time is about more than the clock; it is about creating and fostering an environment in which discipline and hustle rule over carelessness and a casual attitude about time.

### Document Minutes, Days, Weeks, Months, and So On.

In reviewing the details of UCLA practice schedules from prior years, I was looking to see what worked at precise intervals throughout the season. Doing so helped me to keep the team moving forward; I learned from and incorporated past lessons. Those records were most helpful in showing me how not to waste time. Keep good, meaningful records. Use them to help you find ways to improve.

# ON WOODEN

**Eddie Powell:** South Bend Central High School Varsity; Assistant Coach, Indiana State Teachers College and UCLA

### DON'T BE LATE

The team bus was scheduled to leave for our game against the Mishawaka High School Cavemen, our archrivals, at exactly 6 p.m. All the players were in their seats and ready to go except for two guys. They happened to be the co-captains of our team, the South Bend Central Bears.

"Driver, what time did I say we would leave for the game?" Coach Wooden asked as he stepped on board the bus. The driver answered, "6 p.m., Coach. Same as usual."

Coach Wooden asked, "Well, what time is it?" The bus driver looked at his watch and said, "It's exactly 6 p.m., Coach Wooden." Without hesitating, Coach replied, "Well, that's what time my watch says, too. I guess it must be 6 p.m."

He turned and looked down the aisle of the bus—at those two empty seats—and said to the driver, "Let's go." The bus left without the two most important players on the team.

Coach's rule was to be on time or the bus left without you. Even though those two players were important, it didn't matter. Our bus left for Mishawaka on time.

It also didn't matter that one of the players was the son of a vice principal at South Bend Central—the kind of person who could create job problems for Coach Wooden.

From that, we learned Coach wasn't kidding: Be on time. That story was told for years to new players coming in. It sent a message. Coach Wooden wasn't kidding. He meant what he said.

We found out later that the co-captains had skipped our game with Mishawaka to go to a dance.

# 11

# THE CARROT IS MIGHTIER THAN A STICK

*"Punishment invokes fear. I wanted a team whose members were filled with pride, not fear."*

M R. EARL WARRINER, principal of my grade school in Centerton, Indiana, had an old-fashioned motivational tool: the switch. Cut from the hedge running alongside the schoolhouse and trimmed of thorns, it was a strong motivator for young pupils who got out of line.

One morning before our daily song, four of my classmates and I decided we'd play a practical joke on Mr. Warriner by pretending to sing—moving our lips but remaining silent. Of course, once the singing—or lack of it—began, he caught the prank and spotted the mischief makers. Our giggling gave us away.

The singers were asked to stop while Mr. Warrriner slowly walked over to his desk and got out his switch. He then lined us in a row and quietly asked one by one, "Will you sing?" I was fourth in line.

The first boy lost his nerve immediately, almost before Mr. Warriner had finished asking the question. "I'll sing, Mr. Warriner," he blurted.

The second boy held out until he was told to turn around and bend over. That was all it took.

The third boy lasted until he got the switch—one time. Now it was my turn.

"What about you, Johnny, will you sing?" Mr. Warriner asked. "No," I snapped. He asked again, "Are you sure about that?" I shook my head back and forth. I was very sure. I got the switch.

"Will you sing now, Johnny?" he asked. I shook my head again, "No!" Again the switch, and this time it stung; my eyes started watering.

"Johnny, will you sing now?" Mr. Warriner asked patiently. My resolve had weakened but not my attitude. "I'll try," I replied sullenly. That wasn't good enough. Once again I got the switch.

"OK, OK, I'll sing, Mr. Warriner!" I shouted out at the same moment the boy next in line exclaimed, "Me too, Mr. Warriner. I like to sing!"

Never was our morning song sung with more gusto than on that day. Even now I can hear the five of us, highly motivated, filling the classroom with song.


## THE BEST MOTIVATOR?

There are times when threat of penalty is effective for both schoolboys and adults. Most often, however, a leader resorts to punishment because he lacks an understanding of its limitations as well as the skills necessary to create motivation based on pride rather than fear. (Mr. Warriner was skilled in all forms of motivation.)

You might say that a leader has a simple mission: to get those under his supervision to consistently perform at their peak level in ways that benefit the team. Your skills as a motivator determine if, and to what degree, this occurs.

I came to the conclusion that when choosing between the carrot and the stick as a motivational tool, the well-chosen carrot was almost always more powerful and longer lasting than the stick. In fact, simply withholding a properly selected carrot can become a most forceful punishment and powerful motivator. Its denial creates desire; the carrot becomes a stick.

Conventional carrots include money, of course, as well as advancement, awards, a corner office, or a more prominent role on the team or in the organization. Carrots come in many forms. However, I believe the strongest and most meaningful motivators

How To Avoid Grievances

1. Get all the facts. What went wrong — not who is to blame.

2. Stay calm. Find the solution together. Do not permit emotions to take over. We Reason

3. Criticize in private. ~~Criticism is to correct, help, improve, prevent, etc., not to punish.~~ Listen if you want to be heard. ~~Disagree without being disagreeable~~

4. Commend ~~before~~ and perhaps after you criticize. Help save face.

5. Keep your criticism constructive. Cri--- is to correct, help, improve, prevent — <u>not</u> to punish.

= Treat all people with dignity + respect.

— "Any philosophy that can be put in a nutshell belongs there."

are not necessarily the materialistic, but the intangible. In this regard, there is perhaps no better carrot than approval from someone you truly respect, whose recognition you seek. Acknowledgment, a pat on the back, a wink, a nod of recognition or praise from someone you hold in high esteem is most powerful—the most valuable carrot of all. At least, this has been my experience.

Importantly, sincere approval instills pride. Punishment invokes fear. I wanted a team whose members were filled with pride, not fear. Pride in the team and commitment to its mission are fundamental components of competitive greatness. Wise use of the carrot can facilitate this, especially in combination with prudent use of the stick.

## IF YOU DON'T MEAN IT, DON'T SAY IT

Positive acknowledgments have impact only when offered by someone who is held in esteem. Even then, however, positive words become meaningless when offered habitually and excessively.

Frequent and gratuitous praise removes the great value of a sincere compliment. Leaders who dole it out with little thought sacrifice a most powerful motivational ally—the pat on the back. (Of course, occasionally the pat must be a little lower and a little harder.) If you don't really mean it, don't say it.

For example, I avoided the phrase, "That's great!" Instead, I would say, "Good, very good. That's getting better." Or, "That's the idea. Now you're getting it. Good." I kept in mind that how I conveyed information was often as important as the information itself. My tone was measured and my demeanor controlled. And I was honest.

In basketball being allowed to play in the game is a carrot. Taking away playing time—"sentencing" a player to the bench—becomes a fearsome stick. In business the "bench" exists in various forms—denial of privileges, perks, and promotions. (Of course, dismissal from the group—termination—represents the ultimate stick and can have a sobering effect on those remaining with the team. However, firing someone also suggests failure on the part of a leader. Did you originally misjudge the individual? Were your skills lacking when it came to working with that person? Dismissing an individual you brought into the group suggests failure on your part.)

Great leaders—those who achieve consistent and long-term results—are experts in the appropriate use of the carrot and the stick. And they also understand that you discipline those under your supervision to correct, to help, to improve—not to punish. Dictator-style coaches and leaders have their own approach (all sticks, no carrots) and can also rise to great heights. But for me, the fear and ill feelings that arise from intimidation, punishment, and cruel words have far less power than pride.

It is very hard to influence someone in a positive manner over the long haul when you antagonize and alienate that individual. In addition, once you've angered someone and created a feeling of animosity, then you're forced to waste additional time backing up and trying to smooth things over.

## DON'T LIMIT YOUR OPTIONS

Commendations and criticism exist, of course, within a framework of expectations—rules of behavior—from those under your leadership.

When I was just starting out, I had lots of rules and very few suggestions. The rules were spelled out in black and white, and so were the penalties for breaking them. When a player broke one of my rules, the punishment was automatic, enforced without discussion. And the punishment was often severe. I was very strict.

Smoking was cause for immediate dismissal—no questions asked. At South Bend High School, I summarily dismissed a top player from the team for the entire season for smoking. I had a rule. He broke it. That's all there was to it. At the time, I thought this was good, no-nonsense leadership. Of course, it meant I was ignoring extenuating circumstances and ramifications. The boy later quit school because of my actions and lost an athletic scholarship that would have helped him through college. To deprive a young man of a college education because he broke a no-smoking rule is simply inexcusable. I was too inexperienced to understand this.

Eventually I came to recognize that common sense is needed in deciding when and how penalties—that is, discipline—should be applied. Over the years, I changed from having lots of rules and few suggestions to lots of suggestions and fewer rules. To a large degree, I replaced specific rules and penalties with strong suggestions and unspecified consequences. This gave me much greater discretion and allowed for more productive responses to misbehavior.

An individual who knows exactly what the penalty is for a particular act can subconsciously measure the risk against the reward. That person may decide the risk is worth it. By keeping the specific penalty unknown, I may have kept a few individuals from making a bad choice. They couldn't determine if the risk was worth the reward because they didn't know what the penalty was.

## FAVOR FIRM SUGGESTIONS OVER STRICT RULES

Leaders need leeway in dealing with different individuals and situations. Those who use suggestions and teachings rather than being locked into a long list of rigid rules can develop far more productive relationships with members of the team.

## NOT KNOWING IS WORSE THAN KNOWING

Here's a story—fictional—that illustrates my point about keeping the specifics of the penalty unknown: A cowboy hitches his horse outside the local saloon, goes in, and orders a cold mug of beer. When he's finished drinking it, he goes back outside, but his faithful horse is nowhere to be seen.

The cowboy stomps back into the bar, slams his fists on the counter, and yells, "Somebody in here took my horse. Now, I'm going to order another cold mug of beer. When I'm through drinking it, I'm going to slowly walk back outside. I would strongly suggest whoever took my horse bring it back and hitch it to the hitching post. Otherwise, I'm gonna do what I did down in Texas—exactly the same thing as I did down in Texas."

The cowboy orders another mug of beer, drinks it, and walks outside. Sure enough, his horse is at the hitching post. As he prepares to ride away, the bartender comes running out and asks, "Say, fella, that was very impressive. But I've got to ask ya, 'What *did* you do down in Texas when they took your horse?' " The cowboy looks down at the bartender and says, "I *walked* home."

Those under your leadership—like all those cowboys in the saloon—fear the unknown more than the known. As I matured in my coaching, I relied increasingly on strong suggestions with unspecified penalties attached.

At UCLA, especially in the seventies when there was so much turmoil on campus and around the country, I strongly suggested to our players that they neither smoke nor drink. However, if they did drink and as a result behaved in a manner that brought discredit upon the team, action would be taken.

But the specifics of my actions were often not spelled out. Unlike my earlier days as a coach, I allowed myself options—the opportunity to evaluate those ramifications and extenuating circumstances. A leader must preserve options to be effective.

Furthermore, when difficulties arose and strong action—or words—were called for, I made it a policy to criticize in private, not in front of others. The rebuke was done without rancor. I was stern, but I did not get personal—no insults, no berating, no anger, no emotion. There were some occasions, of course, when I broke this rule. Sometimes I intentionally let emotion creep in, for effect. Other times I did it because I'm human and humans make mistakes.

> When mistakes are made, such as missing an easy shot, making a bad pass, overlooking an open man, letting your man get away, or something similar, I insist that the boys never criticize each other but encourage the offender so that it won't happen again. It is up to the coach to do the criticizing and it should be as constructive as possible.

## THE PURPOSE OF CRITICISM

When the discussion or action was over, it was all over. We moved on to other business without lingering anger or animosity. At least, I made every effort to ensure that that occurred.

I never wanted to embarrass or humiliate. The purpose of criticism or discipline is to correct, enhance, educate, modify behavior, or bring about positive change. It takes great skill to do so without incurring ill feelings, animosity, anger, or even hatred. A leader who lacks the skills necessary in this area will often see his or her attempt to offer constructive criticism reduced to *destructive* criticism. You will have damaged your own team by making one or more of its members less effective.

In providing criticism, you must not open wounds that are slow to heal. An individual subjected to personal insults, especially in front of others, can be needlessly impaired.

Of course, my policy of having more suggestions and fewer rules works best when the leader is astute at bringing good people into the organization, individuals who aspire to—and live up to—a solid code of conduct.

Criticism is most effective when made in a positive environment, when something good has occurred—a victory, a well-run play during practice. At those moments, criticism can be given and received with great effect. Likewise, praise is used to great effect when an individual, or the group, has suffered a setback, when they are in need of strong support.

I also attempted to combine a compliment with criticism when possible. Most people don't like criticism, even when it's for their own good. An acknowledgment—praise—offered as part of the criticism reduces their resistance; for example: "I like your aggressiveness on defense. Can I see some of that when you drive to the basket?"

A statement like this is a method of honestly offering a pat on the back while pointing up a problem and how to correct it. The results were usually productive. In business there are ample opportunities to combine compliments with criticism. For example:

Great sales quarter. How can we use that momentum to get us closer to our annual sales budget?

Or

I am sorry you had to let go of your first hire after only six months on the job, but I thought you handled it very well, very professionally.

## ONLY THE LEADER GIVES CRITICISM

I made it clear early on in the season that only the leader gives criticism. I insisted that players never criticize or razz a teammate. The effects of criticism—player to player, employee to employee—can be extremely destructive to the group. I spent decades figuring out how and when to apply commendations and criticism to achieve optimum results with minimum damage. It was not something I wanted left to chance, not something a player was equipped to do. I did not tolerate such behavior.

On those few occasions when a player or two started going after someone else, I would sometimes wait until we got back to the locker room and then remind the group of how the Roman Empire crumbled—not from the outside, but rather from within: *internal* fighting, bickering, and bloodletting. The Roman Empire, I told them, collapsed because of what they did to themselves: "The very same thing can happen to us," I advised. "A team divided against itself will not succeed." The few who didn't heed my message would then be dealt with privately.

**"Opponents are working very hard to defeat us. Let's not do it for them by defeating ourselves from within."**

While I was intolerant of players criticizing one another, I instructed—insisted—that they acknowledge a teammate who assisted them in scoring. In fact, I may have been one of the first coaches to implement this policy.

By encouraging the weak side men and the protectors and complimenting them whenever a play away from them culminates in a score, I try to instil a better team spirit. A scorer must always compliment the passer and all the boys must compliment a scorer, one who does a nice piece of defensive work, who gets the ball off the board, intercepts a pass, or makes some other valuable play--not by a great display, but by a nod, a smile, or a kind word or two.

Praise and criticism are volatile forces *within* an organization, but they also can come from outside the group, from friends, family, and the media. I was aware of the potential for damage this influence could bring and told our team members to ignore what others said or wrote. "You'll like it if it's complimentary and get mad if it's critical. In either circumstance—deserved or not, appreciated or not—ignore it, because when you allow it to affect you, the results are detrimental to the team."

The praise and criticism I wanted to have meaning and positive impact was that which came from me and my assistant coaches. None of the rest—*Sports Illustrated*, newspapers, radio broadcasters, friends, family, or relatives—should matter as it related to UCLA basketball.

Much of my understanding and appreciation of the impact that praise and criticism can have within an organization came from my own experience, from my relationship with my father when I was young. My dad was not averse to giving me or my brothers a whipping on occasion when we got out of line. But it was my great desire to please him that motivated me. I had no fear of physical punishment, but my greatest fear was that my dad would be disappointed in my behavior.

Later, my coaches and mentors were individuals I respected so much. Their approval—commendations, a pat on the back—was like gold to me, more precious, in fact. I came to believe as a coach and leader that if I conducted myself in a manner that earned the respect of those under my leadership, this same powerful motivation would exist. When this was achieved, I would have one of the most powerful tools available to a leader: respect from those I was charged with leading into the competition.

I tried hard to earn that respect, knowing that it gave my words tremendous import. It made my commendations and compliments the greatest carrots of all. Likewise, you may see merit in the following guidelines as they pertain to your own carrots and sticks.

# SUGGESTIONS TO LEAD BY

**Pride Is Easier to Instill with the Carrot.**
The best leaders perhaps understand this fact intuitively. Members of an organization always fearful of penalty and punishment are at a great disadvantage when competing against a team filled with pride. This is so particularly over the long haul.

**Make Sure All Praise Is Genuine and Appropriate.**
Just as damaging as biting personal criticism is the compliment given but not meant. Your praise will have impact only to the extent that it is given honestly and in good faith. Anything else is usually perceived as such and becomes counterproductive.

**Do Not Tolerate Internal Carping and Criticism.**
Leaders should be solely responsible for critiquing and criticizing members of the team. The purpose of criticism is to correct, improve, and change. It is not to humiliate, demean, or punish. It is a task that requires great skill and judgment and is best left in the hands of able management and coaches.

**Don't Lock Yourself into Rigid Penalties.**
Successful leaders understand that it is important to have options. This allows you to tailor the response to each situation. Still, when it comes to the most important rules, it is wise to have clearly understood penalties attached. Common sense, however, must always have a place in your decisions. What is fair is more important than what is right.

# ON WOODEN
**Bill Hicks:** UCLA Varsity, 1960–1962

## FLEXIBILITY IN ENFORCING RULES

One of our top players—maybe our best—got upset about something during practice one day and stormed off the court. This put Coach Wooden in an awkward position because he didn't want to lose the guy. We didn't exactly have a lot of talent to spare.

Coach solved the problem by telling the player who had blown up and walked off the court that he was suspended. However, he then informed the suspended player that our whole team would be allowed to vote on whether or not to let him return. This allowed everybody to save face. It also empowered the team, because it felt like we got in on the decision. Of course, we voted to let him back.

Coach had solved his problem, disciplined the player, and strengthened our team all at the same time. This was typical of his leadership—very innovative.

He treated all the players the same—no favorites—but said he was only human and would probably like some of us more than others. However, he promised to be absolutely fair in his evaluation of us as players. Coach Wooden wanted us to know that there would be no favoritism on his part. We all had an equal chance.

Coach Wooden always had a passion for the little things. He wanted us to tie our shoes the correct way, pivot the correct way. There was a correct way to do everything, and he wanted us to know how.

So he taught us how.

# 12

# MAKE GREATNESS
# ATTAINABLE BY ALL

*"Each member of your team has a potential for personal greatness;
the leader's job is to help them achieve it."*

MICHAEL JORDAN IS REGARDED as the greatest player in the history of the NBA by pundits and experts alike, those who make a living speculating on who's number one? The best? The greatest?

While I was teaching basketball at UCLA, several of our players, including Bill Walton, Lewis Alcindor, Jr. (Kareem Abdul-Jabbar), Keith Erickson, Sidney Wicks, Walt Hazard, Keith (Jamaal) Wilkes, Gail Goodrich, and David Meyers, also received a great many accolades: MVP trophies, selection to All-Conference teams, media honors, and All-American awards.

Thus, I am often asked, "Who is the greatest player you ever coached?" Although I have heard this question hundreds of times, I've never answered—picked a *greatest* player—because I do not like this whole business of who's number one?

Speculation of this kind may be harmless amusement for outsiders, but identifying an individual under my leadership as being better than the others—the "greatest"—runs contrary to my bedrock belief about success. I believe that personal greatness is measured against one's own potential, not against that of someone else on the team or elsewhere.

## ATTAINABLE GREATNESS

I wanted the individuals under my leadership—players, assistant coaches, student managers, the trainer—to know that the kind of greatness I sought was available to each one of them. How? By performing his specific job to the highest level of his ability. I wanted every individual connected with the team to fully comprehend that when this was being accomplished, he had achieved the kind of greatness I valued most.

I didn't ask our student manager, Les Friedman, to do Bill Walton's job, and I didn't ask Bill Walton to do my job. Each of us needed to be concerned only with doing our specific job to the very best of our ability. Therein lies our personal greatness.

As leader, my job was to do everything possible to help those I allowed to join our team achieve this—to create an environment and attitude that brought out the very best in each of them. Personal greatness for any leader is measured by effectiveness in bringing out the greatness of those you lead. Thus, personal greatness is within the grasp of each member of an organization, regardless of role and responsibilities—whether a CEO or secretary, starter or nonstarter, head manager or head coach.

I am not naïve. I knew that an All-American such as Bill Walton should have much greater impact than the player sitting at the end of UCLA's bench. But my expectation (*demand* is a more accurate word) was that all those under my leadership seek greatness—their *own*, not that of anyone else.

I also knew that Bill Walton would be unable to achieve his own potential greatness unless others on the team achieved theirs. Everyone had to do his job; everyone had to seek and achieve his own personal best for our team to be as good as it could be.

When leaders instill the genuine belief that the opportunity for making great things happen is possible in every job, they have achieved something extraordinary. They have created an organization that fosters and breeds achievers, a superior team filled with people striving to reach 100 percent of their potential in ways that serve the team. It becomes a force with exponential power and productivity.

Some of those achievers will be more talented or intelligent, score more points or close more sales than others. But will a particular individual be *greater* than all the others on the team? No. This is not a measurement or evaluation of *primary* concern to me. Rather, my first goal was to do everything possible to ensure that all members of our team were committed to doing their job to the best of their ability—to attaining personal greatness. Accordingly, I avoided using the term *substitutes* for those who were not on the starting team. *Substitute* is a demeaning term for one who is fully executing his role on the team. A player was a starter or nonstarter, but never a substitute.

Thus, as you'll see in Part III, the postseason awards I encouraged alumni and university groups to bestow on individual players never acknowledged the top scorer. Instead, such qualities as "mental attitude," "most unselfish team player," and "improvement" were recognized and saluted.

Singling out an individual as the "greatest"—which in sports "top scorer" perhaps suggests—devalues the roles and jobs of all others on the team, makes them second-class citizens. It takes 10 hands to make a basket; I believe this principle deeply. Anything that gets in the way of this cooperative attitude is counterproductive and can lead to a caste system within your organization.

## NO INDIVIDUAL OWNS THE NUMBER

That's why I have always been strongly against retiring a player's number. Doing so, in effect, declares a particular individual to be the greatest—better than someone else on the team.

When UCLA decided to retire the numbers of Bill Walton and Lewis Alcindor, Jr.—numbers 32 and 33, respectively—I strongly objected and joined the ceremony at Pauley Pavilion only as a courtesy to my former players. It would have been an insult to them to do otherwise. But, I was against it. They both understood why I felt the way I did, in part because they were consummate team players.

Both Lewis and Bill always put the team ahead of personal glory. Certainly there is no question about the contribution each one of them made to his respective team. But others also wore those same numbers and contributed to their own teams, working hard to give everything they had for the welfare of UCLA basketball. Others achieved personal greatness wearing numbers 32 and 33. All those other players, in contributing to their fullest capacity, achieved personal and competitive greatness just as Bill and Lewis did.

For example, Steve Patterson played at center on two UCLA national championship teams in 1970 and 1971. He wore number 32, just before Bill Walton was assigned that number as a varsity player in 1972. How could number 32 eventually become Bill's exclusive property?

Likewise, Lewis's number 33 was worn previously by Willie Naulls, who was a UCLA All-American in 1956. Nolan Johnson was not an All-American, but he wore number 33 the following year.

The number on a uniform always belongs to the team, never to an individual, just as all glory belongs to the team, not the coach, not the player. I sought to build a team of individuals, each seeking greatness in his own role—big and small—in whatever way it best served the team. I clearly stated in my teaching how this goal is accomplished: "In whatever role I assign you, accept and execute your responsibilities to the very best of your ability."

Whether a player served as a nonstarter or was a star, I called on him to seek his *own* potential. For an organization to succeed, all

## CHOOSE YOUR AWARDS CAREFULLY

Recognition for individual productivity certainly has a place in your list of potential award categories. But it must be valued equally with awards for "improvement," "attitude," "contribution to the team," and other acts that strengthen the organization. "Employee of the month" is often most effective as a motivating tool when it recognizes behavior that, in turn, allows your "top scorer" to excel.

members must be great, each in her or his own particular way. All members must fulfill the requirements of their own specific jobs, each striving to give those jobs the best they have. It is the responsibility of the leader to teach and instill this desire.

## GREATNESS IN A SUPPORTING ROLE

Swen Nater understood that his greatness came in practice rather than in games. He served his team as a backup center behind the significant skills of Bill Walton. This positioning allowed Bill to sharpen his abilities in practice against a center, Swen, who was also tall and talented. (Swen could have been a starter on almost any other team in the country.)

Before Swen joined us, I clearly explained to him what specific role he would play on the team and how valuable it would be to the team. He took on the task, eagerly accepted his role, and helped UCLA win two national championships.

Was Bill Walton greater than Swen Nater? It's a question that has little relevance to me in the context of leadership and team productivity. Both young men attained greatness in performing their specific and important roles as it best served their team. That is what mattered most to me.

It is your responsibility as leader to educate those within the organization that each role offers the opportunity to achieve personal greatness. When all members of your organization strive for personal greatness—

> **"Personal greatness is not determined by the size of the job, but by the size of the effort one puts into the job. This applies to *everyone* on the team."**

and derive pride from what they contribute to the group—you will unleash powerful forces that will make your unit more effective and, ultimately, more competitive.

## ENCOURAGE AMBITION

In any competitive environment, there are ambitious and talented individuals who may be great team players but are also looking for ways to expand their role in the group. This goal cannot always be attained immediately, but you must not destroy their desire or diminish their ambition. Ambition, properly controlled and directed, is vital.

Let the ambitious individuals know that before advancing they must first perform their assigned roles with great skill. Before calculus comes geometry; before geometry comes addition and subtraction. Each must be mastered in its turn before the individual advances to the next level. Before a player on our team could move to an expanded role, he must have demonstrated complete mastery of the role he had been given.

Remind your most ambitious people that they must have patience, and if proficiency at their current job continues unabated, their chance will come, often when least expected. I cautioned ambitious players: "Be ready when your opportunity arrives, or it may not arrive again."

> ## MAKE IT CLEAR TO ALL THAT "PROMOTIONS" DEPEND ON MASTERY OF CURRENT ROLES AND ASSIGNMENTS
>
> Never discourage ambition, but do let people know that they need to keep their eye on the ball in their current jobs. Their time may come, but only if they exercise patience and demonstrate continuous improvement.

## MY MOST SUCCESSFUL PLAYERS

Conrad Burke showed little promise as a player when he arrived at UCLA. When I first saw him scrimmaging as a freshman, I shook my head and thought, "My, he's hopeless. If this young man makes the varsity team when he's a sophomore, it'll mean the varsity is pretty terrible."

Imagine my surprise and delight when the very next season he became a starter on a varsity team that was anything but terrible. We won the conference title with a 16–0 record. Even though Conrad lacked the physical skills a coach likes to see, he made up for it with a great mind and very hard work. He came extremely close to achieving his potential, his own greatness.

For example, even though he couldn't jump very well and was relatively short for a center, he learned through constant practice and observation how to gain position under the basket. Of course, gaining position is vital in rebounding.

Conrad worked relentlessly to bring out all he had, and he came very close to doing that. He figured out how to make a contribution to the team—a big contribution. The key lesson is that anyone with the ambition, properly channeled and focused, has the potential to achieve more than anyone would have imagined. The key is for leaders to help individuals understand their strengths and weaknesses, and enhance the former while finding a way to at least neutralize the latter.

Another individual who came close to achieving 100 percent of his potential—personal greatness, as I define it—is Doug McIntosh, who also showed little promise as a freshman. When he first scrimmaged at the Men's Gym, I thought, "This fellow will never play a meaningful minute on the UCLA varsity squad."

Once again, I misjudged how hard a player would work to bring out his best in his quest to achieve personal greatness. The following year, Doug came off the bench and played 30 crucial minutes in helping UCLA defeat Duke and win our first national championship.

In assessing Doug's potential, I had not perceived his resolve to work constantly to bring forth his best performance. It was that unbridled determination that helped our team win a national title. A little-known player had achieved competitive greatness. (Doug wore number 32, just as Bill Walton did eight years later. You can see why awarding this number to someone else is inappropriate in the context of the team.)

Neither Doug nor Conrad received much attention or played in the NBA; neither was declared by pundits to be the greatest, the best, or anything close to it. But both, in my opinion, were as successful as any player I've ever coached—the kind of player I prized most highly.

Each came so close to realizing his full potential through hard work and good thinking. Both were as focused as any I have coached in helping the team to win in any way they could. To my own credit, I am proud that as their leader I had created an environment that fostered this attitude.

A leader can get the unseen potential of individuals to blossom when she or he leads the *entire* team and not just the star players. This type of leader creates an environment in which every job matters and every member of the organization counts. In this atmosphere, everyone knows that the team's success rests, in part, on their efforts to seek personal greatness.

Whether Doug and Conrad were as great as Kareem Abdul-Jabbar and Bill Walton and others doesn't matter. It goes to my father's advice: Don't worry about being better than someone else, but never cease trying to be the best you can become. Doug and Conrad did that.

> Each player, however, must have the proper mental outlook and mental attitude. He must be unselfish and want, not just be willing, to sacrifice individual glory for the welfare of the team. He should be industrious and "bubbling over" with enthusiasm. As I stated earlier, each player should feel that, although others may have more ability, may be larger, faster, quicker, able to jump better, etc., no one should be his superior in team spirit, loyalty, enthusiasm, cooperation, determination, industriousness, fight and character.
>
> Each player should have an intense desire to improve. He should be studying and working toward further development at all times. In the majority of cases, the only difference between a truly star performer and just a good player is merely the perfection of a few minor details or fundamentals. This doesn't occur by chance or accident, but by study and hard work.
>
> There is no substitute for being prepared and preparedness can be acquired only through study and hard work. Those who are prepared are never lacking in courage and confidence, and it is real, not false.

It is most valuable for a leader to understand and teach that greatness is attainable by everyone who is a part of the organization. When you unleash the desire in those you lead to attain their own personal greatness—day after day, month after month—you'll find unexpected talent springing up all around you, just as I did with Conrad and Doug and very many others. A winning organization, a successful team, is made up of many individuals, each of whom, in his or her own way, has attained personal greatness.

*Who's the greatest?* is always the wrong question to ask. *How many of those under my leadership have achieved personal greatness?* will always be the right one. That's what matters most; that's what creates a great organization.

# RULES TO LEAD BY

### Each Job Counts.
All roles on a team offer the opportunity for individual greatness. This idea will be understood and accepted only if the leader reinforces it on a consistent basis. Everyone must feel that his or her contributions count and affect the success, or lack thereof, of the team.

### Encourage, but Manage, Ambition.
Ambition can be a valuable characteristic in a team member. However, those who aspire to advancement and greater responsibility should be cautioned that it will occur only if they master their current position. No member of the team should be allowed to let future opportunities distract from present responsibilities.

### Teach Your Players to Expect Unexpected Opportunity.
Unforeseen opportunity may arise for many reasons. In basketball, it might be because a starter fouls out or is injured. In business, it may occur when the company wins a new account or acquires a competitor, or because an employee leaves the firm. The key is to make sure that those under your supervision are ready, mentally and physically, when that opportunity avails itself. Let everyone know that advancement often comes with little or no warning. They must be prepared to seize the opportunity when it presents itself (or it may not present itself again).

### Believe in the Hidden Potential of All.
Create an environment that rewards hard work and improvement and you unleash the unseen talents of those you lead. Employees—team members—who feel they can better themselves by doing a great job and helping the team will work at the highest level. Often it will come from a member of your organization from whom you

may least expect it. Your job as a leader is to get the best from each member of your unit, to tap into that concealed reservoir of talent. A leader who effectively taps into potential is potent.

---

# ON WOODEN

**Doug McIntosh:** UCLA Varsity, 1964–1966;
two national championships

---

## THE POWER OF POTENTIAL

"You can always do more than you think you can." That's the biggest thing I got from Coach Wooden's teaching. There's always more inside if you're willing to work hard enough to bring it out.

Most of the time we don't recognize we have great potential inside. Coach brought out the potential in people. He taught mental readiness: "Be ready and your chance may come. If you're not ready, it may not come again."

Thus, he made me see there are no *small* opportunities. Every opportunity is big. If you only play for two minutes, make it the best two minutes possible. That's your opportunity, whether in basketball or in life. Be ready; make the most of it. It may not come again.

In 1964 I was on the UCLA bench at the start of 29 consecutive games. The thirtieth game was against Duke for the national championship. When it started, I was on the bench just like the previous 29 games. And I was ready. Everybody on Coach Wooden's bench was ready.

Five minutes into the championship game, Coach gave me

an opportunity. I went in at center, replacing Fred Slaughter, who'd gotten off to a slow start. I stayed in until the game was decided and UCLA had won its first national championship.

The next year, 1965, UCLA played Michigan in the championship game. This time I wasn't on the bench. I was a starter and played the best 10 minutes of basketball I'd ever played—running up and down the court blocking shots and getting rebounds. Then Coach took me out for a breather and put in Mike Lynn.

Mike played out of his mind—brilliantly. I spent most of the rest of the game on the bench. Mike was ready when his opportunity came, just as I had been the previous year. Either way was fine with me, if it's good for the team.

The year before, Fred Slaughter was OK with me coming in and replacing him. Fred also believed that what was best for the team was best for him.

Where'd we get that concept? Coach Wooden. He taught that across the board to everybody. There's always resentment by some guys who want more playing time, a bigger role, but Coach was very effective in getting people to understand that the team's interests came first, that doing what was best for the team—even if it meant sitting on the bench—was best for us. Now that's a tough lesson to teach. But he did it.

At UCLA we had five guys on the court playing basketball and seven guys on the sidelines forming a cheerleading squad. When I was on the bench, I was a cheerleader, and I felt that it mattered; I needed to be a great cheerleader, because it could help our team.

In 1966, after UCLA won two consecutive national championships, many picked the Bruins to win a third. We didn't, mainly because of injuries. Through it all, Coach Wooden wasn't any different from the year before, when UCLA won a championship, and the year before that, when UCLA won its first title.

He didn't turn into a raving maniac when we started losing games. His demeanor was about the same, championship season or not. No "woe is me"; never a word about bad breaks and injuries.

He built great teams in practice. He was a "practice coach," and he conducted practices at a very high level. How you practice is how you play is what he believed.

He was strict, but there was no sense of fear of him by players. We knew there was nothing personal in his criticism or comments. What he did was always for the common good and welfare of the team. We all knew that and wanted the same.

He taught that discipline is the mark of a good team. And Coach Wooden was disciplined. And part of that meant keeping emotions under control.

I don't know that there was a "secret" to his success. It was just those three things he stressed: fundamentals, condition, and team spirit.

The drills he ran at UCLA were mostly the same drills I had run back in high school—the very same drills. Coach Wooden just did them more repetitively and with more speed and precision. He just demanded a higher level of execution when it came to fundamentals. There was no secret formula.

He was very intense, but not to the point of screaming or pulling out his hair. Coach was dignified and didn't let his emotions show very much. But we all knew what was going on in his mind.

He kept those emotions under control, but sometimes it was right on the edge. The maddest I ever saw him was against Oregon State, when I went up high for a basket and my legs got cut out from under me. I hit the floor and was knocked unconscious. When I woke up, I saw Coach standing there absolutely livid and demanding that the referee throw out the Oregon State player for the cheap shot.

And he wouldn't tolerate cheap shots by us either—no dirty play. If one of his players threw an elbow in anger, he'd pull you and put you on the bench. Then, when it was convenient, he'd let you have it real good.

He was more upset that we'd lost our temper than anything else. He absolutely wanted emotions to be controlled. If you lost it out there, he'd make you pay a price. He knew that when you lost it—when emotions took over—your performance suffered, your potential was locked inside. He wanted that potential out where it could help the team.

# 13

# SEEK SIGNIFICANT CHANGE

*"Be uncomfortable being comfortable,
discontent being content."*

THE 1961–1962 SEASON would be a turning point for UCLA basketball, one that eventually produced 10 NCAA championships including seven in consecutive years and an 88-game winning
streak. I had no idea it was all about to happen.

At the beginning of the season, I'd been coaching basketball at
UCLA for 13 years in conditions I would describe as harsh, perhaps as bad as any major university in the country. Our practice facility, the Men's Gym, was cramped and poorly ventilated and
often jammed with student-athletes participating in other sport-
ing activities during our basketball practices. There was constant
commotion and distraction—hardly a place to teach or learn the
finer points of basketball.

Additionally, the seating area for fans was so limited that it was
declared a fire hazard and "home" games were subsequently played
at other local schools. The facility also hurt us when it came to at-
tracting players with exceptional talent. Many, no doubt, chose
programs that offered decent facilities.

I was confronted with this situation immediately upon my arrival at UCLA and soon concluded it was virtually impossible to

achieve my teaching goals under such conditions. It also had an impact on my assessment of the possibility of winning a national championship; specifically, in the back of my mind I just felt there was no chance that UCLA would ever be able to go all the way. Unfortunately, some of my attitude may have carried over to those under my supervision. The leader's attitude, conscious and subconscious, inevitably becomes the attitude of those he leads. Winston Churchill's resolution, courage, and defiance nourished an entire nation in the worst of times; *his* attitude became the attitude of those he led. The same thing happens with effective basketball coaches and business leaders.

While I didn't like the great disadvantages imposed on us by our practice facility, I accepted it as the way things were going to be. We might do fairly well on occasion, but we would never get all the way to the top.

How did all of this affect my coaching? I can't be sure, but I know this: The events of the 1961–1962 season changed my perspective completely, took the blinders off my eyes, and removed a barrier I had imposed on myself—one that should never have existed in the first place. What subsequently happened is a good lesson in how we can limit ourselves and our organization without even knowing it—how we can say "no" when we should be asking "how?"

## SO CLOSE TO THE CHAMPIONSHIP

Much to the complete surprise of everyone, our unheralded 1961–1962 UCLA basketball team advanced all the way to the Final Four before we lost 72–70 to Cincinnati in the final seconds of the game. It was the first time in history the Bruins had ever reached the Final Four.

Games decided on a last-second basket obviously can go either way, and this game was no exception. With 2:27 remaining on the clock, John Green made two free throws for us and tied the game at 70–70. UCLA then committed an offensive foul and turned the ball over to Cincinnati. The Bearcats ran the clock down to 10 seconds and called for a timeout.

When play resumed, Cincinnati's Tom Thacker, a player who hadn't scored a single point in the whole game, took a pass from Tom Sizer who, with three seconds left to play, dribbled to his right, stopped, and from 25 feet away made the final basket of the game. UCLA was outscored 72–70. The following night Cincinnati won their second consecutive national championship.

We had come within a whisker of winning it all. Our near-victory was a revelation to me.

Much to my surprise, UCLA had nearly won the 1962 NCAA basketball championship. Suddenly—shockingly—it became clear that our inadequate basketball facility, the Men's Gym, did *not* mean we couldn't win the national title. Walt Hazzard, Pete Blackman, Gary Cunningham, Billy Hicks, Fred Slaughter, Kim Stewart, Dave Waxman, John Green, Jim Milhorn, and Jim Rosvall, our assistant coaches, student managers, and our trainer Ducky Drake had just about done it despite the great disadvantages forced on us by our practice facility.

If I had been using the Men's Gym as a rationale for poor performance in past NCAA playoff appearances—we had lost in the first round three straight times—I couldn't use it any more. A subconscious barrier had been removed; a light went on.

No longer could I tell myself "no"; no longer could I be comfortable with the status quo. I now knew what I should have understood long before, namely, UCLA could go all the way to the top despite the Men's Gym. It was up to me to figure out how to do it.

## REMOVE EXCUSES TO BE SATISFIED

Once I realized our practice facility did not preclude a national championship, it shook me out of some form of complacency or perhaps subconscious excuse making. It's hard to describe except to say that I came to recognize that issues I couldn't control—the Men's Gym and what it forced upon us—had interfered with those things I could control, such as ceaselessly and creatively searching for ways to improve and reach the next level of competition.

By giving myself that crutch, I may have gotten comfortable with the way things were—not happy, but comfortable. I would never again allow myself to be satisfied that UCLA had gotten as good as we could get, improved as much as we could improve.

Never be satisfied. Work constantly to improve. Perfection is a goal that can never be reached, but it must be the objective. The uphill climb is slow, but the downhill road is fast.

There would be no excuses in the future, only a ceaseless search for solutions. Following that startling breakthrough in 1962, I began an intense and comprehensive review of what I was doing and how I could do it better. Meticulously I began searching for changes that would allow UCLA to consistently be more competitive in postseason play with the sure belief that the answers would take us to the next level. Those answers came both from within and from outside.

I reviewed absolutely everything going back to day 1 at UCLA—my notebooks, my 3 × 5 cards, practice and game statistics, and much more—in an attempt to determine if there were things I had done that were holding us back. Soon enough, I found them.

## NEVER ASSUME YOUR TEAM IS AS GOOD AS IT CAN BE

The old UCLA Men's Gym gave me an excuse for accepting our performance results. Think about your workplace and the people under your leadership. Are you holding your team back with misconceived notions and false limitations? Identify and then eliminate them. Seek solutions rather than excuses.

## CHANGES THAT COULD HAVE BEEN MADE SOONER

Throughout my coaching career, I had always attempted to operate in a democratic way. One player described me as being "egalitarian." He was correct in the sense that I disliked anything that singled out a player for special attention, and this included awarding playing time. Instead, I tried to share it in a somewhat democratic manner.

In practice and in many games, my records from those previous years showed that I was trying to appease players by working everyone into the rotation. Of course, the five starters got most of the time, but from the sixth through the twelfth player—almost 60 percent of the team—I tended to try and work each player into the rotation equally, both in practice and in games. This was not possible in a literal sense, of course, but I made the attempt to let everyone share as much as possible in playing time.

After review, however, I came to the conclusion that while this objective may have been democratic, it also hurt the team. During games when I benched a starter in favor of the sixth or seventh man, our cohesion and quality of play dropped off. More mistakes were made and things ran less smoothly.

Starting in 1962–1963, my new policy was to go primarily with seven main players—virtually, seven starters—in both practice and games. My previous goal of doling out playing time in a democratic manner was discarded. I changed a fundamental policy for how I did things.

Once I decided on this new plan, it was reflected in how I organized practice. I would have five starters on the court, and rotate in the "extra" starting guard and front line player after the starters had made a designated number of free throws. I followed this formula during the roughly one-third of the practice time devoted to five-on-five work. The "starting" players who were being replaced would come out of the five-on-five scrimmage until the replacements, in turn, had made a specific number of consecutive free throws. This pattern continued throughout the practice.

I didn't intend to ignore the eighth to twelfth players, obviously, but I let them know very clearly what their roles in the group would be and for what purpose. More important, I tried very hard to make them understand the great value of their role and how it would contribute to the overall welfare of the team.

In part, this meant they would be the stone that sharpened the sword, that is, the starting lineup. But it also meant being fully prepared to step into a more prominent role if the opportunity arose. Of course, this plan would be effective only if individuals put the team's welfare first—if team spirit really existed.

An extensive review of my notebook also revealed that when UCLA qualified for the NCAA postseason tournament, I intensified our already grueling practices, working players even harder—so hard, in fact, that by tournament time they were physically and mentally spent. Once I saw evidence of this fact in my notes, I became very prudent in conserving players' energy prior to the playoffs.

Additionally, my notes showed that in preparation for the NCAA tournament, I added new plays and piled on more information. Instead of staying with what had worked during the regular season—a clear and uncomplicated strategy—I unintentionally made things complicated. I resolved that in the future I would keep it simple going into postseason play just as I did during the regular season.

These changes—concentrating on a "starting seven," not overworking players prior to the tournament, and keeping it simple—came about from my personal observations and reflections following the revelation of the 1962 season, the fateful year that almost produced a surprise national championship for UCLA.

The changes I have described came about because I had stopped giving myself an excuse for accepting the status quo, for staying at the same level. But change was only beginning.

## LOOK FOR "YES" MEN WHO WILL SAY "NO"

I believe one of the requirements of good leadership is the ability to listen—really listen—to those in your organization. Being a good listener, however, is only half of the equation. As a leader, you must be confident enough to employ individuals who aren't afraid to speak up and voice their opinion. If you're willing to listen, it means little if nobody is willing to talk in a substantive manner.

> "An effective leader is very good at listening. And it's difficult to listen when you're talking."

It's also important that those individuals under your leadership embrace your overall philosophy, your system or way of doing things. It's one of the reasons I sought assistant coaches who understood, believed in, and agreed with my fast-play style of basketball. For example, when Minnesota initially insisted on telling me that Dave McMillan was going to be my assistant coach, I refused, in part, because I wanted to bring along someone who accepted—said yes to—my overall system (although I was willing to consider changes within my system). Coach McMillan's system was more deliberate and focused on ball control—totally different from what I taught, which was a fast and furious attack style of basketball.

I wanted individuals as assistant coaches who understood and embraced my system—people such as Eddie Powell, Gary Cunningham, Jerry Norman, and Denny Crum. All of them were astute analysts and unafraid to tell me exactly what they thought.

All those people mentioned were very familiar with the kind of basketball I taught; they were all former players. In fact, Eddie Powell had played basketball on the South Bend Central High School team that I coached back in Indiana and then had been my assistant at Indiana State Teachers College.

Their input was valuable because they understood my overall basketball philosophy and were able to see ways to improve it as we went along.

## GOOD EARS ARE PART OF LEADERSHIP

Following the 1962 Final Four appearance and my renewed determination to review everything I was doing, it happened again—input from an assistant coach sparked a change that would positively impact UCLA's fortunes for the next 13 seasons.

On the plane ride back from the tournament in Louisville, assistant coach Jerry Norman began making his case for us going to the full-court defense—known as the "Press"—in the upcoming season and beyond. This system imposed an intensive defense on the opponent from the moment they attempted to put the ball in play at their end of the court. (Conventional defensive systems waited until the opponent reached half-court. In effect, this allowed them to move the ball without interference for almost 40 feet up the court.) The Press put opponents under immediate pressure but required great conditioning, athleticism, coordination of players, and intelligence.

The system he was recommending was not new to me. I had installed it almost 25 years earlier when I was coaching at South Bend High School and used it later with good results at Indiana State Teachers College. In fact, I was eager to use it on my first day as head coach at UCLA—and did (or tried to). However, I abandoned it before the first game of the season.

The Press is difficult and time consuming to teach. It had worked at Indiana State, but only because I had coached many of the players before, at South Bend. They knew the system and my style of coaching. At UCLA it just didn't click in soon enough— perhaps because of my own shortcomings in teaching amidst all the other distractions of the Men's Gym. Whatever the reasons, I simply lost patience and got rid of it.

*Assistant – avoid a "yes man," work with him, give him responsibility and authority, give credit but not blame.*

During our flight back to California, Coach Norman made a very convincing argument for trying the Press again. He reminded me that two new players were joining the varsity team whose intelligence, athleticism, and competitiveness were perfectly suited to the demands of this style of defense—Keith Erickson and Gail Goodrich. My assistant coach was convinced that now was the time to install a system I had abandoned 14 years before.

I listened carefully to what he said, even though I had heard and ignored it before from others. This time, because of our near win against Cincinnati and the clarifying effect it had on my thinking, I said yes instead of no.

As soon as practice began six months later, I began teaching the Press. It ultimately became a trademark of UCLA basketball and contributed to our run of championships. The Press would not have been used if Jerry Norman had been content to keep his ideas to himself.

Equally important, it would not have been used if the person responsible for making the final decision had not been listening with an open mind. That person, of course, was me.*

## THE NEXT LEVEL ARRIVES

During the 1962–1963 season, the changes I have described were implemented, and the results were quickly apparent. We tied for first place in our conference and began preparations for the NCAA playoffs. Led by Gail Goodrich, the Press was in place; our "seven-man starter" system was ready; my new plan to keep the players fresh mentally and physically was in place; and I made sure to keep it simple—no new plays or tactics were introduced in preparation for the tournament.

It was now time to see how these major changes worked—all of them brought on by the revelation that UCLA could win a national championship in spite of the Men's Gym and my subsequent commitment to figuring how to do it.

A few days later, in the first round of the NCAA tournament at Provo, Utah, the UCLA Bruins took on the University of Arizona. It wasn't even close. We lost 93–75. Nevertheless, I had seen

---

* I have often wondered what might have happened if I had installed the Press earlier, for example, when Olympic gold medalist Rafer Johnson was a member of our team in 1958–1959. His intelligence, competitiveness, and athleticism made him a perfect player to run the Press. I didn't have to think about it very much. I knew I had waited too long.

enough to know that the future for UCLA basketball in NCAA tournament play was going to be very good. The changes I installed had put UCLA on the verge of reaching the next level.

The tournament loss to Arizona—red hot in the game against us—couldn't change what I came to believe during the 1963 regular season. I felt strongly that in the following year, 1964, UCLA could be a very strong contender for the NCAA national championship. And we were. One year later, on March 21, 1964, UCLA outscored Duke and won the national title.

It all began when Walt Hazzard, Fred Slaughter, Billy Hicks, and their teammates forced me to stop saying "no" and start asking "how?" With that new mindset, I began seeking significant change and putting new ideas to work with the Bruins.

The changes were directly responsible for UCLA's national championships in 1964 and 1965. In turn, those two titles set in place conditions that helped produce eight championships: Pauley Pavilion was built to replace the Men's Gym; top talent such as Lewis Alcindor, Jr. (Kareem Abdul-Jabbar) and others began signing on to the team; and, importantly, UCLA basketball acquired a reputation for excellence—a winning tradition.

## SURROUND YOURSELF WITH PEOPLE STRONG ENOUGH TO CHANGE YOUR MIND

I believe that you must have people around you willing to ask questions and express opinions, people who seek improvement for the organization rather than merely gaining favor with the boss. Look for these people when hiring and making promotion decisions. Remember: Failure is not fatal, but failure to change might be.

The events of that 1962 season changed me as a leader—forced me to dig deep to look for ways to break through to a higher competitive level. Some of the changes resulted from my own reflections and research, but important changes came from the minds of others.

## ALWAYS QUESTION, ALWAYS PROBE

Denny Crum, a former player and assistant coach who went on to win two national championships as head coach of Louisville, asked more questions than anyone I've ever met. When he worked with me, he never stopped asking why I made the choices I did.

But Denny did it in a way that was usually appropriate—neither contentious nor confrontational—and always intelligently. He always wanted to know the logic behind what I was doing, and he never stopped probing. The kinds of questions he asked, and the recommendations he offered, consistently revealed great insight and understanding of the game. In the process of asking all his questions, he made me a better coach and teacher because he forced me to think even harder about the logic of the decisions I was making.

> Although it is a sign of weakness and uncertainty to be constantly changing, it is an equal fault to stand still and not progress with the game. You must be prepared to meet all emergencies and be able to make necessary changes when the occasion calls for them.

All this is possible only when the leader—you—is willing to listen with open ears and an open mind. Coach Crum impressed me even then with the intelligence of his questions. I knew he would do quite well if he chose to become a head basketball coach, and I was right. At Louisville, Denny Crum appeared in the Final Four six times, won two national titles, and was elected to the Naismith Basketball Hall of Fame.

Think of all I would have denied myself if I'd been too close minded to listen to and evaluate the opinions of Denny Crum, Gary Cunningham, Jerry Norman, and others. They were my leadership team, and team members must not only work together, they must *listen to one another*.

In my opinion, being an effective leader—one who can build a winning organization—requires being an effective listener. The most productive leaders are usually those who are consistently willing to listen and learn. Perhaps it stems from their understanding that success is more often attained by asking "how?" than by saying "no."

## RULES TO LEAD BY

**Success Breeds Satisfaction; Satisfaction Breeds Failure.**
A leader must set realistic goals, but once they are achieved, you must not become satisfied. Achievement will continue at the same or a greater level only if you do not permit the infection of success to take hold of you and your organization. The symptom of that infection is called complacency. Contentment with past accomplishments or acceptance of the status quo can derail an organization quickly. In sports or business, getting to the top is difficult. One of the reasons staying there is so rare is because the infection sets in.

**Identify and Remove Excuses for Not Getting to the Next Level.**
Only when I realized that it was me—and not the Men's Gym—that was holding the team back was I able to raise the level of our effort in all areas. What is your "Men's Gym"?

**Stop Saying "No" and Start Asking "How?"**
Assume improvement is always possible and force yourself—and others—to find out how. A leader who thinks he or she has all the

answers has stopped asking questions. When you've asked, "How can I help our team to improve?" a thousand times, ask it again.

### Welcome Contrary Ideas, but Not Contrarians.

New ideas and perspective from those under your leadership are essential for achieving and maintaining a competitive edge. Welcome those people strong enough to speak up and offer alternatives and ideas. Beware those who do it in a manner that crosses the line, who challenge your overall philosophy or your leadership itself. Look for solid leaders like coaches Crum, Powell, Norman, and Cunningham, who knew how to engage in a robust exchange of ideas and opinion without causing disruption or challenging authority.

---

# ON WOODEN

**Gary Cunningham:** UCLA Varsity, 1960–1962;
Assistant Coach, 1966–1975; six national championships

---

## BE WILLING TO CHANGE

Coach Wooden was strongly opposed, in principle, to the 3–2 zone defense—a half-court defensive system. Nevertheless, Denny Crum and I, assistant coaches, thought it could be very effective for the Bruins to install it. We recommended that he make the change.

Keep in mind, at this point Coach Wooden's teams had just won five national championships in six years. He could easily have told us, "If it ain't broke, don't fix it." However, Coach was always willing to listen, to evaluate new ideas, to seek ways to improve our team. He was never satisfied—never satisfied.

So, despite the fact that UCLA was undefeated at that point in the season, 20–0, Denny and I convinced him to install the 3–2 zone defense for a series up at Oregon.

UCLA won the first game against the University of Oregon, 75–58, but the next night, using the same 3–2 zone against Oregon State, we got beaten, 78–65, and it was apparent the new system wasn't all we thought it might be.

That was the last time we brought up the 3–2 zone defense.

But Coach Wooden had listened and given it—and us—a chance. He wasn't afraid to make a change. And when it didn't work, there were no recriminations. He moved on without making us feel we had led him down the wrong path.

He did not want "yes men" around him. We were encouraged to argue our points, knowing he'd come back at us strong with his own opinions. That was his way of testing how much we believed in what we were telling him and how much we knew about it.

For example, we'd debate the pivot—what was the best way to do it—for 45 minutes during a morning meeting. But he listened with an open mind, let us contribute—insisted on it. During those meetings, we didn't just sit and take notes. He wanted interaction, ideas back and forth. And he got it. And, of course, he taught us to pay attention and teach details—the little things, like the correct way to pivot.

Those little things that got a lot of attention are one of the secrets to his great strength, namely, organization. We planned practices down to the exact minute.

He had us address the team before games and made sure the assistant coaches talked to the players in the huddle during time-outs. He was very inclusive and gave us both authority and respect.

When we fouled up, he never criticized us in front of the team, nor would he allow the players to challenge us. He insisted on having them address us as Coach Cunningham or Coach Crum rather than by a nickname or informally as Gary or Denny.

In the locker room talks there was no yelling, no pounding on the wall. It was focused and intense, and always at the end he'd say: "Now go out there and do your best so you can come back in here with your heads up. Let's make sure you can do that."

He was very efficient in his teaching and kept it simple— broke it down into parts, taught each part, then built the whole back up. Always he used the laws of learning: explanation, demonstration, imitation, and repetition. Lots of repetition. You can't believe the repetition.

Coach Wooden didn't believe in lengthy discussions. He was very succinct, clear, substantive. When I first started with him as an assistant, if I took more than 10 seconds to say something during practice he'd say, "C'mon, let's get going. C'mon." Not rude, just a great sense of urgency.

I learned to keep it short and say it right. Every word counted, because he believed every minute mattered.

The way he conducted himself embodied the Pyramid. It wasn't until later that I realized he was teaching the Pyramid all the time with the model of his behavior.

Teamwork was so important. He kept saying that it doesn't matter who gets credit. If we play together as a team, each player doing his job, we'll like the results. We'll all get credit.

He was prepared, and he got us prepared. People can see when you're not prepared. UCLA was always prepared.

Coach Wooden was an intense competitor and loved to

win. But, win or lose, it was always on an even keel. He didn't want us to get too excited about winning even if it was a national championship.

He was a strong disciplinarian, but he demanded discipline in a very controlled way. "Goodness gracious sakes" was real angry for him. He was a master at analyzing personalities. Player A might just need an explanation. Player B might need some push. He knew what everybody needed to learn his lessons, and he supplied it.

Like with Sidney Wicks. Sidney loved the practices, so the worst possible thing he could do to Sidney was say, "Sidney, you're not with it today. Take a shower." No screaming, yelling. That was it, "Take a shower."

He kept it simple—but intense; not emotional, just very intense.

# 14

# DON'T LOOK AT THE
# SCOREBOARD

*"Things turn out best for those who make the best of
the way things turn out."*

SOME MIGHT THINK THAT a least a few of my coaching habits
were a bit unusual. For example, I kept a sealed envelope in
my UCLA office that contained a slip of paper with predictions on
it. No one was allowed to see those predictions until the Bruins'
regular season was over—and then only a select few.

Each year in the weeks before practice began, I would study the
upcoming basketball schedule, evaluate teams, players, coaches,
past outcomes, and officials, where the games would be played, and
the day and time of those games. Then I would get out my yellow
pencil and make an educated guess on what the upcoming season
would hold for the UCLA Bruins basketball team, specifically, in
which games we would outscore opponents and in which games
opponents would outscore UCLA.

When my predictions were complete, I'd put them in the envelope, seal it, and then file it away until our regular season was over.
Most of the time, my guesses were pretty close to UCLA's final win-
loss record, although occasionally I'd be off on a game or two.

In 1959, when all the experts predicted a losing season for the
UCLA Bruins—and with good reason—I thought differently. The

number I wrote down and put in the jar was 14–12. My prediction turned to be right on the button.

Of UCLA's four undefeated seasons, however, I predicted only one of them: 1973. In each of the other three I always spotted one opponent who would outscore us for various reasons (for example, playing Notre Dame at Notre Dame was a pretty good reason).

I was wrong all three times; the game I thought we'd lose, we won.

This little ritual was not intended to motivate me or establish goals or guidelines such as so-and-so should be an easy win or this particular opponent required special preparation. My basic philosophy was to prepare for each opponent with the same intensity and respect regardless of whether they were undefeated or hadn't won a single game. Respect all; fear none; concentrate on improving and executing our own system to the highest level possible. That was always my approach.

Therefore, I never scouted other teams. We were better off, I believed, letting them adjust to us. My belief was that we'd be stronger executing our system at the highest possible level than trying to change each week depending on who the opponent was. (There were exceptions to this approach, of course, but not many.)

## FORGET THE FUTURE, WATCH THE BALL

My predictions at the beginning of each season were done primarily for fun. Some people enjoy doing crossword puzzles; I liked predicting the outcomes of a season's worth of games. And just like a crossword puzzle, they were forgotten once I finished them and locked them away.

With very few exceptions those predictions, filed away in a drawer, were as close as I came to worrying about what the scoreboard would show when the buzzer sounded at the end of a game—whether we would beat some other team.

I wanted our players to do likewise—to forget about the scoreboard, the standings, and what might happen in the future and just focus on doing their jobs to the best of their ability, both in practice and in games.

*Success is not a destination, it is a journey.*

A good leader determines what occupies the team's attention, what they work on and worry about. This process begins with what you, the leader, are preoccupied with.

The scoreboard? Championships? A sales quota? The bottom line? As goals, predictions, hopes, or dreams to be sealed up and filed away, fine. But as a day-to-day preoccupation they're a waste of time, stealing attention and effort from the present and squandering it on the future. You control the former, not the latter.

An organization—a team—that's always looking up at the scoreboard will find a worthy opponent stealing the ball right out from under you. You must keep your eye on the ball, not up on the scoreboard or somewhere out in the distant future. This task, however, is not always easy to do.

> "If you want to extend a winning streak—forget about it. If you want to break a losing streak— forget about it. Forget about everything except concentrating on hard work and intelligent planning."

## HOW NOT TO WIN 94 STRAIGHT GAMES

A sportswriter for the *Los Angeles Times* wrote an article on the Bruins at one point speculating that if the Bruins would win two more games that season and all 30 games in each of the next two seasons,

UCLA would have a winning steak of 94, thus surpassing the national collegiate record of 60 in a row set in 1954–55–56 by Bill Russell and K. C. Jones's University of San Francisco team.

This article illustrates just how out of control expectations had become: Pundits were predicting perfect season after perfect season—looking years ahead—and those prognostications were making their way into the national media.

Against that backdrop, the greatest task I faced was to stay focused on the job of teaching the team how to improve a little each day and forgetting about scoreboards, predictions, and the assumptions of others. This job is difficult enough, but I also faced the greater challenge of getting those I coached to do the same—to ignore all the external "noise" that had the potential to derail the team's focus during the season.

The lesson I learned was inescapable: The surest way not to win 94 games in a row (or even two games in a row) is to start thinking about it—to be looking up at that scoreboard and out into the future.

## THINKING BACK FROM BROADWAY

My personal hope—my goal—at the beginning of each season was to win our conference title, the Pac-10 Conference, as it's called today. This included teams from Stanford, the University of Southern California (USC), Washington, and Oregon.

Even during the years when we were NCAA defending national champions, my goal was not to repeat as national champions but to secure our conference title. For me, this was just a practical way of approaching things. Back then, only conference champions were eligible for the NCAA tournament—March Madness.

Winning the conference title was a formidable task in itself, but it presented a good deal of information to me in advance. Specifically, I knew about the schedule, whom we would play, coaches, venues, even the referees. I knew when we would be playing and where the game would be. The landscape was all familiar.

This situation stood in marked contrast to the NCAA tournament. I knew nothing about who the opponents would be until the season concluded. So instead of thinking about it—worrying about it—I dismissed it from my mind.

Mentally, I worked backward from my long-term goal—the conference championship—to the very short-term goal of taking full advantage of each practice. To help accomplish this, I drew on my background as a high school English teacher and compared the basketball season to a theater play, perhaps a Shakespearean tale. The off-season was for evaluating and talking to potential players, not unlike assembling a cast of actors for a stage play. In fact, in the theater actors are usually listed in the program as "the players."

On October 15 when our practices started, it was like the tryouts for the roles in *Othello* or *King Lear*. Like any director, I needed to decide who would play what part and which individuals would serve as understudies to the featured performers. Basketball practices were like rehearsals in the theater, with players performing different roles for which they were most suited.

The early games, preseason and nonconference, were like off-Broadway dress rehearsals, where we evaluated our casting choices and made adjustments in the performances—who worked well together, who tried to steal scenes at the expense of others, which players made for the best ensemble. Finding the best ensemble is the most important task for the director, the head coach, or the leader.

I always kept in mind that the best actors might not create the best stage play and the five best athletes do not necessarily make the best team. Everyone had to work well together for the show to be a success. In other words, the interaction between and among the "cast" was as important as the talent of the individual players.

The "play" opened in January, with the start of our conference season. That's when all tryouts and casting were complete and off-Broadway dress rehearsals done.

> Strive to accomplish the very best that you are capable of. Nothing less than your best will suffice. You may fool others, but you can never fool yourself. Self-satisfaction will come from the knowledge that you left no stone unturned in an effort to accomplish everything possible under the circumstances.

## ENCORES START WITH A GOOD DAY OF REHEARSAL

I explained to the team that this was an incremental process where our attention had to be focused on producing the best stage play possible by focusing like a laser on each day's rehearsal, our practice sessions. As director, I would try to teach them how to give the best performance possible during those rehearsals. That's what we were striving for—to put on the best stage play of which we were capable.

Would the audience applaud? Would we get a standing ovation and great reviews? I told our team we couldn't control that—only the effort to perform at our highest level. If we accomplished that, our efforts might merit an encore.

The encore in basketball is the NCAA tournament playoffs—March Madness. I reminded players that the best way we could re-

> You can do nothing about yesterday, and the only way to improve tomorrow is by what you do right now.

## FOCUS ON "REHEARSALS"

Like any skilled director or sports coach, a manager needs to make sure that her or his team is properly prepared for the performance. In business, every day is a performance day, so everybody must be prepared. This means that enough time needs to be allocated to training, brainstorming, exchanging ideas, and the like in an effort to produce the most prepared "cast of characters."

ceive that encore opportunity was to work hard in practice right now, today. "Let's get to work. Let's have a good practice, fellas," I'd say. Then I'd blow my whistle and we'd get started.

Forget about the encore, forget about Broadway, forget about dress rehearsals, ignore reviews, and don't dream about a standing ovation. Forget about winning and get back to work—right now, this minute. And we did.

As their leader, my job was to help them accomplish the goal of blocking out the future, the standings, and what they hoped the scoreboard might show at the end of the game.

All we have is the opportunity to prepare in the present. It is impossible to do this when and if you're peering into the future. Whatever peering needed to be done, I would do for the team. And even that was tightly contained, sealed in an envelope and filed away.

Success is possible only when everybody is paying attention to their jobs. The best way to achieve dreams is to ignore them. The best way to attain long-term goals is to put them in an envelope. My first goal and priority was never long term, it was very short term: helping the team improve right now in practice.

This was a goal I never sealed in an envelope and filed away. It was a goal that had nothing do with looking up at the scoreboard, but rather with keeping our eye on the ball. It's one of the reasons I never talked about winning to our players. When you start thinking about winning, you stop thinking about doing your job.

## RULES TO LEAD BY

### Identify Team Goals, Then File Them Away.

As leader, it is most challenging to keep yourself and your team from becoming distracted by future challenges, opportunities, rewards, and consequences. I rarely mentioned the upcoming opponent in my comments to the team during the week. The same was true of the standings or playoff possibilities. All that existed in the future. Improvement exists in the present, not the future.

### Give Full Respect to Each Competitor.

While I seldom altered our practice or game plan based on the competition, I wanted players to have respect for the abilities of all opponents. I never took any game or opponent for granted. The same should hold in business. Respect all; fear none. This is not easy to do. When you're down looking up, fear is natural. When you're up looking down—leading the competition—respect for all is often most elusive.

### Long-Term Success Requires Short-Term Focus.

This goes to the heart of my "don't look at the scoreboard" imperative. It is key to my leadership methodology. Focus on improvement—now. Not tomorrow; not next week. Let's get it done today.

# ON WOODEN

**Dave Meyers:** UCLA Varsity; 1973–1975;
two national championships

## WIN, WIN, WIN? NO, NO, NO.

I retired from the pros when I was 26 after being drafted by Los Angeles as part of a trade that sent me to Milwaukee. On the first day of practice there, I think I heard the "F" word 150 times. Quite a change from Coach Wooden. But that wasn't the only change—just the most inconsequential.

As a pro, absolutely nothing else mattered but winning. If you missed a shot or made a mistake, you were made to feel so bad about it because all eyes were on the scoreboard. Winning was all that mattered and all anybody talked about: "We've gotta win this game," or "We shoulda won that game," or "How can we win the next game?" Win. Win. Win.

Coach Wooden didn't talk about winning—ever. His message was to give the game the best you've got. "That's the goal," he would tell us. "Do that and you should be happy. If enough of you do it, our team will be a success." He teaches this, he believes it, and he taught me to believe it.

Winning was not mentioned, ever—only the effort, the preparation, doing what it takes to bring out our best in practice and games. Let winning take care of itself.

When I was a senior playing forward at UCLA, none of the experts really thought we'd do much. The Walton Gang—Bill Walton, Keith Wilkes, and others—had just graduated after winning two national championships and extending a streak that got up to 88 straight victories before a loss to Notre Dame. I was the only returning starter on the 1974–1975 Bruins.

Coach went to work with us—fundamentals, drills, teamwork, self-sacrifice. Play hard, don't get down, wait for your chance, try to improve each day. Don't worry about the scoreboard. Never a single word about winning. We won the national championship that year.

At the time I didn't quite see it, but his behavior was basically the Pyramid of Success—hard work, energy and enthusiasm, self-control, and the rest of it. That's him. And he taught it by being himself.

In fact, I kind of thought of him as a professor. When I interviewed with him while I was in high school at Sonora, California, I remember, his office at UCLA was full of books, memorabilia, papers, plaques, certificates, lots of stuff. It seemed like the office of an English professor.

On the wall he had pictures of his own coaches—"Piggy" Lambert at Purdue, Glenn Curtis at Martinsville High School, and Earl Warriner from his grade school days in Centerton. There was a large drawing of his Pyramid of Success next to them.

Before practice, he'd often be standing there as we walked on to the court: "How's your mother, David? Have you called her?" "You over that cold, Jim?" "How's the math class coming?" He knew us as people. You could tell he cared. And you could tell that he really knew how to teach—just like a professor.

And, in a certain kind of way he was a professor. What he taught was how to win. And he did it without ever once mentioning winning.

# 15

# ADVERSITY IS YOUR ASSET

*"Things turn out best for those who make the
best of how things turn out."*

J UST BEFORE I WAS DUE to ship out on the U.S.S. *Franklin* during
World War II, I got appendicitis and was rushed to the hospital
for emergency surgery in Iowa City. While I was recovering from the
operation, the *Franklin* shipped out and left me behind. The sailor
who took my place on board was a friend of mine, Freddie Stalcup,
a fraternity brother and former football player at Purdue.

Weeks later news came back that the *Franklin* had taken a disastrous hit from a kamikaze while on patrol somewhere out in the
South Pacific. Freddie's battle station, the one I would have been
manning had fate not put me in the hospital, was destroyed when
the kamikaze crashed directly into it. Freddie was killed instantly.

A tragedy like that gets you thinking. For reasons unknown, fate
had smiled on me but taken my friend's life. With the loss came
the clearest comprehension that so often our destiny lies beyond
our control. And while we can't control fate, we must do all things
possible to control our response to it.

That response becomes all important because fate plays such a
profound role in much of what we do in life and in leadership. Circumstances we can't foresee, understand, or desire can be—and

are—imposed on us without warning; random acts happen to people and organizations out of the blue. In my experience, this is not the exception to the rule, but the rule.

You may have noticed that when unexpected good fortune arrives at our doorstep, we often accept it without thought, not even a tip of the hat. In trying times, however, we are quick to conclude that the fates are working directly and unfairly against us—to find an excuse to let up, lose heart, and then quit.

George Moriarty described it like this:

*Sometimes I think the fates must grin*
*As we denounce them and insist,*
*The only reason we can't win*
*Is because the fates themselves have missed.*

But it is not the fates that have "missed," rather the fortitude of a leader who says "woe is me" moments before giving up in the face of misfortune. Do not let "woe is me" become your theme song. It is a tune sung only by weak leaders.

Shakespeare expressed it well. Shortly before Hamlet faces likely death in a fencing match arranged by the man who murdered his father, his friend Horatio tries to offer him an excuse to run, hide, or quit. Hamlet refuses. He has come to believe that all things happen for a reason and tells Horatio, "There is special providence in the fall of a sparrow." Hamlet saw divine guidance and care in all events—big and small—and was determined to face his destiny with courage and skill.

**"Although you may not be able to control what fate brings your way, you can control how you react and respond to it. At least, you *should* be able to."**

I believe the same. I was taught to make the best of whatever the fates—providence—brought forth into my life. This belief has been of great benefit to me, most particularly when it came to leading others.

When the going gets tough, the tough get going. Don't beg, cry, alibi, sulk, or lose your self-control; but do maintain poise, condition, alertness, confidence, industriousness, enthusiasm, fight, and desire.

## DAD'S RESPONSE BECAME MY MODEL

When my father, Joshua, lost our farm because contaminated hog vaccine killed the animals, he blamed neither fate nor the merchant who sold the serum. Even though Dad had been hit hard by misfortune, he was resolute, optimistic, and uncomplaining.

As difficult as it was, he left the land he loved, moved to Martinsville, and found work in a sanitarium to support his family. Not once did I hear him express anger, bitterness, or dismay about his misfortune. Never did he envy nor compare himself to those who seemed to have been treated better by the fates. Dad took what life offered and made the very best of it. This was a powerful example to me.

When things go bad for reasons beyond your control, it is tempting to first blame and then embrace fate as the cause of your failure. An effective leader ignores the temptation—the easy excuse—of using bad luck to become disheartened, disillusioned, and defeatist.

Adversity can make us stronger, smarter, better, tougher. Blaming your troubles on bad luck makes you weaker. Most worthwhile things in the competitive world come wrapped in adversity. Good leaders understand this and are inclined to see the truth in this verse:

*Looking back it seems to me,*
*All the grief that had to be.*
*Left me when the pain was o'er,*
*Stronger than I was before.*
*—Anon.*

We do not control the unwelcome twists and turns that are part of our leadership. At those difficult moments I have drawn strength from Dad's strong example as well as his suggestion to worry only about those things over which I have control. We can't control fate, only our response to it.

## PLAY THE HAND YOU ARE DEALT

Fate played the cruelest trick on me—not for the first or last time—soon after I moved into the college ranks as a coach in 1946 at Indiana State Teachers College. During my second season, the phone started to ring with coaching offers from schools such as UCLA and the University of Minnesota.

At the time, UCLA was just four letters in the alphabet that meant almost nothing to me. Minnesota was another story entirely because it was in the Big 10 conference.

In addition to having allegiance to the Big 10 because I'd played basketball at Purdue, there was a more practical reason involved: I knew—and was known by—so many high school coaches around the territory. All of them—several hundred—would be potential recruiters for my program. It's hard to overstate how important this could be in developing and maintaining a superior basketball program. It was an asset of almost indescribable value to a coach. I wanted that asset very much.

There was also the issue of my family. Nell and the children didn't want to move far from Indiana and, in truth, neither did I. We loved everything about the Midwest, including the winter weather. For many reasons I had the greatest desire to become head coach of the Minnesota Gophers basketball team in the Twin Cities.

I visited UCLA only as a favor to a former teammate of mine at Purdue, Dutch Fehring, football line coach of the Bruins. He and a local broadcaster, Bob Kelly, had recommended me to the selection committee that subsequently invited me to come out for a visit. What I saw wasn't very impressive.

As soon as I got back to Indiana from my trip out West, I announced to Nell, "We're going to Minnesota." But I spoke too soon. Fate was going to have the last word.

Gopher officials and I had agreed to every single term of the contract except one; specifically, they wanted me to keep the head coach I was replacing, Dave McMillan, on staff as my assistant. I was unwilling to do this, because it was unfair to both of us; each had his own system and way of doing things. I didn't want to constantly be second-guessed by a former head coach who had a different philosophy of teaching and playing basketball.

After several weeks of calls back and forth, Minnesota told me their final decision would be made on the following Saturday and they would call with the results at exactly 6 p.m. In the meantime, I phoned UCLA to inform them that in all likelihood I would be turning down their offer because I expected Minnesota officials to grant my request and allow me to appoint my own assistant. In the unlikely event this did not occur, I told UCLA I'd be willing to become head coach of the Bruins. What I didn't mention is how much I hoped this would not happen.

On Saturday night, Nell and I sat in our living room in Terre Haute waiting for the phone call from Minnesota. But it didn't come—not at 6:00, and not at 6:30. We were becoming increasingly concerned until finally, at 7 p.m., the telephone rang. We were both relieved and very eager to hear the news that would soon take us to Minnesota.

Unfortunately, the call was from California. The voice on the other end of the line was UCLA athletic director Wilbur Johns: "Coach Wooden, what's your decision?"

It was hard for me to say the words, but I replied, "Minnesota didn't call, Wilbur. I guess they wouldn't budge on my request after all. I accept your offer."

What I didn't know was that Minnesota had budged and decided after long discussions to let me pick my own assistant coach and to find Dave McMillan an acceptable job elsewhere in the athletic department.

However, when officials tried to call me at exactly 6 p.m. with the good news that I was going to be the next head coach of the Minnesota Gophers, their phone lines were dead.

A spring blizzard had knocked out all telephone service in the Twin Cities. By the time service was restored again and Minnesota was able to get through to me—about 7:30 p.m.—it was too late. Fate had made the first and final call. I had already given my word to UCLA that I would be the next Bruins head basketball coach.

As much as I wished the conversation with Wilbur Johns had not taken place, I couldn't go back on my word. If your word is nothing, you're not much better. I remembered Dad's simple advice in his Two Sets of Three: "Don't lie, don't cheat, don't steal; never whine, never complain, never make excuses."

I followed his advice and example the night a fateful blizzard moved me in a direction I didn't want to go—California. I knew exactly what Dad would have done in similar circumstance. I had seen it when he lost the farm, when he took fate and made it his friend.

## YOU ARE YOUR WORD

When you say you'll do it, do it. Don't give your word unless you intend to keep it. A leader whose promise means something is trusted. Trust counts for everything in leadership.

As a leader, you must play the hand you're dealt even when you don't like the cards—even when fate frowns on you. A few months after those Saturday night phone calls, the Woodens were in California and I was conducting practice as the newly arrived head coach of the UCLA Bruins. But fate soon intervened again, this time in an ironic way—good fortune became misfortune.

## MAKE THE BEST OF IT

When overflow crowds began showing up for UCLA's games in the cramped quarters of the third floor court of the Men's Gym, the fire marshal forced us to pack up and play home games elsewhere: Venice High School, Long Beach Municipal Auditorium, Long Beach City College, Pan Pacific Auditorium, Santa Monica City College, and others. We even played a home game at Bakersfield Junior College, which is 100 miles north of Los Angeles.

For many years we had no home court or the advantages that come with it. I tried to turn the disadvantage to our advantage, to do the best I could under the circumstances that fate—a fire marshal—had imposed.

I told our players, "This will make you stronger when you play opponents on their own home court, because we'll be conditioned to the disruption and distractions of traveling." And it did. The players made fate their friend. (I had been assured when I came to UCLA that the tiny Men's Gym would soon be replaced by an adequate facility. Seventeen years later it finally got done.)

Later, misfortune hit us again when the Bruins began practice in 1965–1966 as defending national champions. I felt we would start the year with an even stronger team than the one that had just won the NCAA title seven months earlier; so much experienced talent was returning to play for another year. However, while talent and experience is a potent package, it is not as potent as fate.

Almost from the start of the season, injuries and illness began to hamstring our team. Everything seemed to change practically overnight: Edgar Lacey broke a kneecap; Freddie Goss went down with a mysterious flulike condition; Kenny Washington pulled a groin muscle, an injury from which he never fully recovered. In a matter of weeks, fate dished up more misfortune than in the two previous years combined.

Not only didn't we defend our national championship, with a 10–4 record we didn't even win our conference title. So many circumstances had worked against us that were beyond our control. Nevertheless, you make the best of what you're given. I reminded myself that during the two preceding seasons fate had smiled on our program.

## FATE REMOVES A WEAPON

When officials outlawed the dunk in 1967 it was ostensibly to stop players from hanging on to the rim and occasionally shattering the backboard. However, it also had a direct effect on Lewis Alcindor, Jr.; specifically, it took away one of his strong offensive weapons. Certainly it would be easy to bemoan what happened.

Although I supported outlawing the dunk for several reasons, including the fact that it turned into a showboating device, Lewis felt the action might have been directed specifically at him. I told him, "Lewis, this will make you a better player because you'll have to develop additional aspects of your game. And, don't worry, when you go to the NBA you'll still remember how to dunk." And I was right.

He subsequently developed possibly the greatest offensive weapon in the NBA: Kareem's sky hook. He turned a negative into a positive, a disadvantage into a great advantage. (A few years after Lewis and Bill Walton left college basketball, the dunk was allowed back in the game.)

# YOUR OWN SPECIAL PROVIDENCE

I mention these obstacles and setbacks not to suggest I faced greater or more frequent challenges than others or that fate had been unduly hard on me. Just the opposite, in fact. Leadership in any context comes with such adversity. Fate seems, at times, to single out the leader for testing, as if it wants to know whether that leader is strong enough, resilient enough to be the one trusted with leadership.

Early on I had come to believe that events in life usually work out as they should, for a reason, even if that reason is not readily apparent. Perhaps it was because of my faith, the example of my parents, or my own experiences along the way. I don't know exactly why, but I began accepting what fate offered and tried to make the best of the situation—to move forward with optimism and the determination to make the most of the hand I was dealt, whether it was good or bad.

Losing the coaching job I longed for at Minnesota, being forced to play UCLA's home games on the road for many years, waiting so long for an adequate gym, watching a potential national championship team become decimated with injuries—all these setbacks and more are what coaches and leaders deal with every day. We are paid to deal with fate.

Those who prevail look fate in the eye and say, "Welcome," and then move ahead without complaint, excuse, or whining. While we can't control fate, we are—or should be—able to control our response to it. In leadership, your response becomes crucially important, because ultimately it is the response of your organization.

When you have found an excuse to let up or quit, so will your team. When you press on with enthusiasm regardless of the circumstance, your organization—if you have chosen good people and taught them well—will follow you as you continue to fight on. Quit or fight? It's the leader who decides for the organization.

*"You are not a failure, until you start blaming someone else for your weaknesses and mistakes."*

As a coach and leader I tried hard to avoid letting those things I couldn't control affect the things I could control. In more than nine decades I have yet to control fate. Neither have you, I'm sure.

Prepare to the utmost of your ability; teach your team to do the same. Ignore the fates with the sure knowledge that adversity will only make you and your team stronger if you resist self-pity. How you handle bad luck, setbacks, and the vagaries of the competitive environment is one of the major differences between the champion and the also-ran. Be a realistic optimist and remind yourself that things turn out best for those who make the best of the way things turn out.

## RULES TO LEAD BY

### Always Assume Adversity.

All leaders and organizations are blind-sided by bad luck and misfortune in various ways at various times. The best leaders understand this and are seldom thrown off stride when it occurs. They recognize the opportunity it presents, namely, that your response can separate you and your organization from the competition whose leader is stunned and then disheartened when fate frowns. Expect the rough patches and allow them to make you stronger.

### Don't Make "Woe Is Me" Your Fight Song.

Leaders cannot allow themselves to be sidetracked by self-pity. Accurate self-assessment and team assessment is linked to success. This activity is impossible when you are bogged down in feeling sorrow for yourself, in denouncing misfortune. Make the best of what you've got; play the cards you are dealt. Walt Disney once said, "There is no education like adversity." However, to gain this education you must be tough enough to overcome adversity rather than allowing adversity to overcome you.

**Don't Blame Failure on Fate.**
You can stumble and fall, make errors and mistakes, but you are not a failure until you start blaming others, including fate, for your results. Always believe there is a positive to be found in the negative. Things usually happen for a reason, even when you are unable to discern the reason. Remember, "there is providence even in the fall of a sparrow."

# ON WOODEN

**Ken Washington:** UCLA Varsity, 1964–1966; two national championships

---

## THE FICKLE FINGER OF FATE

The great lesson I take from Coach Wooden is this: The best thing you can do in life is your best. You're a winner when you do that, even if you're on the short end of the score.

Too many factors can affect the final results; the fickle finger of fate can suddenly take over. The best talent doesn't always win, but the individual or team that goes out and does their best is a winner. That's his philosophy. It's what he teaches.

We had a perfect season and won the national championship in 1964. We repeated as national champions in 1965. There was no question in my mind that in 1966 we could become the first team in college basketball history to win three championships in a row. Then the fickle finger of fate pointed at us.

Injuries, sickness, and all kinds of stuff were hitting us. We didn't even win our conference title in 1966—we had a 10–4 record and weren't even eligible to play in the NCAA tournament and defend our title.

Through all the misfortune I never heard a single complaint or excuse from Coach Wooden. He fought hard and kept telling us to keep working, never give up, and do our best. And we did in spite of the fickle finger of fate.

We were winners in 1966 because of that.

In retrospect, I believe it was probably fantastic for me as a person that we didn't win that third consecutive national championship. It showed me what life is really like, what fate can do—why you can't base your success just on results.

Of course, this is what I had been taught by my coach. More than anyone I've ever known, he comes closest to practicing what he preaches. He was so consistent in what he said and did in both principles and standards. In fact, I began to think it was normal behavior in a leader. But it's not normal. Holding to those high standards and principles is rare out in the world.

At the end of my four years at UCLA I still needed additional credits to graduate. Coach Wooden was all over me to make sure I came back for that fifth year to earn my degree in Economics.

Even though my playing days were over at UCLA, he cared a great deal about my welfare. "This is very important for you, Kenneth. Let's get that diploma." And he kept checking in on me during the year to make sure I got it. And I did.

Coach Wooden didn't teach character; he nurtured it. He chose individuals to be on the team based on talent, of course, but not talent alone. He wanted a certain kind of individual—the team player, a person with integrity and values.

Then he nurtured those values just like he nurtured your talent as an athlete. Honesty, being unselfish, caring about your teammates, a good work ethic, all these things were stressed constantly.

Along with this he would never degrade, abuse, or humiliate individuals, even though he had the power to do it. After all, he was the boss. But he gave respect even when discipline was doled out.

Coach is a master psychologist who understands the differences in people. Certain things he insisted on, like no swearing, being on time, no showboating, all of that. But when it came to working with us, he treated everybody as an individual, approached each of us in a way that worked.

Jack Hirsch, for example, was a free spirit, very flippant, and the only guy on the team who addressed Coach Wooden as John. Coach understood that it was not being done in a disrespectful manner and let him do it. Coach knew Jack wasn't crossing the line. It was just Jack being Jack.

When he crossed the line, however, there was a price to pay. One day we were eating dinner at the training table and Jack got up and said, "I can't eat this slop." Coach very calmly, but firmly, suspended Jack—told him not to come back until he could apologize as well as eat what all the other players were eating.

Coach understood the disrespect that was carried in Jack's remarks about our food. Disrespect by anyone for anyone was simply not allowed.

Now, where Jack came from maybe our training table food didn't taste good. As far I was concerned, it was fine. Coach understood he could not let Jack say what he said. It was not acceptable, disrespectful. Jack remained off the team until he changed his attitude and apologized.

Two weeks later Jack was back at the training table, not exactly wolfing it down, but not complaining either.

Athletics is like life. Sometime you can do everything right and still lose. It's all a journey. You do your best, and then you have to let it go. Lots of people preach that, but come crunch time—oops, not so easy to do. Coach practiced what he preached. Even when the fickle finger of fate took over.

Re: Criticism

## PART 3

1. If the coach "bawls you ___ cons___ ___t as a compli___
   He is trying to teach you an_ ___ ___oint upon you_
   If he were not interested in you, he wo___ not bother
   player is criticized only to improve h_m and not for __
   personal reasons.

# LESSONS
## FROM MY
# NOTEBOOK

F2 passes back out
G1 and forms double
reen with C render
~ G2
G1 looks for F1 on
de post or for G2 coming out
ind double screen.

S A, B, C, + D - G to F

Same optim
___ G1 + G2 _
changed ___ g___

G to F - "Bac

## INTRODUCTION

What follows are pages or excerpts of pages from notebooks I used through the years in my teaching—notes, observations, reminders, suggestions, and lists of relevant goals and how to achieve them. They include rules for behavior, preseason priorities, minute-by-minute practice schedules, awards, varsity captains, and more. I've tried to select material that has application to leadership beyond just basketball or sports and to suggest how it might apply to your own organization.

I don't believe there is a "one size fits all" methodology or philosophy when it comes to effective leadership and winning organizations. Nevertheless, in sharing these pages from my notebooks along with the Pyramid of Success and my Lessons in Leadership, I hope you find some ideas that can be successfully incorporated into your own approach to building a winning organization—a team that knows how to succeed in a competitive environment.

A good leader never stops learning. A great leader never stops teaching. When you've finished reading this book, I sincerely hope you'll have found information that will help you become an even better teacher and leader, one capable of building an organization characterized by Competitive Greatness.

What follows are some relevant pages and notes I kept to help me achieve that goal with the UCLA Bruins basketball team.

## DIAGRAMS DON'T WIN CHAMPIONSHIPS

In sports it is easy to become consumed with diagrams of plays, *X*s and *O*s, patterns, and systems of offense and defense. To a large de-

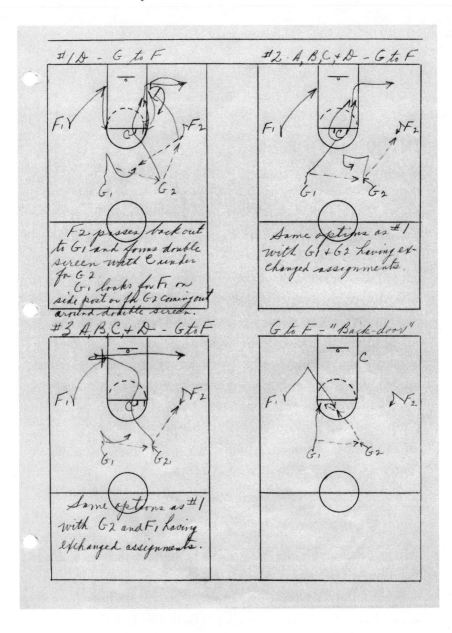

#1 D - G to F

#2 A, B, C, + D - G to F

F2 passes back out to G1 and forms double screen with C under for G2.
G1 looks for F1 on side post or for G2 coming out around double screen.

Same options as #1 with G1 + G2 having exchanged assignments.

#3 A, B, C, + D - G to F

G to F - "Back-door"

Same options as #1 with G2 and F1 having exchanged assignments.

gree this involves the mechanics of how things can or should be done.

I believe the same is true in most organizations. There is a certain way that a leader wants and expects things done, whether it's selling, producing, constructing, designing, or anything else. In one way or another, you draw up the plans and your team carries them out with varying degrees of effectiveness.

Here are some of the plans that I drew up as head coach of the Bruins. I share them here because looking at them flat on the page gives a sense, perhaps, of how useless they are without all the other vital elements that go into building a successful team.

For any leader, any organization, the plans are a starting point. That's why I put them at the beginning of Part Three. The much more difficult task for anyone in a leadership position is to create an environment, a way of thinking, a set of beliefs, that ultimately gets everyone working *eagerly* and to the best of their ability to make those plans result in a winning organization.

Drawing up plans such as these diagrams is the easy part. I did it thousands of times. Creating a successful organization with people who execute the plans at a level of Competitive Greatness—now, that's the challenge of leadership.

For me, it started, in large part, at our first team meeting.

## MY FIRST SPEECH TO THE TEAM: SETTING THE STANDARD

Getting off to a good start is important. It sets the tone for your team in many ways—expectations, values, attitude, behavior, rules, and much more. This is especially true with individuals who are new to your organization, but it also applies to the others under your leadership who may need a reminder from time to time of how you expect things to be done.

At UCLA I began each season with introductory remarks in a room that served as a "classroom." During that meeting I made a conscientious attempt to let everyone in attendance know what I expected of them and what they could expect from me. Among other things, I reviewed my philosophy of success and how you achieve it.

Rafer Johnson, a starter on the varsity team in 1959 and winner of an Olympic gold medal in 1960, said that my opening remarks gave him the confidence that he could succeed as a member of the Bruins. And he did.

While my speeches at the start of the season were never recorded or written down, a few years ago the Indiana Basketball Hall of Fame asked me to approximate what I said for a 3-D video presentation at their excellent facility in New Castle.

What I wrote down and recorded for them is included here. Obviously, my remarks changed a bit from year to year, but this is a pretty good example of the basic tone and philosophy that I presented at the start of a new season at UCLA.

I think it's important that everyone in an organization be on the same page. And, from my perspective it's the leader who decides what that page will be. Here's a page from my speech to the players at the start of a new season.

Please let me have your attention, young men. I would like to say a few words about this coming season. We all want it to be very successful, but for our success to become a reality you must first accept my concept of what success truly is. True success in basketball shouldn't be based on individual statistics or the percentage of victories, any more than success in life should be based on material possessions or a position of power and prestige. Success must be based on how close you come to reaching your own particular level of competency.

Outscoring an opponent is important, and we must make an honest effort to do that, but you must keep things in proper perspective. Our efforts on the court are only building blocks for achieving success in life, and that should be our main purpose in being here.

Even though it can never be attained, perfection should be our goal. Giving less than your best effort toward attaining perfection is not success - regardless of winning percentages or how successful others may perceive you to be.

You cannot be truly successful without the peace of mind, and that only comes through the self-satisfaction that comes from knowing you made the effort to become the best that you are capable of becoming. You and only you will know whether or not you have done that. You can fool others, but you cannot fool yourself.

We must not become too concerned about the things over which we have no control, but we must make every effort to utilize to the best of our ability the things over which we have control.

Everyone is different. There will always be others who are bigger or stronger, or quicker, or better jumpers, or better in some other areas, but there are other qualities in which you can be second to none.

Among these are - your dedication to the development of your own potential, your industriousness, your physical condition, your integrity, self-control, team spirit and cooperation. If you acquire and keep these traits, I can assure you that you will be successful, not just in basketball, but in life, which is of far greater importance.

Now for some final thoughts. You are here to get an education which will provide you with the foundation for a productive and pleasant life for all the years to follow. Your education and academic progress must be your first priority. No one else can do it for you. Your second priority is basketball, and here again, it is entirely up to you - under my direction, of course - to make the effort to reach your potential. Do not try to be better than someone else, but make every effort to become the very best you can be. For a team, at practice and at games, your concentration must be completely on basketball. But the rest of the time you are not a basketball player, you're a student - a student who should neither want nor expect any special privileges.

Are there any questions? Good!

## THE ABCs OF SUCCESS

"What's the secret of success?" is a question most of us have asked ourselves at one time or another. My conclusion, shown here, may disappoint you; namely, there is no secret. In other words, you and your team must master the old-fashioned ABCs of success, whether it involves making baskets, meeting sales quotas, or most anything else. For me, it's execution, not some secret, that gets the job done right. Execution of fundamentals by individuals who integrate their talents in a smoothly working unit matters most.

Over the decades I've noticed that teams and leaders who attain great heights have one thing in common: The ABCs of success.

A. No secrets. It is not what you do, but how well you do it.
B. No system will be successful unless the players are well grounded in the fundamentals.
C. System or team play comes from integrating individuals, who have mastered the fundamentals, into a smooth working unit. This applies to both the offensive and defensive point of view.

## A LEADER'S LIST OF SELF-IMPROVEMENTS

I am something of a list maker. Perhaps it comes from the knowledge that when you have a goal, it makes sense to determine what will help you get there. For me, making a list of those things was a logical way to proceed. Thus, I had lots of lists over the years.

The list you see here includes secondary traits I believe are valuable for a leader to have (the primary traits are listed in the Pyramid of Success). Some of the secondary traits are obvious (although often the most obvious things are overlooked) and others may seem trivial—for example, "voice." However, I don't assume anything is obvious or that something relevant is trivial, especially when it comes to a leader's personal improvement.

I had a simple approach; namely, if I could think of something that would bring about improvement, I tried to do it. These accompanying traits are a list of things I believe would help me, or any leader, be more effective.

You will also see that "Alertness" is included here as well as within the second tier of the Pyramid. Perhaps I was unconsciously following the fourth law of learning: Repetition.

```
Secondary Traits

1. Affability - Friendly, likable, cordial.

2. Appearance - Clean, neat.

3. Voice - Proper use of tone and pitch.

4. Adaptability - Adjust to the environment.

5. Cooperativeness - Harmonious co-worker with faculty, team, and community.

6. Forcefulness - Back up your ideas with firmness, not "bull-headedness."

            "The man who once most wisely said,
            'Be sure you are right, then go ahead.'
            Might well have added this to it,
            Be sure you are wrong before you quit."

7. Accuracy - In choice of men, in judgement, in techniques, and reacting
   quickly to emergencies.

8. Alertness - Be alert to observe weak spots in the opposition, in your
   own team, note fatigue, etc., and be quick to make the necessary
   corrections.

9. Reliability - The boys must know that they can depend upon you.

10. Cheerful, optimistic disposition - Think positively rather than
    negatively. Sincere optimism builds confidence and courage.

11. Resourcefulness - Each individual and each team is a separate problem--
    mentally, physically, socially, and spiritually. Use the right
    appeal for each.

12. Vision - Provide the incentive, a picture of the possible.
```

## SQUEEZING MORE FROM A MINUTE

As you see in these notes, I ran full-court scrimmages almost every day in practice prior to the first game of the season. (The last full-court scrimmage actually occurred one week prior to the opening game.) After that, we used them much less frequently.

> Full court scrimmage – Use almost
> every day prior to the first game, then –
> 1. Occasionally as needed for first seven
> or eight men.
> 2. Every Monday for those who did
> not get to play too much in the games.

In the weeks leading up to our first game, UCLA's full-court scrimmages served three purposes: (1) physical conditioning; (2) preparing players for what they would face in games, that is, the dynamics of full-court basketball; and (3) evaluating players.

Once the season got underway, the full-court scrimmage was incorporated only occasionally, because physical conditioning was attained through our intense and constant drills. There was also no longer a need to get the team acclimated to full-court play, because each week's games took care of that. My evaluation of players continued in practice and games throughout the entire year. All this effort reduced the need for utilizing full-court scrimmages.

The primary reason I stopped using full-court scrimmages regularly once our season began was that I viewed them as an inefficient format for good teaching. Why? They wasted time. While players ran from one end of the court to the other, time was being squandered.

My preferred method of instruction was the whole-part system, which broke the "whole," that is, playing basketball, down into small pieces that could be worked on selectively and perfected. Those pieces included how to execute a shot correctly, eye movement, hand placement, passing, pivoting, catching, running routes on plays, the specifics of rebounding, defensive systems, and more.

After practicing them individually, we put the "parts" back together as a whole. Running the full court wasted time that could be spent working on those details—the parts. Thus, while full-court scrimmaging served three specific purposes prior to the beginning of the season, it served very little purpose after that. Our goals could be accomplished by more efficient means: half-court scrimmages and drills.

Efficient use of time was extremely important to me, as you read in Chapter 10, "Make Each Day Your Masterpiece." Eliminating full-court scrimmages was one small way of using time more efficiently for squeezing more out of a minute. I give this example only because it might get you to thinking of ways to make your own organization use time better.

## DEFINE YOUR RULES CLEARLY

Chapter 11, "The Carrot Is Mightier Than a Stick," described how I evolved over the years from having lots of rules and few suggestions to lots of suggestions and fewer rules. Nevertheless, I still had my fair share of rules, especially during practice. Here is a list with a few of those rules. I considered them "normal expectations" to be observed by all players.

Of course, balance in every area is critical to a leader and to the team. Finding the correct balance in the area of rules is very challenging. When do the lists of dos and don'ts become so numerous they overwhelm you and your organization? Equally important, which rules make a positive difference? Which are simply a nuisance? I don't know the answer to those questions. Each coach, each leader, tries to figure it out for his or her organization.

For several years I handed out a hefty-sized book of information at the beginning of each season to each player. When I began to realize that the vast amount of material was overwhelming to them,

I started delivering it in smaller amounts, day by day, both verbally and on mimeographed pages such as the one you see here.

This page from my notebook may strike you as having too much or too little information; too broad or too detailed. And that's my point: Each leader must figure out the best balance and timing for delivering information within the organization.

---

Practice

1. Be dressed, on the floor, and ready for practice on time every day. There is no substitute for industriousness and enthusiasm.

2. Warm up and then work on your weaknesses and shoot some free throws when you take the floor and until organized practice begins.

3. Work hard to improve yourself without having to be forced. Be serious. Have fun without clowning. You develop only by doing your best.

4. No cliques, no complaining, no criticizing, no jealousy, no egotism, no envy, no alibis. Earn the respect of all.

5. Never leave the floor without permission.

6. When a coach blows the whistle, all give him your undivided attention and respond immediately without disconcerting in any manner.

7. Move quickly to get in position to start a new drill.

8. Keep a neat practice appearance with shirt tails in, socks pulled up, ~~and~~ hair cut short, *clean shaven, & finger nails trimmed.*

9. Take excellent care of your equipment and keep your locker neat and orderly.

10. Record your weight in and out every day.

11. Do things the way you have been told and do not have to be told every day. Correct habits are formed only through continued repetition of the perfect model.

12. Be clever, not fancy. Good, clever play brings praise while fancy play brings ridicule and criticism.

13. When group activity is stopped to correct one individual, all pay close attention in order that you will not require the same correction.

14. Condition comes from hard work during practice and proper mental and moral conduct.

15. Poise, confidence, and self-control comes from being prepared.

# TEACHING OTHERS TO TAKE CRITICISM

Giving criticism is an essential part of being a leader. While compliments, correctly conveyed, are a powerful motivational force—perhaps the most powerful force of all when given by someone who is trusted and respected—criticism serves a similar purpose in a different way.

While criticism *should* have productive results, it is very easy for the opposite thing to happen. Thus, I have tried hard to be businesslike in delivering criticism and have avoided personal remarks that could create embarrassment or ill will. But that's not enough.

I believe those under your leadership must be taught how to respond properly to your criticism. I did not assume that just because I didn't get personal, the recipient of my critical remarks took them the right way. Thus, I gave the following instructions informing—teaching—players how they should respond when criticized.

```
Re:  Criticism

    1.  If the coach "bawls you out", consider it as a compliment.
        He is trying to teach you and impress a point upon you.
        If he were not interested in you, he would not bother.  A
        player is criticized only to improve him and not for any
        personal reasons.

    2.  Take your criticism in a constructive way without alibis
        or sulking.  If the coach was wrong, he will find it out
        in due time.

    3.  Do not nag or razz or criticize a teammate at any time.
        It may lead to a bad feeling, which can only hurt the team.
        We must avoid cliques and all work toward the best interest
        of the team.
```

As you see, I was also very clear in explaining that at no time were they allowed to deliver criticism to a teammate.

An effective leader achieves positive and productive results with criticism. The leader who is less effective uses criticism in a heavy-handed manner that only compounds the problem. Thus, a leader must both know how to deliver criticism and teach others how to receive criticism.

## NOTES PRIOR TO UCLA'S FIRST NATIONAL CHAMPIONSHIP

Prior to the opening game of the 1963–1964 season that produced UCLA's first national championship, I realized we had the makings of a formidable team. All our starters were returning, and they were extremely well suited to the demands of executing the Press, a full-court system of playing defense which we had installed the previous season. Coupled with UCLA's fast-break offense, I felt that our players would be strong contenders for a national championship.

In fact, I even wrote a little poem about my feelings and the team's future:

> *With every starter coming back,*
> *Yes, Walt and Gail and Keith and Jack*
> *And Fred and Freddie\* and some more*
> *We could be champs in sixty-four.*

Going into the 1963–1964 season, I wrote these notes to myself as reminders of where I wanted emphasis and improvement. As much as I believed in the potential of our team, I realized it would not be realized without continued—ceaseless—efforts to improve.

The notes you see here are a preseason list of things I intended to work on and, if possible, perfect. It includes "work a lot" (number 3) on the various systems of the zone press; "work a lot on the

---

\* Walt Hazzard, Gail Goodrich, Keith Erickson, Jack Hirsch, Fred Slaughter, and Freddie Goss.

team fast break: Go. Go. Go!!!" (number 4); and "really strive for team play" (number 12).

These elements had already been deeply ingrained in our team's play and practice. I mention them to demonstrate my intense desire and intention to target areas for improvement *even* when the level of execution was already quite high.

Accepting the status quo means a leader feels no further improvement can be made. I never reached a point in 40 years of teaching basketball where I felt no further improvement could be made. And that applied to every area of the game, including my own leadership skills.

*Practice Schedule*

*For The*

*1963-1964 Season*

Suggestions #

1. Close each early practice with wind sprints.
2. Run special parts of our offense against live defense after permitting the first pass. This forces adjustments when necessary.
3. Work a lot on "pressing defense. Try Zone presses. 2-2-1, 2-1-2, 1-3-1, 1-2-1-1
4. Work a lot on team fast break. !!!
5. Use the 3 on 2 conditioner a lot - every day. Also other off. drills.
6. Use weak side post without a shot a lot.
7. Coaches do more individual and detail coaching.
8. Play the strong hand more on defense. Employ defense on man without the ball.
9. On the press - when two-timing a man, do not permit to dribble out or throw a direct pass. Come in high to force a lob or bounce and be alert to cover his potential outlets. Keep some one between the ball and the opposite corner of penetration.
10. Emphasize personal pride - on defense in particular.
11. Teach more <u>talking</u> on <u>defense</u> and offense.
12. Really strive for team play.

Let me also highlight two other items on the accompanying list worth comment: Point number 1, "Close each early practice with wind sprints," was never used. I didn't like wind sprints during practice because they were designed simply for conditioning. I felt I could get our team in condition by running drills at high speed. Thus, we could accomplish two things at once. That item may be on the list because I was thinking about giving it a try. In any case, it was never incorporated into our practices.

But point number 11, "Teach more *talking* on *defense* and offense," was very important—a reminder to me that communication between players is essential. During a game, teammates must constantly be talking to one another, warning one another, encouraging one another in all areas of the game. I even designated the number 5 player (a guard) as "the director," the individual most responsible for initiating communication on plays, both offensively and defensively.

Communication is essential in sports. The same is perhaps true with your team. Do you stress and teach good communication? Of course, it starts with the leader. Are you a good communicator?

## SOME DETAILS OF A VERY GOOD SEASON

As I mentioned in Chapter 14, "Don't Look at the Scoreboard," at the beginning of each season I would write down my predictions for UCLA's upcoming games. Those predictions were based on many things, including what you see here: the starting time of the game, day and date, opponent, final score, location, and the names of the officials.

All this and more was factored in before I wrote down my "best guess" on the outcomes of UCLA's games for the coming year. Then I would seal my predictions in an envelope and forget about them until the season concluded. Obviously, I didn't *literally* forget about

1963-64 Season    Won 30    Conf.

✓ NCAA Champs –    Lost 0    (15-0)

UPI #1   AP #1    100%

| Time | Date | Opponent | Score | Location | Players |
|---|---|---|---|---|---|
| 8:00 | F 11/29 | UCLA Freshman | | SMCC | Perry – Miletich |
| 9:15 | F 12/6 | Brigham Young Univ | +113-71 | L.A. Arena | Frivaldsky – Henley |
| 7:00 | S 12/7 | Butler | +80-65 | " | Frivaldsky – Filberti |
| 7:30 | F 12/13 | Kansas State | +78-75 | Lawrence, Kan | Alex George – Ken Bryan |
| 7:30 | S 12/14 | Kansas | +74-54 | Manhattan, Kan. | Tom Glennon – Pat Haggerty |
| 7:00 | F 12/20 | Baylor | +112-61 | Long Beach Arena | Doug Harvey – Jack Taylor |
| 9:15 | S 12/21 | Creighton | +95-79 | " | Jackie White – Jack Taylor |
| 1:15 | Th 12/26 | Yale ⎫ L A | +95-65 | L.A. Arena | Bill Fonts – Jack Taylor |
| 7:00 | F 12/27 | Michigan ⎬ | +98-80 | " | Jim Tunney – Joe Weigel |
| 9:00 | S 12/28 | Illinois ⎭ Classic | +83-79 | " | Bill Fonts – Joe Weigel |
| 8:00 | F 1/3 | ⎫ Wash. State | +88-83 | Pullman, Wash | Louie Soriano – Chas Moffett |
| 8:00 | S 1/4 | ⎭ | +121-79 | " | Burt Burr – Chas Moffett |
| 8:00 | F 1/10 | ⎫ U. So. Calif. | +79-59 | L A Arena | Louie Soriano – Bill Fonts |
| 8:00 | S 1/11 | ⎭ | +78-71 | " | Louie Soriano – Bill Fonts |
| 9:15 | F 1/17 | Stanford | +84-71 | " | Bill Bussenius – Joe Frivaldsky |
| 8:00 | S 1/18 | Stanford | +80-61 | SMCC | Bill Bussenius – Joe Frivaldsky |
| 8:00 | F 1/31 | Santa Barbara | +107-76 | Santa Barbara | Jackie White – Joe Frivaldsky |
| 8:00 | S 2/1 | Santa Barbara | +87-59 | SMCC | Doug Harvey – Jim Tunney |
| 8:00 | F 2/7 | UCB | +87-67 | Berkeley | Mel Ross – Jim Tunney |
| 8:00 | S 2/8 | UCB | +58-56 | " | Mel Ross – Jim Tunney |
| 7:00 | F 2/14 | Washington | +73-58 | L A Arena | Ernie Filberti – Mel Ross |
| 9:15 | S 2/15 | Washington | +88-60 | " | Ernie Filberti – Jim Tunney |
| 8:00 | S 2/22 | Stanford | +100-88 | Palo Alto | Ernie Filberti – Jack Taylor |
| 8:00 | M 2/24 | Washington | +78-64 | Seattle | Chas Moffett – Wm Kendrick |
| 8:00 | S 2/29 | Wash. State | +93-56 | L A Arena | Bill Bussenius – Jim Tunney |
| 7:00 | M 3/2 | UCB | +87-57 | " | Ernie Filberti – Jackie White |
| 8:00 | F 3/6 | U. So. Calif. | +91-81 | " | Louie Soriano – Joe Frivaldsky |
| 9:30 | F 3/13 | Seattle ⎫ NCAA | +95-90 | Corvallis, Ore. | Alex George – Lloyd Magnussen |
| 9:00 | S 3/14 | U. San Fran ⎬ WEST. REG | +76-72 | " | Tom Glennon – Don Watson |
| 9:30 | F 3/20 | Kan. State ⎫ NCAA | +90-84 | Kansas City | Red Mihilic – Hoggo |
| 9:00 | S 3/21 | Duke ⎭ Finals | +98-83 | " | Red Mihilic – Tom Glennon |

all of the information I had reviewed, because some of it was helpful in reminding me of certain situations that we might face again. For example, some officials might be tougher on calling fouls than others; some arenas (and the fans) are more challenging for a visiting team; I wanted to know if UCLA had problems with games that were played on the road, or at night, or on a particular day of the week—Friday or Saturday.

I think accurate and detailed record keeping is most important in leadership. I was always looking for clues that would help us improve individually and as a team. To help me accomplish this, I also kept extensive and detailed accounts of practices and games. My No. 2 yellow pencil was used even more than my whistle.

The page you see here is for the 1963–1964 season, which produced UCLA's first national basketball championship and a 30–0 record. Its format is similar to those of previous seasons and shows the kind of specific facts I reviewed at the beginning of the year.

## INOCULATING AGAINST INFECTION

UCLA won the NCAA national championship in 1964 and 1965. At the start of the 1966 season I wrote this brief note to myself—an urgent reminder to teach a very important lesson to the returning squad.

My message sounded an alarm; specifically: "Don't assume that past success will happen again in the future." I wanted each player to be very aware that UCLA's two recent national championships did not guarantee them *anything* in the coming season. The championships belonged to previous teams—not them. They needed to create their own identity, to work very hard and perhaps win their own championships.

This message—an admonition—was delivered verbally at various times in various ways. It was my attempt to help the players avoid overconfidence and complacency—the infection of success. It is an infection that is often fatal.

I knew from my own experience as a player that getting to the top was tough. Staying there was also tough, because we tend to let down, relax, and rest on our laurels when a little success comes our way.

Past achievements for any leader or organization will occur again in the future only with equal, or greater, effort. The leader whose teams achieve success must work hard to eliminate complacency among those in the organization. Otherwise, initial success is unlikely to become long-term success. This note—a reminder of the message I would repeat over and over to the team—was an attempt to inoculate them against the infection of success.

## TWO LISTS WITH ONE GOAL: IMPROVEMENT

The lists I created over the years dealt with everything from avoiding blisters to making jump shots. I was concerned with the physical mechanics of the game as well as the emotions and mental part of it.

Here are two lists, one entitled "Coaching Methods," the other called "Coaching—Important Principles to Keep in Mind." In both lists you could substitute the word *leadership* for *coaching*. The 27 instructions, in my opinion, have almost direct application to effective leadership in almost any organization.

UCIA  BASKETBALL

John Wooden, Head Coach

Coaching Methods

1. Be a teacher. Follow the laws of learning--explanation and demonstration, imitation, criticism of the imitation, repetition until habit is formed.

2. Use lectures, photographs, movies, diagrams, mimeographed material, etc., to supplement your daily practices.

3. Insist on punctuality and proper dress for practice.

4. Insist on strict attention.

5. Permit no "horse play." Practice is preparation.

6. Show patience.

7. Give new things early in the practice period and then repeat daily until learned.

8. Avoid harsh, public criticism. Use praise as well as censure.

9. Encourage teamwork and unselfishness.

10. Do considerable individual coaching of individuals.

11. Use small, carefully organized groups.

12. Have a definite practice plan--and follow it.

John Wooden, Head Coach

<u>Coaching</u> - Important principles to keep in mind

1. Basketball is a game of habits.

2. Never become satisfied.

3. Don't give them too much, but teach well.

4. Don't tie them down so rigidly that they lose their initiative.

5. Have an offense that gives equal opportunity to all.

6. Don't overlook little details. You must prepare to win to be a winner.

7. Convince your players of the importance of condition - mental, moral, and physical.

8. Nothing is as important as proper execution of the fundamentals.

9. Confidence comes from being prepared and properly conditioned.

10. Development of team spirit is a must and selfishness, envy, and egotism must be eliminated.

11. Both coach and players must be industrious and enthusiastic if success is to be achieved.

12. Teach respect for all and fear for none.

13. Use the positive approach and develop pride in your own game.

14. Have one team, not regulars and substitutes.

15. Give public credit to your playmakers and defensive men at every opportunity.

254 Wooden on Leadership

# A GOOD FACILITY IMPROVES EFFICIENCY

By 1967, UCLA's modern basketball facility, Pauley Pavilion, had been in use for one year, and it allowed my practices to reach a much higher level of efficiency and effectiveness.

You see some evidence of that in these suggestions—reminders to myself—for 1966–1967, specifically, number 3: "Shooting" (free throws).

Previously, our teams practiced at the Men's Gym, with all its limitations, including just two baskets. With Pauley Pavilion's expanded facilities—including six baskets (more were available)—I was able to conduct drills and scrimmages while simultaneously having pairs of players isolated on other baskets practicing free throws.

In fact, even then I doubled up on baskets and had one pair of players shooting free throws while another pair practiced shots from the outside perimeter. While players shot free throws, a manager would record the percentage of shots that were successful.

Even with all the backboards and baskets available at Pauley Pavilion, I rarely assigned one player to a basket. Basketball is a team sport, and I felt it was unwise to allow players to practice by themselves. Always I wanted them to be interacting with their teammates.

You'll also see in my notes a reminder that players be on the court for practice no later that 3:15 p.m. A relatively unsupervised warmup occurred between 3:00 p.m. and 3:30 p.m. I had noticed players take advantage of that situation to some degree by arriving later and later. I wanted to correct this tendency in the coming season. The warmup was important. Everything was important.

## EIGHT STEPS TO GOOD RELATIONS

The relationship between a leader and those in the organization determines in many ways whether success will occur. It's easy to overanalyze such things as relationships. I tried to avoid that and stuck to common sense instead.

Here are eight specific "commonsense" steps that I tried to incorporate into my coaching so that the relationship I had with those on our team would be as productive as possible.

You will recall that I included the first three steps in Chapter 5, "Use the Most Powerful Four-Letter Word." I feel that all eight steps are worth repeating here. You'll notice that everything here is based on plain old common sense.

```
         John Wooden, Head Coach
                    and
          - Coach your player relationship
```

1. Keep a close personal player relationship, but keep their
   respect. Be sincerely interested in their personal problems
   and easy to approach.

2. Maintain discipline without being dictatorial. Be fair and
   lead rather than drive.

3. Study and respect the individuality of each player and handle
   them accordingly. Treat each man as he deserves to be treated.

4. Try to develop the same sense of responsibility in all.

5. Analyze yourself as well as your players and be governed
   accordingly.

6. Approval is a great motivator. Use the "pat on the back,"
   especially after severe criticism.

7. If you teach loyalty, honesty, and respect for the rights
   of others, you will be taking a big step toward a cooperative
   team with proper team spirit. Jealousy, egotism, envy, criticism and razzing of each other can ruin this.

8. Consider the team first, but don't sacrifice a boy just to
   prove a point.

## GOOD RECORD KEEPING

Here is the day's practice schedule for Monday, December 12,
1969. Besides breaking down the time into our usual 5-, 10-, and
15-minute blocks of instruction, it notes the absence of one player,
Steve Patterson. I include this because it perhaps shows how we
tracked various elements of our practice schedule. In this case,
Steve Patterson missed all but 30 minutes of that day's practice because he had a final exam.

With the graduation of Lewis Alcindor Jr. (Kareem Abdul-
Jabbar), Steve had become UCLA's starting center. These notes reminded me that he was absent, gave the reason for his absence, and
showed what part of the practice he missed.

It was important to me to keep track of these things—who was where, when, and for how long. Everything and everyone was accounted for.

## NORMAL EXPECTATIONS

When I was coaching, I had a pretty good memory for facts and figures, names and faces, *and* the rules of behavior that members of the team were expected to follow. Nevertheless, I wrote things down, including lists of personal qualities that I wanted our players to have or develop—the ingredients necessary for a successful team. While my memory served me very well, I took no chances that something would be overlooked or forgotten. Lists. Lots of lists resulted.

My overall description of those lists as they pertained to players came under the general heading "Normal Expectations." In other words, I did not consider the rules a hardship or particularly unusual. Here's one list of those rules of conduct that players were given and expected to observe.

The leader of any organization who has individuals on the team who adhere to these "Normal Expectations" has the makings of a very good team.

---

Normal Expectations

Our chances of having a successful team may be in direct proportion to the ability of each player to live up to the following sets of suggestions:

1. Be a gentleman at all times.

2. Be a team player always.

3. Be on time whenever time is involved.

4. Be a good student in all subjects - not just in basketball.

5. Be enthusiastic, industrious, dependable, loyal, and cooperative.

6. Be in the best possible condition -- physically, mentally, and morally.

7. Earn the right to be proud and confident.

8. Keep emotions under control without losing fight or aggressiveness.

9. Work constantly to improve without becoming satisfied.

10. Acquire peace of mind by becoming the best that you are capable of becoming.

* * * *

1. Never criticize, nag or razz a teammate.

2. Never miss or be late for any class or appointment.

3. Never be selfish, jealous, envious, or egotistical.

4. Never expect favors.

5. Never waste time.

6. Never alibi or make excuese.

7. Never require repeated criticism for the same mistake.

8. Never lose faith or patience.

9. Never grandstand, loaf, sulk, or boast.

10. Never have reason to be sorry afterwards.

# A LESSON FROM WILT

In the late 1960s, Wilt Chamberlain was traded to the Los Angeles Lakers. At the press conference that introduced him to local writers and broadcasters, a reporter asked, "Wilt, do you think Lakers' Coach Van Breda Kolff can handle you? It's been said that you're hard to handle."

I was at that press conference, and Wilt's answer had a strong impact on me. He told the reporter, "You 'handle' farm animals. You work with people. I am a person. I can work with anyone."

Hearing his words reminded me that my book on coaching basketball, *Practical Modern Basketball*, which had recently been published, included a section called, "Handling of Players."

I immediately rushed home, got out my notes, and changed the title of that section to "*Working* with Players." For me that change in wording was extremely important because I believe an effective leader works *with* those individuals on the team. *Handling* suggests a much different, and, in my opinion, less productive, relationship. You see evidence of my change in wording on this page from my notebook. It's a very small thing, but it goes to something very big, namely, your perspective on the relationship you have with those under your leadership.

*Working with*
Handling of players - be impartial, but remember that no two are alike and each must receive the treatment that he earns and deserves; *remember that you cannot antagonize and influence at the same time;* praise as well as censure - no one truly likes to be criticized; be easily approached, but maintain respect; publicly commend your play makers, rebounders, and key defensive work; permit no razzing, criticizing among the players; players must thank and praise each other; have one team - not regulars and subs; try to get across the idea that doing their best will bring desirable results in every way; hold no post mortems immediately after games, but learn and improve; do the job at hand as we can do nothing to change the past, but can help prepare for the future.

## CATNIP AND THE IMAGINARY BALL

Practice—that is, the process of your preparation—is where championships in any context are won. How you practice is how you "play."

One of the challenges I faced with the Bruins during practice was dealing with the distraction caused by a player's natural instinct and desire to score baskets or grab rebounds. Either urge is such a powerful siren song that it's hard to make them pay attention and learn the "dull" fundamentals that ensure success in scoring and rebounding—such things as pivoting, hand and arm movement, and routes on plays.

The same is perhaps true with your team. It's only natural for those under your leadership—perhaps even you—to focus on the end result rather than learning and doing what it takes to get there.

I attempted to solve this particular problem at UCLA by occasionally removing the siren song; specifically, I made them practice and play basketball without the ball. Without the basketball, a player can neither score baskets nor grab rebounds. Without those distractions, he was better able to fully concentrate on what I was teaching.

You'll see that in these notes to myself on "Rebounding," I listed such things as three-on-three drills, the three-man pass-and-move, the five-man back and forth over basket, and other drills.

You'll also see listed at number 8: "Imaginary ball." That was the drill that removed the siren song and made players concentrate on the fundamentals of scoring and rebounding.

I've also included a list of Practice Drills: "jump shots" (number 7) and "offensive tipping and defensive rebounds" (number 8) are both done with an imaginary basketball. In these instances, we worked on the fundamentals of jump shots and rebounds free from the distraction of a ball.

Rebounding - use some every day.
1. Five man rebound and passing.
2. Five man back and forth over basket.
3. Three man pass and move.
4. Moving straight line for timing
5. 3 on 3 inside with outside shooters.
6. 5 on 5 full team from various shots
7. 1 on 1, 2 on 2, and 3 on 3
8. Imaginary ball.
9. Individual tipping - three and in
10. Flankers covering the bank shots

For a player, the basketball is like catnip to a cat—irresistible. So, I occasionally removed the "catnip" during practice. In fact, I occasionally started practice without a basketball on the court. Players ran patterns and executed moves without having to worry about the ball. Forcing them to make imaginary passes helped to

Practice Drills
Start the organized practice each day by devoting 10 minutes to some combination of the following:
1. Easy rushing + stretching
2. Change of pace + direction
3. Push ups (5)
4. Defensive sliding
5. One on One (Cutter)
6. One on One (Dribbler)
7. Imaginary jump shots
8. Imaginary Off. tipping - Def. Reb.
9. Defensing the passer + cutter
10. Squad sliding to signal
11. Five man weave
12. Inside turn
13. Reversing without ball
14. Reversing with ball
15. Loose ball recovery (2 lines, one becomes defensive man)
16. Five man reb + passing
17. Offensive Cutting without shot
18. Review stop and turn
19. Jumping
20. Hopping

instill good habits and improve timing, footwork, elbow and hand position, and balance.

I suppose it's similar to shadowboxing, where a fighter concentrates on the moves rather than the target. Without the right moves it's hard to hit your target. The same is true for basketball teams and most organizations. Figuring out "the right moves" and teaching them is up to the leader. Perhaps there's a version of the "imaginary ball" that would be useful in your own quest for improving your team.

## TEAM CAPTAIN?
## NO POPULARITY CONTESTS

I did not like the idea of appointing a team captain for an entire season, nor did I permit players to elect one. Part of the reason went back to something that happened during my first year as head coach at South Bend Central High School in Indiana. Before I arrived, the basketball team's custom was as follows: At the conclusion of each season the players would elect their captain for the next year—almost eight months in advance.

When I began coaching the team, Sebastian Nowicki was already in place as captain of the Bears—elected before I even arrived in South Bend. Unfortunately, Sebastian did not earn a starting position on the Bears basketball team during my first year as coach. It became a little awkward to have him represent the Bears as team captain in pregame duties and then go sit on the bench during the game itself.

That event reinforced my opinion that *electing* a captain could be more of a popularity contest than having anything to do with a player's leadership ability. While Sebastian accepted his role in good spirit, I saw the potential for trouble in the future. Electing a captain based on popularity didn't seem like a particularly productive exercise when it came to creating a successful team.

I could have solved the problem by appointing each year's captain myself and not leaving it up to the players. In fact, that's what I began doing—with one major change; specifically, the team captain was selected, by me, on a game-to-game basis rather than for the entire year.

While there were four notable exceptions to this policy at UCLA, I recognized the great benefit of passing an "honorary" team captaincy around on a game-to-game basis. It was a very good "carrot" that I could use in rewarding players for various productive and unsung contributions to the team—for example, hard work and hustle during practice, a good attitude, and other less glamorous but important acts.

Even though the pregame duties were negligible, every player took pride in being chosen to stand up and represent his team as its captain. The reward of being selected captain for a game by the head coach was a great motivational tool.

At the conclusion of my first season at South Bend Central, the players were informed there would be no election for captain of the following year's team. I began personally appointing the player who would serve as that game's captain and announcing the selection in the locker room shortly before the tipoff for each game.

When I arrived at UCLA, the same situation existed—a team captain, Ron Pearson, had been elected by the players at the conclusion of the previous season. At the conclusion of my first year of coaching the Bruins, I instituted my South Bend policy—a team captain would be selected by *me* before each game.

There were four exceptions to this rule in the ensuing 26 seasons at UCLA. Four times I felt it would be productive to appoint a team captain for the entire season because of special circumstances. In 1950, I chose Eddie Sheldrake because he was the only returning starter and also had the additional qualifications of hustle and setting a good example. In 1966–1967, I appointed Mike Warren to serve as team captain for the season because, again, he was the only returning starter, he had great on-court intelligence and hustle, and he set a good example.

Mike Warren's younger teammates included Lewis Alcindor, Jr. (Kareem Abdul-Jabbar), Lynn Shackleford, Lucius Allen, and Ken Heitz, an extremely talented but inexperienced group. I felt Mike would provide a stabilizing influence on them. When he and his teammates won the NCAA national championship that year, I saw no reason to make a change: Mike Warren was renamed captain of the Bruins for the 1967–1968 season, and again they won a national championship.

The fourth time I appointed a player as captain for the entire season was in my final year as coach, 1974–1975. Again, there was only one returning starter, Dave Meyers, and, like Mike Warren and Eddie Sheldrake, he possessed the other important qualifications, namely, hustle and setting a good example.

You'll see on the accompanying list entitled "Varsity Captains" that each season has a name listed for a particular year. The list is misleading in that it suggests we had a "captain" who served for the entire year. In fact, the player was elected by popular vote only *after* the season concluded. At that point, I didn't mind a popularity contest.

## Varsity Captains

1949 - * Ronnie Pearson
1950 - * Alan Sawyer
1951 - Eddie Sheldrake
1952 - * Don Johnson + * Jerry Norman
1953 - * Barry Porter
1954 * - Ron Livingston
1955 * John Moore + * Don Bragg
1956 - * William Naulls
1957 - * Dick Banton
1958 - * Ben Rogers
1959 - * Walt Torrence
1960 - * Clifford Brandon
1961 - * John Berberich + * Bill Ellis
1962 - * Gary Cunningham + * John Green
1963 - * Jim Milhorn
1964 - * Walt Hazzard + * Jack Hirsch
1965 * - Keith Erickson - * Gail Goodrich
1966 * - Freddie Goss
1967 - * Mike Warren
1968 - * Mike Warren

1969 * Lewis Alcindor + Lynn Shackelford
1970 * John Vallely
1971 * Steve Patterson, Curtis Rowe, Sidney Wicks
1972 * Henry Bibby
1973 * Larry Farmer
1974 * Bill Walton + Keith Wilkes
1975   David Meyers

## REWARD THE QUALITIES THAT COUNT

I have always believed that glory belongs to the group rather than to any single individual. Nevertheless, it is important to recognize contributions that those within your organizations make to the welfare of the team. Usually that recognition goes to your most visible producer—for example, a top scorer in basketball or a top salesperson in business.

While I coached at UCLA, there were a number of awards given to players by alumni groups and local boosters for various accomplishments. While I couldn't control what those groups chose to give an award for, I strongly encouraged them to honor personal qualities, characteristics, and contributions that were less prominent than scoring points.

Scoring points is important, but recognition comes automatically to those who are top producers in this area. I wanted recognition given to top producers in other important, but less obvious, areas.

The names of award winners I've included here are less important than the categories they represent: the Glendale Bruin Club Award ("service to his team and to the university"); the Bruin Bench Award ("mental attitude"); the Bruin Hoopster Award ("most unselfish team player"); the Armand Award ("scholastic attainment"); and the "Caddy" Works Award ("competitive spirit").

In any organization, individuals who possess qualities such as unselfishness, competitive spirit, and the others I've mentioned are most valuable to the team. The UCLA alumni groups and booster clubs provided the Bruins a great service in recognizing players who were top performers in these areas. In your own organization, make every effort to ensure that individuals who contribute big things in little ways get the recognition they deserve.

As I observed in Chapter 8, "It Takes 10 Hands to Make a Basket," don't just reward the two hands scoring points. Recognize the additional hands that make the points possible. They are crucial underpinnings of a winning organization.

> *Glendale Bruin Club Award*
>
> Annual award to member of U.C.L.A. basketball team for outstanding service to his team and to the University.
>
> Perpetual trophy in Trophy Room of Kerckhoff Hall. The small trophy for the recipient is ordered by the club.
>
> Presentation made at the basketball banquet by the chairman of the Glendale Bruin Club.

**268**   Wooden on Leadership

## Bruin Bench Award

Presented annually to a U.C.L.A. varsity basketball player who has shown the most improvement in over-all play and mental attitude from a previous varsity year.

|  |  |
|------|------|
| 1954 | Ronald Bane |
| 1955 | Morris Taft |
| 1956 | Conrad Burke |
| 1957 | Jim Halsten |
| 1958 | Roland Underhill |
| 1959 | Denny Crum |
| 1960 | Clifford Brandon |
| 1961 | John Berberich |
| 1962 | John Green |
| 1963 | Jim Milhorn & Dave Waxman |
| 1964 | Gail Goodrich & Keith Erickson |
| 1965 | Keith Erickson |
| 1966 | Mike Lynn |
| 1967 | Lynn Shackelford & Bill Sweek |
| 1968 | Jim Nielsen |
| 1969 | Bill Sweek |
| 1970 | Sidney Wicks |
| 1972 | Larry Farmer |
| 1973 | Larry Hollyfield |
| 1974 | David Meyers |

## Bruin Hoopster Award

Originated for the 1960-1961 season.

Annual award to the member of the U.C.L.A. varsity basketball team considered to be the most unselfish team player.

The winner will be selected by a committee of Hoopsters appointed by the president.

Presentation will be made at the annual basketball banquet by some appointed Hoopster.

1961 - Bill Ellis
1962 - Pete Blackman
1963 - Fred Slaughter
1964 - Jack Hirsch & Fred Slaughter
1965 - Kenny Washington & Freddie Goss
1966 - Doug McIntosh & Kenny Leavy
1967 - Mike Warren
1968 - Mike Warren
1969 - Lynn Shackelford
1970 - Steve Patterson
1971 - Steve Patterson & Kenny Booker
1972 - Keith Wilkes

1973 - Tommy Curtis
1974 - Ralph Drollinger
1975 - Ralph Drollinger

*Armand Award*    (Originated 1956)

To freshman basketball player rating high in playing time, scholastic attainment to date.

1956 - Robert Archer        1975 - Ray Townsend & Brett Vroman

1957 - Brian Kniff

1958 - Kent Miller

1959 - Gary Cunningham + Pete Blackman

1960 - Ronnie Lawson

1961 - Fred Slaughter

1962 - Gail Goodrich & Fred Goss

1963 - Doug McIntosh & Ken Washington

1964 - Edgar Lacey + Mike Lynn

1965 - Mike Warren

1966 - Lew Alcindor

1967 - Steve Patterson

1968 - Curtis Rowe

1969 - Henry Bibby & Andy Hill

1970 - Larry Farmer

1971 - Bill Walton

1972 - David Meyers

1973 - Ralph Drollinger

1974 - Marques Johnson

## "Caddy" Works Award

Awarded annually to member of U.C.L.A. basketball team for his competitive spirit, inspiration, and unselfish contribution to the team.

The recipient is chosen by the basketball coach + Dir. of Ath.

Presentation is made at the basketball banquet by the recipient of the award the previous year.

1945 - Dick Hough
1946 -
1947 - John Stanich
1948 - Dave Minor
1949 - George Stanich
1950 - Carl Kraushaar
1951 - Ed Sheldrake
1952 - Don Johnson
1953 - John Moore
1954 - Don Bragg
1955 - John Moore
1956 - Allen Herring
1957 - Dick Banton
1958 - Jim Halsten
1959 - Walt Torrence
1960 - Pete Blackman
1961 - John Berberich
1962 - Gary Cunningham
1963 - Walt Hazzard

1964 - Walter Hazzard
1965 - Gail Goodrich
1966 - Freddie Goss
1967 - Discontinued

## BAD HABITS ARE HARD TO BREAK

The Bob "Ace" Calkins Memorial Award was given to the Bruin basketball player who made the highest percentage of free throws each season. Free throws were, and are, an important element of overall scoring, and, at crucial moments in the game, making or missing them can often have a disproportionate impact.

Thus, I paid a lot of attention to free throw practice (as you'll see in other notes presented here). But, looking at these statistics of the winners of the Ace Calkins Award reminds me of this surprising fact: As a *team*, the players I coached at South Bend Central High School were generally better free throw shooters than those I coached at UCLA. This fact may surprise you, but the reason is fairly simple.

At South Bend I taught and insisted on one method of shooting the free throw, namely, the two-hand underhand style. Today nobody anywhere uses it, but I still think it's the most structurally sound method.

I was also able to convince junior high school coaches in South Bend to teach the same method to their players. So, by the time a young man arrived at South Bend High School, he had already been taught the method I believed in. In effect, the high school player had no bad habits or home-grown style that I had to untangle. My job was simply to help them refine the method they had already been taught—a method I felt was most productive.

At UCLA the situation was just the opposite. By then, free throw shooting had taken on many forms and each player developed his own style going through junior high and senior high school programs. By the time they arrived at UCLA, it was a difficult chore to make changes. The habits—often bad habits—were too deeply ingrained.

Bad habits are tough to break in free throws. They are even tougher to break when it comes to character issues such as those I placed in the Pyramid of Success and discuss in Chapter 4, "Good

Values Attract Good People." I didn't kid myself into thinking that just because a player had great athletic talent, I could change his bad habits in these more important areas.

I believe effective leadership is very cautious about bringing individuals with bad habits into the group. More often than not, before you can break their bad habits, they have taught those habits to others on your team.

<u>Ace Calkins Award</u>
<u>Sigma Pi Fraternity – Free Throw Trophy</u>

Awarded to the varsity player who makes the highest percentage of his free throws. The winner must average at least one shot per game.
Presentation at the basketball banquet by a representative of Sigma Pi.

|  |  | | |
|---|---|---|---|
| 1949 - | Paul Saunders | 27 out of 36 | = 75. % |
| 1950 - | Jerry Norman | 30 out of 37 | = 81.1% |
| 1951 - | Richard Ridgway | 153 out of 188 | = 81.4% |
| 1952 - | Ronnie Livingston | 85 out of 102 | = 83.3% |
| 1953 - | Richard Ridgway | 42 out of 53 | = 79.24% |
| 1954 - | Eddie White | 27 out of 30 | = 90. % |
| 1955 - | Eddie White / Dave Hall | 55 out of 69 / 22 out of 25 | = 79.7% / = 88.% |
| 1956 - | Willie Naulls | 185 out of 236 | = 78.4% |
| 1957 - | Ben Rogers | 109 out of 134 | = 81.3% |
| 1958 - | Ben Rogers | 74 out of 99 | = 74.7% |
| 1959 - | Walt Torrence | 165 out of 218 | = 75.7% |
| 1960 - | Gary Cunningham | 45 out of 54 | = 83.3% |
| 1961 - | Gary Cunningham | 70 out of 86 | = 81.4% |
| 1962 - | Gary Cunningham | 86 out of 104 | = 82.7% |
| 1963 - | Jack Hirsch | 69 out of 95 | = 72.6% |
| 1964 - | Walter Hazzard | 150 out of 209 | = 71.8% |
| 1965 - | Doug McIntosh | 56 out of 76 | = 73.9% |
| 1966 - | Kenny Washington | 78 out of 104 | = 75.0% |
| 1967 - | Lynn Shackelford | 55 out of 67 | = 82.1% |

## MOST VALUABLE? LET THE TEAM DECIDE

As I mentioned in Chapter 12, "Make Greatness Attainable by All," I was against naming any single player as "the greatest." Even now I won't name the greatest player I ever coached. In fact, I am reluctant to admit there is any such thing as a *greatest* player or a *greatest* team.

For reasons stated earlier, I would never retire a player's number, because it suggests that a single individual is the greatest to ever wear it. Retiring the number in their name dismisses the great effort and contributions of all others who have worn that same number. This approach is wrong. It goes against my philosophy of leadership and team spirit. Nevertheless, there is great pressure to single out individuals within teams and organizations as the greatest.

At UCLA I handled the situation as follows: At the conclusion of the season the entire team was allowed to vote for the player they felt was most valuable. As you'll see in my notes, the award was started in 1967 (replacing the "Caddy" Works Award) and was given to Lewis Alcindor, Jr. (Kareem Abdul-Jabbar), then Sidney Wicks, Bill Walton, and David Meyers—all good choices.

Doing it this way allowed a top producer—an All-American—to be acknowledged in a manner that brought his teammates into the process. They made the determination of "most valuable" and announced it to the public. I felt that doing it this way perhaps reduced envy or even jealousy within the team. It gave the whole squad the power to identify and select the player who was, in *their* view, "most valuable."

The manager of a large company in the shipping business recently expressed her concern that "in spite of doing everything we're supposed to do there is still no real connection or commitment by most of our employees to the organization." She was talking about the lack of Loyalty within her company and wanted to know how to fix it.

Well, this manager is not alone in facing this problem—getting those in the organization to think "we" rather than "me." It is not an easy problem to fix. In fact, it often is the biggest challenge of leadership.

Loyalty is a big thing, and I felt that one of the small ways it could be nurtured is by allowing team members to select the person they felt was most valuable to the group.

Contrast that with having the head coach, or boss, select and announce the most valuable individual. Even though the team might agree with your choice, doing it this way would certainly rankle more than a few people.

Every good organization has top producers within it. A leader's challenge is to find the balance, giving that individual deserved recognition without stirring up ill will with the rest of the group. In part, I tried to meet the challenge by letting the group select and honor a top producer—the "greatest" player.

UCLA - Most Valuable Player Award

( First awarded in 1967 to replace the Caddy Works Trophy)

1967 - Lewis Alcindor
1968 -      "           "
1969 -      "           "
1970 - Sidney Wicks
1971 -      "
1972 - Bill Walton
1973 - Bill Walton
1974 - Bill Walton
1975 - David Meyers

## MY REPLACEMENT WAS IN PLACE

During the eighth week of UCLA's 1972 basketball season I developed some heart problems and had to go into the hospital. It was an unexpected development and caught us all by surprise.

I am rather proud of the fact that our team didn't miss a beat while I was absent for two weeks. This continued level of high performance was possible because my assistant coaches, Gary Cunningham and Frank Arnold, had been given leadership responsibilities along the way. They knew my system and how it ran.

I designated Gary as my replacement as temporary head coach. Included here is a practice schedule that was put together for one of the days I was gone. You'll see that the handwriting is different, but the content and substance are very similar to my own. A leader truly dedicated to the team's welfare doesn't make himself irreplaceable. Gary was appointed UCLA's head basketball coach in 1977 and did an outstanding job.

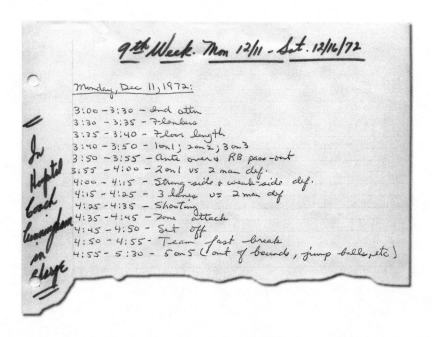

Obviously, I had no idea that I would suddenly need to be replaced for a time, but the way I fully incorporated my assistant "leaders" into the process of my coaching meant the team could continue performing at a consistent level. Things did not fall apart just because I was gone.

Who are your assistant leaders? Are you allowing them the opportunity to learn and grow as leaders? Is there someone ready to take the reins of leadership in case something happens to you? Or do you feel threatened by having someone in the organization potentially be your replacement?

## PUT A LID ON IT

The "imaginary ball" drill, you'll recall, involved running plays or shooting baskets without the ball. Players would be forced with this drill to concentrate exclusively on perfecting fundamentals rather than on the outcome of those fundamentals, such as scoring baskets.

I also used a somewhat unusual approach in helping individuals learn correct habits—the fundamentals—for rebounding. Again, it stemmed from my desire to use time as efficiently as possible. A typical rebound drill might involve six players—three defensive players against three offensive players. They would be positioned under the basket while a coach took a shot from the outside perimeter.

Obviously, it's difficult to practice rebounding if there's no rebound—if the shot goes through the hoop. Thus, at times we practiced rebounding with a cover over the basket, which meant that *every* shot produced a rebound opportunity. (The cover was sold commercially, and since I was very cost-conscious, I got kidded by some for spending money on it: "Coach, if you want rebounds just let so-and-so shoot." Of course, "so-and-so" would be a teammate who was less proficient when it came to making baskets.)

Obviously, our rebound drills began with a shot at the basket. With the cover over the hoop, a rebound was guaranteed and the drill could proceed without disruption. No time was wasted resetting, so we could try it again. Theoretically, we had a situation that was pure teaching and learning, with no false starts or resets necessitated by a successful shot.

In Chapter 10, "Make Each Day Your Masterpiece," I emphasized the importance of good time management. In my experience, this objective is usually accomplished through a series of small efficiencies rather than in one big chunk. Therefore, I kept looking for those little opportunities that would help the Bruins become most efficient in using our limited time to best advantage. Putting a cover over the hoop was an example of how we tried to squeeze more out of each minute.

In truth, we used the drill with a cover over the hoop only for a short time. I found that the quality of the rebound coming off the cover was not similar to what actually happens when a ball comes off the backboard or the basket. However, I cite this example only as further evidence of my desire to seek ways to use time better, to increase teaching results, to improve.

Often those types of opportunities exist within an organization, but we fail to seize on them because we're not looking hard enough, we're not creative in our approach. Never stop looking for an opportunity to put more value into each minute of your organization's time. Those small opportunities, one by one, eventually make a big difference.

Have the courage—the Initiative—to experiment when you're seeking answers to a leader's most important question: "How can we improve?" Some of those answers, like the "imaginary ball," will be useful. Others will soon be discarded, just as I discarded the cover that went over our hoop.

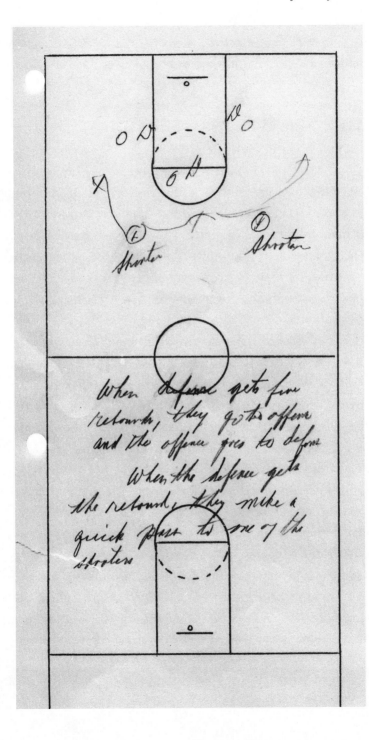

What was never discarded was my desire for improvement and the effort we made to find ways to bring it about.

## NOTES FOR MY FINAL SEASON

When I look back at the notes for UCLA practices from early in my coaching career and compare them to those notes many years later, I'm surprised we accomplished as much as we did in the beginning.

Over the years I greatly increased my ability to extract more improvement from each UCLA practice, knowing exactly where work was needed, including not only the physical but also the emotional and mental. I also was increasingly effective in knowing how to make the necessary improvements in those areas using the least amount of time.

Here is a page of notes for my final season as head coach at UCLA, 1974–1975. To put them in context, the preceding three seasons had been characterized by some people in the media as featuring "The Walton Gang," namely, Bill Walton and his teammates. During their years on the varsity team, UCLA had won two national championships and extended the winning streak to 88 games before losing to Notre Dame.

Thus, when Bill and his fellow seniors graduated, many onlookers suggested that UCLA would not be a contender for the national championship in 1974–1975. For one reason, we would have only one returning starter, David Meyers.

Going into my final season, I felt the team's potential was greater than commonly believed. Of course, *potential* means little unless it's realized. As the notes show, going into the 1974–1975 season, I viewed some areas as needing attention so that our potential would become a reality.

Those areas included supporting and building confidence with Pete Trgovich and Ralph Drollinger; helping Andre McCarter in-

*To Consider for 1974-75 season*

1. Build up confidence in Drollinger and Trgovich.
2. Get McCarter under control. He "hurries" too much.
3. Develop our pressing defense with patience. Try - 1-2-1-1, 2-2-1, 1-2-2, and 2-1-2.
4. Use 3 on 2 conditioner three times a week.
5. Defense the passing game more.
6. Work more against zones and pressure man to man.
7. Use our weak side post drill without shooting more frequently. Could be used in pre-game warmup.
8. Organize our time-outs better.
9. Try out the "4 corner" as a lead protector. Use McCarter and Spillane in they key spot.
10. Make David Meyers captain with responsibilities.
11. Be very cautious with Marques Johnson — hepatitis.
12. Forget the last season and concentrate on each day of practice. Don't take anything for granted — analyze, plan, work, evaluate, prepare.
13. Prepare Richard Washington for both high and low post play as well as forward.
14. Be patient with players on floor, but be firm in discipline both on and off the floor.

corporate my maxim, "Be quick, but don't hurry"; appointing David Meyers captain for the year (for reasons explained earlier); recognizing the physical status of Marques Johnson, who was recovering from a months-long illness; reminding myself to be patient but firm when it came to discipline (this, in part, because I had a suspicion that during the previous season I may have been too lax in this area); and the vital reminder to forget the past, concentrate on the present, and always plan, work, evaluate, and prepare.

These notes were for my use only, and they served as a starting point, a guide, to specific day-to-day practices. The schedule for our first day of practice in 1974 is shown next.

Most effective coaches that I've known or studied have a similar approach to charting out plans. Like most leaders, I wish I'd known in the beginning what I knew at the end. Perhaps something here will save you some time and unpleasant experience when it comes to creating a winning organization. A good leader always seeks improvement—always. This list is an example of the answers I came up with when I asked myself the question, "How can we improve this year?"

In a way, they provided a starting point—a guide—to my last year at UCLA. It would produce a championship.

## THE FIRST DAY OF MY LAST YEAR

Traditionally, October 15 was the first day of UCLA's basketball practice each season. October 15, *1974*, was the first day of my final season of basketball practice as head coach of the Bruins. Although I didn't know it at the time, I would retire at the end of the year.

Here are my notes for the first day of my last year. In reviewing them, I am pleased with the obvious continued concentration on identifying and perfecting relevant details. Reading through the many specifics here may give you a headache, but it brings a smile of satisfaction to my face.

Free throws, always in need of improvement, were given time and individual attention. Additionally, we included imaginary jump shots and rebounds; change of pace and direction drills; quick starts and stops drills; three-on-two work; dribbling (right and left handed); 1-3-1 offensive patterns, and much more.

First Week of Practice

Tuesday, Oct. 15, 1974

300-330 - Individual attention and free throws.
Wooden with guards, Cunningham with forwards

330-335 - Stretching, twisting, bending, squatting, running in place; Imaginary — jump shots (quick set, fake drive and set), offensive rebounding (right and left hand tip, two hand-jump-power); defensive rebounding (jump and jerk, cross over + turn or reverse turn for checkout and go); defensive sliding  (5 lines of 3)

335-340 - Change of pace + direction; quick starts + stops (with + without ball); defensive sliding with quick turns and catch up; one on one (with + without ball). (3 lines)

340-350 - Dribbling (right + left handed) - speed, control, maneuvering; stops + turns (both feet) with pass back. (3 lines)

350-355 - Auto-over; Rebound + pass out (5 at a basket)

355-405 - 3 man lane - parallel line, thru middle, front + side

405-415 - Jump shooting ( base line, board, key area, fake the drive + pull up ) (3 groups - 2 balls with each)

415-425 - 3 on 2 work for 15 foot jumpers.

425-440 - 1-3-1 offensive patterns

440-445 - Get ready for scrimmage

445-530 - Full court scrimmage with officials.
3 games of 15 minutes each (1 vs 2, 1 vs 3, 2 vs 3) Keep complete statistics. Those not scrimmaging shooting free throws.

530 - To shower on a happy note.

I also included a full-court scrimmage *with* officials because I believed it helped prepare the players for the upcoming first game of the season. As noted earlier, once we had played that first game, full-court scrimmages were used much less often.

Also, these notes show that I included a reminder to myself to end practice at 5:30 on a "happy note." I wanted players leaving the court with a good feeling, and I would devise a drill to achieve that. For example, I might select one player to make five free throws in a row before the team was allowed to go to the showers.

Of course, all the players gathered around and cheered or jeered, depending on how the free throw shooter was performing. It was very spirited and a happy way to close the day's practice. It also was an effective way of getting a weak free throw shooter to practice free throws under some pressure.

This was drawn from what I described in Chapter 11, "The Carrot Is Mightier Than a Stick." I wanted the players to leave with a good feeling about the day's hard work, and a happy ending was a nice carrot.

Of course, on occasion—when I felt they had not really been producing—I dispensed with a "happy" ending to the practice. Instead, I would deliver a message, perhaps a stern admonition, that would *stick* with them overnight.

## MEETING CHANGING CHALLENGES

As time progresses, the challenges change. An effective leader recognizes the new circumstance and moves quickly to meet it effectively.

These notes from the sixteenth week of UCLA practice during my final season, specifically, January 28, 1975, show my attempt to identify challenges and problems that needed attention.

As you see, I broke the practice time into 5- and 10-minute increments to focus on a four-man fast break (4:30–4:35); attacking

<u>16<sup>th</sup> Week of Practice</u> at USC on Sat. Feb 1.

<u>Tuesday, January 28, 1975</u>

300-330 - As usual. Cunningham work with Washington + Drollinger; Wooden - with press.

330-335 - Loosen up as usual. Same as Monday

335-340 - Front + side with flanker shot. 3 man lane.

340-345 - Center over (3); Rebound + pass out (4)

345-350 - Rebounding - 3 on 3 inside. 2's break for 2 on 1

350-405 - Defense - the USC passing game.

405-420 - Set Offense - high + low post. Stress "backdoor" reverses, guard to inside, + other options against overplay.

420-430 - Position shooting. Cunningham with forwards; Wooden with guards and centers.

430-435 - 4 man fast break - no protector.

435-440 - Attack the 1-2-1-1 press after made free throw

440-450 - 3-1-1 trap vs delay and "4 corner"

450-500 - Half court scrimmage - Attack 1-2-2 and 2-3 zones.

500-515 - Half court scrimmage Offense vs tight man to man overplay Press after a score.

515-530 - Half court scrimmage! Defense the USC passing game offense. Fast break on possession.

530 - Make 2 consecutive free throws and go to shower.

the 1-2-1-1 press after a successful free throw (4:35–4:40); the 3-1-1 trap versus the delay and "four-corner" (4:40–4:50); and a half-court scrimmage attacking 1-2-2 and 2-3 zone (4:50–5:00).

If you're not a basketball fan, those designations mean little to you. My point here is that the process of constantly seeking to analyze performance with an eye toward improvement means addressing new problems and issues on a daily basis. That's what this page from my notebook shows, namely, the identification of issues I wanted to focus on and improve.

You will also see that at 5:30—at the close of practice—I instructed players to make two consecutive free throws. Only then could they go to the showers. At that point in the practice, every player had been through a very rigorous two hours or more of exertion and wanted to get to the locker room. Of course, I knew this and took advantage of the situation by insisting that they make two *consecutive* free throws before they could leave the court. It was a way of forcing them to make two free throws under pressure when they were very tired—the exact kind of situation that they might face in the last seconds of a championship game.

## NOTES TO MYSELF ABOUT IMPORTANT THINGS

I gave much thought to those qualities and characteristics that were most necessary for strong leadership. Of course, my Pyramid of Success set in place those I felt were primary, but along the way I kept evaluating other qualities that mattered. I also kept track of phrases or thoughts that were insightful and related to qualities of importance. I drew great strength and direction from the writing of Abraham Lincoln and Mother Teresa and have included some of their wisdom in this book.

The jottings on this final page are from my notebook and offer a look at some ideas that I recorded many years ago.

*Giving - Receiving*
*Living - Receiving*

Conquer fear of mistakes

## Words of Giving

Love — "So faith hope, love abide, these three; but the greatest of these is love"

Courtesy }
Politeness } Are a small price to pay for the good will and affection of others

Sympathy — True concern for others

Friendship — mutual esteem, respect, & devotion

Cooperation — meeting more than halfway

Loyalty

Thanks

Mercy — "Merchant of Venice" — is twice blest; it blesseth him that gives, and him that takes

Sharing — "everenough & enough"
It's not what we give, but what we share,
For the gift without the giver is bare,
Who gives of himself with his alms feeds three —
Himself, his hungering neighbor, and me."
Widow's mite.
Respect

Square your life away by getting the
following things in order  1. Your faith
                            2. Your family
                            3. Your education
                            4. Your basketball
                            5. Your social life

# EPILOGUE

# TALENT TO SPARE, OR SPARE ON TALENT, A LEADER'S GOAL REMAINS THE SAME

MOST LEADERS DEFINE SUCCESS as winning—beating an opponent, gaining supremacy over the competition in the marketplace, achieving production quotas or sales goals. However, for any of these objectives to be met, talent must be present within your organization. A leader can't create a competitive team out of nothing. No coach can win consistently and no leader can succeed in the marketplace without good material.

You need talent on your team to prevail in the competitive arena. However, many leaders don't know how to win even when they have great talent in their organization. Furthermore, leaders are frequently forced to compete when the talent matchup isn't in their favor. What do you do then?

While a book can't replace talent, it can provide productive insights on how to get the most out of the talent you have available. And that, in my opinion, is the first goal of leadership—namely, getting the very best out of the people in your organization, whether they have talent to spare or are spare on talent.

Your ability to bring forth—maximize—the potential and abilities of those under your leadership marks you as a great competitor and leader. Some years, the teams I taught were blessed with significant talent. Other years, this was not the case. But in all years—with all levels of talent—my goal was the same, namely, to get the most out of what we had. This book has attempted to share my philosophy for doing that.

I also wish to say again how much my dad's practical wisdom affected me in my leadership. His example and words were—and still are—powerful. Earlier, I listed his Two Sets of Three and quoted his advice about success and winning the race. He also gave me a little card when I graduated from elementary school on which he written out his own personal Seven Point Creed.

Without mentioning it specifically, I have incorporated it throughout this book. But let me share it with you now in its entirety:

1. Be true to yourself.
2. Make each day your masterpiece.
3. Help others.
4. Drink deeply from good books including the Good Book.
5. Make friendship a fine art.
6. Build a shelter against a rainy day.
7. Pray for guidance and give thanks for your blessings every day.

When Dad handed me the little 3 × 5 card he said, "Johnny, try and follow this advice and you'll do fine." I've tried to live up to Dad's advice in my personal life and in my teaching, coaching, and leadership responsibilities. Dad is everywhere in this book.

I know that "one size fits all" doesn't apply when it comes to leadership. Leaders come in all shapes, sizes, and styles with a wide range of talents and temperaments. Nevertheless, I hope you've found something in my own experience and conclusions that will benefit you and your organization.

Abraham Lincoln used to say, "I never met a person from whom I didn't learn something, although most the time it was something *not* to do." Well, that's still learning. No doubt, this book is the same, namely, ideas and experiences from my life as a teacher, coach, and leader that you can learn from—even, at times, if it's what *not* to do. I've made my share of mistakes, but along the way I kept trying to improve. Maybe something here can make a difference in your own efforts to seek improvement as a leader.

It was with that goal that Steve Jamison and I began work on this comprehensive presentation of my philosophy of leadership. It stood me in good stead during nearly half a century in the competitive arena, and, in spite of all of the changes we see around us, I believe it can be equally effective in the twenty-first century. Some things don't change. Some rules remain the same.

# INDEX

# ABOUT THE AUTHORS

JOHN WOODEN and his legendary UCLA dynasty won 10 NCAA national championships in 12 years, including 88 straight games and four perfect seasons. Named Coach of The Century by ESPN, Wooden has been elected to the Basketball Hall of Fame as both a player and a coach. Recently, he was awarded the Presidential Medal of Freedom. Other books by Coach Wooden include *My Personal Best*, *WOODEN: A Lifetime of Reflections On and Off the Court*, *INCH and MILES*, *The Journey to Success*, and *They Call Me Coach*. For more, visit www.coachwooden.net.

STEVE JAMISON is a best-selling author, keynote speaker, and John Wooden's longtime collaborator and confidant. Jamison and Coach Wooden have worked together on several acclaimed books as well as an award-winning PBS documentary. Visit www.stevejamison.com.